FORCE & FEAR

ROBBERY IN CANADA

Frederick J. Desroches
St. Jerome's University
University of Waterloo

Canadian Scholars' Press Inc.
Toronto

Force and Fear: Robbery in Canada
Frederick J. Desroches

First published in 1995 by Nelson Canada

Published in 2002 by
Canadian Scholars' Press Inc.
180 Bloor Street West, Suite 801
Toronto, Ontario
M5S 2V6

www.cspi.org

CSPI gratefully acknowledges the financial support of the Government of
Canada through the Book Publishing Industry Development Program for
our publishing activities.

National Library of Canada Cataloguing in Publication Data

Desroches, Frederick John
   Force and fear : robbery in Canada / Frederick J. Desroches.

Includes bibliographical references and index.
ISBN 978-1-55130-218-8

1. Robbery—Canada. I. Title.

HV6665.C3D47 2002   364.15'52'0971   C2002-903050-1

Cover design by George Kirkpatrick

Printed and bound in Canada by Webcom

MIX
Paper from
responsible sources
FSC
www.fsc.org   FSC® C004071

Contents

Preface

The purpose of this book is to provide a review of research and theory on robbery with a primary focus on Canada's experience with this crime. I have attempted to clarify issues dealing with robbery and relate these to past and current theories in criminology. This book is based in part on research carried out over the past decade with the assistance of most major police departments in Canada, the Canadian Penitentiary Service, and 80 convicted bank robbers. The text examines the characteristics of robbery, the social background and motivation of offenders, the interaction of robbers and their victims, and the criminal justice system's response to this crime. Chapter One, *Robbery and the Law*, discusses issues related to the reporting of holdups, sociological definitions of crime, and an analysis of the laws surrounding robbery. Chapter Two, *An Overview of Robbery*, examines diverse topics including the planning of a holdup, financial gains, interactions between victims and offenders, age and gender variables, the urban context of robbery, and racial, ethnic, socioeconomic, educational, occupational, and marital characteristics of offenders. Also included is an analysis of typologies of robbery and of offenders. Chapter Three, *The Motivation to Robbery*, focuses on rational choice theory and discusses initial motivation and the motivation to continue, justifications for the crime, the influence of the mass media and the influence of other criminals, and the role of drug usage and unemployment. A discussion of how robbers perceive and deal with risk completes this section. Chapter Four, *Modus Operandi*, examines the various techniques employed by offenders to secure the money, overcome resistance, and make good their escape. Included is an analysis of the use of weapons and violence as techniques for handling victims, heroes, and the police. A typology of three types of bank robbery is presented. Chapter Five, *The Victims of Robbery*, discusses how targets are selected and characteristics of victim/offender interactions. This section also focuses on the potential trauma and physical injury victims face and on techniques to prevent robbery or minimize its impact and risk for victims. Chapter Six, *The Police and Judicial Response to Robbery*, analyzes the manner in which police respond to the problem of robbery in their community. In particular, the organization and operation of the Hold-Up

Squad in large, urban centres is examined. Chapter Seven, *Crime and Social Policy*, is a summary of what research and theory tells us about robbery. Included is a discussion of how society can best deal with the problems posed by this crime and an analysis of various principles of sentencing.

Many people have helped make this book possible. Thanks must go to the reviewers, Walter DeKeseredy (Carleton University), Desmond Ellis (York University), Doug Skoog (The University of Winnipeg), Chris McCormick (Saint Mary's University), and Carl Keane (Queen's University). Special thanks to Des Rowland for opening doors that allowed the research to take place. Thanks also to the Canadian Penitentiary Staff who organized the interviews of inmates for my study on bank robbery. Thanks to the inmates themselves for patiently answering the many and detailed questions put to them. Thanks also to the Hold-Up Squad detectives who took an interest in the project, shared their investigative knowledge, and recommended subjects for interviews.

I also wish to acknowledge the generous financial support of the Social Sciences and Humanities Research Council of Canada for my study on bank robbery, of which this book is a part.

Frederick J. Desroches
St. Jerome's College
University of Waterloo

Robbery and the Law

INTRODUCTION

Because of its sudden nature and the threat of death or serious injury, robbery is one of the most feared crimes common to large urban centres. Robbery is typically a stranger-to-stranger and face-to-face confrontation in which the criminal seizes the victim's money or property by using threats or outright violence. It is a more serious crime than theft because it involves the use of force against an individual. The media have often portrayed robbers as romantic adventurers and rebels but this image is quickly changing. Current research shows that the robber is not a skilled and daring criminal but a young, unskilled, and sometimes vicious predator who exploits vulnerable persons and businesses. Increasing concern for victims and their experiences gives us a more realistic perspective on this phenomenon. Robbery is a serious crime that often traumatizes and/or physically injures the victim. The increase in the robbery rate over the past several decades is seen not only as a threat to life and private property, but also to the public's sense of security. Fear of robbery creates a climate of distrust that keeps some people prisoners in their own homes, threatens the livelihood of small businesses, and undermines community life.

The behaviour included in this criminal category ranges from street muggings and convenience-store robberies, to bank and armoured-vehicle holdups. Weapons may or may not be used, and robbers may be skilled or unskilled and operate by themselves or with others. Robbery is a crime that involves small sums of money, possible resistance from victims and witnesses, an immediate police response, a high rate of capture, and severe penalties from the courts. Even though the police are mobile and use sophisticated communication equipment, robbery is committed with relative ease and is a common occurrence in many cities. Part of the attraction to robbery is the speed with which money is obtained. Furthermore, the act itself requires little planning, few skills, little or no investment of time or resources, and can be committed alone.

Robbery behaviour is a complex phenomenon that presents the sociologist with a number of questions to resolve. How accurately do official statistics reflect the true rate of robbery? Why do individuals commit a crime for which the proceeds are small, the arrest rate is high, and the jail sentences are long? Why do offenders give little thought and planning to their holdups, assume they will not get caught, and view the crime as nonserious? Why is robbery so common in urban areas? What types of robberies occur? Who are the offenders and what motivates them? How do they justify their conduct? What variables are related to robbery? What actually happens in a robbery and how do the robber and victim interact? Who are the victims, how do they respond, and what can someone do in self-defence? What insight does sociological theory and research shed on this phenomenon? And finally, how do the police and courts respond to these dangerous and frightening crimes and how effective are official policies and programs? These are some of the questions that this book attempts to answer.

Despite the frequency with which robbery is committed and the threat that it poses to victims, there are few detailed studies of this crime. In the following chapters, we will refer to research conducted in England, the United States, and Canada that deals with the problem of robbery, as well as official statistics, biographies, and crime prevention literature. Although research on robbery tells us a great deal about some topics, data for other problems are scarce. Thus, some of the generalizations in this text rely on solid empirical evidence but others are suggestive, impressionistic, and based on data that are dated, fragmented, or incomplete. Part of the reason for the shortcomings in the available data relates to the nature of the crime. There are obvious difficulties in gaining the cooperation of incarcerated offenders and insurmountable problems in identifying persons currently involved in crime. Furthermore, researchers are confronted with the issue of confidentiality relating to police and correctional files, the covert nature of criminal activity, and the difficulty of penetrating criminal networks. These factors make it difficult to identify and contact criminals and ex-criminals. Even when subjects are found, researchers must verify their responses and estimate their representativeness. Researchers also face the usual shortcomings related to a subject's faulty memory and ignorance of or inability to articulate his or her motivation.

A review of the research literature is supplemented with data compiled by the author from a study of Canadian bank robbers. Materials from this study will be presented throughout the text to illustrate some of the ideas, concepts, and theories that are discussed. The study was conducted over an eight-year period through interviews with 80 convicted male bank robbers in prisons across Canada. The research is exploratory in nature and focuses on a wide range of topics including the following: the offender's motivation; life circumstances prior to robbery; educational, occupational, and family background; previous criminal involvement; robbery experiences; modus operandi; the influence of the mass media; lifestyle and spending; and the offender's experiences with the police and courts. Additional data were gathered from media reports of robbery, police files and occurrences, and interviews with investigating officers. The research explores the values, attitudes, and beliefs of offenders while they commit or contemplate their crimes. These personal accounts give insight into the life experiences and value systems of the people who rob banks, their decision-making processes, and the manner in which they handle the risks involved.

REPORTING ROBBERY

Many crimes go unreported and/or undetected because they are unseen, nonthreatening, cause little or no harm, or have no true victim. Robbery, however, is visible, physically threatening, emotionally traumatizing, and causes financial loss to the victim. Convenience stores and financial institutions report most robberies and attempted robberies to the police, often through the use of silent alarm systems connected directly to the police station or to a security firm. Bank robbery, in fact, may be the most fully reported crime. The Canadian Bankers' Association policy is to report all robberies and attempted robberies and to cooperate fully with the police investigation. In the United States, by law, all bank robberies must be reported to the FBI.

Although robbery is frequently reported, not all victims of crime notify the police. Surveys indicate that robberies against individuals, known as muggings, are frequently unreported. Criminologists have long been aware that police data cannot measure the true extent and distribution of crime in society, regardless of how conscientiously or reliably the data have been collected. Official statistics are based upon reports received from victims of, or witnesses to, the crime and represent an unknown fraction of all crimes. Victims and witnesses screen out criminal events and only report certain ones. A victim may be aware that he or she has been robbed, for instance, but defines the incident as not warranting police notification or intervention. Gottfredson and Gottfredson (1988) describe citizens as gatekeepers and argue that the decision to report crimes, because it initiates official action, may be the most influential one made in the criminal justice system.

Victimization surveys are designed to shed light on the "dark figure" of crime—crime that is unreported and that does not come to police attention and consequently fails to appear in official statistics. These studies are usually self-reported questionnaire surveys administered to large samples, focusing on experiences of victimization, and filled out anonymously by respondents. This type of research provides us with important alternative measures of certain crimes, which can help us to understand and define the circumstances that inhibit victims from reporting crime to the police. With respect to robbery, victimization studies tend to focus on muggings since commercial robberies are usually reported. Victimization surveys generally indicate that most serious crimes are reported and that the risk of being a victim of serious crime is remarkably small. The vast majority of unreported offences uncovered by the British Crime Surveys, for example, were petty thefts, acts of vandalism, and minor assaults. Although serious offences are cause for concern, crimes such as murder, rape, and robbery represent a small minority of the total that goes unreported. The British survey found that victims were unlikely to report a crime if they judge it as too trivial to justify calling the police (55 percent); they believe that police are unable to do anything (16 percent); they consider the incident is not a police matter (10 percent); or they believe it is too inconvenient to report the offence (2 percent) (Hough and Mayhew, 1983:33–34).

Skogan's review of research dealing with victimization and the reporting of crime to the police indicates that the median "around the world" rate for robbery reporting was about 56 percent and the U.S. figure ranged from 52 percent to 56 percent (1984:117). One potential reason for low rates of robbery reporting, he suggests, is that in all of the cities studied, including cities in the United States, robbery generally did not involve a weapon and only rarely involved a gun. The presence of a weapon of any kind is an indicator of incident seriousness, and the use of a gun is a significant predictor of reporting (Skogan, 1984:120). Because patterns of firearm use will vary enormously across nations, we can expect significant cross-cultural variations in the reporting of robbery incidents.

The Canadian Urban Victimization Survey (Solicitor General of Canada 1984:8) of 61,000 persons age 15 and older from randomly selected telephone numbers in seven Canadian cities found that half the estimated 49,200 robbery incidents were attempted robberies and half were completed, that is, a theft occurred. While 62 percent of robberies that were completed were reported, only 28 percent of attempted robberies came to police attention. Certain factors increased the likelihood of reporting. For example, the presence of a gun dramatically increased reporting to the police (83 percent reported). Similarly, robberies committed against female victims were more likely to come to police attention (53 percent) than those against male victims (36 percent). For both sexes, chances of reporting increased with the number of offenders involved in an incident, though for men, reporting still remained below 50 percent, even with multiple offenders. The sample excluded robberies of commercial establishments. This study was repeated in Edmonton through telephone interviews of 9,200 persons age 16 and over. The study showed that only one-third of violent incidents were reported to the police, ranging from 32 percent of assaults, 39 percent of sexual assaults, and 42 percent of robberies. The most commonly cited reasons for not reporting crimes of violence to the police were that the incident was "too minor" or that "the police couldn't do anything about it" (Solicitor General of Canada, 1987).

Research on citizen crime-reporting suggests that most of the variance in reporting relates to characteristics of the incident. The most common motive for nonreporting is that the crime was "not serious enough." A variant of this rationale is either the primary or secondary reason cited by victims for nonreporting in most surveys. Overall, crime victimization surveys indicate that this rationale is often cited in cases involving attempted rather than completed crimes, those not involving a weapon, crimes without financial loss, and those resulting in no injury (Skogan, 1984:120–21; Hindelang and Gottfredson, 1978). It is reasonable to conclude that the victims' discretion is appropriate since not all crimes need to be reported to the police. Some less serious crimes can probably be handled as effectively by the victim as by the police.

A contradictory observation and conclusion, however, can be drawn from the data on violent crimes, which show that serious victimizations also go unreported. The Canadian Urban Victimization Survey (Solicitor General of Canada, 1984), for instance, found that some victims chose to avoid criminal justice intervention for incidents that most people would judge to be quite serious. When victims were asked their reasons for nonreporting even when weapons had been used, they cited the same reasons as those for the less serious incidents: police couldn't do anything about it (60 percent); the incident was too minor (48 percent); or, especially for young males, reporting was too inconvenient (32 percent) (Solicitor General of Canada, 1984:8). Jock Young argues that although a large part of the unreported crime as shown in victim surveys is unreported because it is of a trivial nature, many victims view the crime as nontrivial yet perceive the police as unable to do anything (Young, 1988:167). This does not necessarily mean, as Young suggests, that the victim has no confidence in the police, but only that evidence may not be available, there are no suspects, or the victim cannot provide adequate information to assist the investigation. Victim reports indicate that attitudes toward the police play a surprisingly limited role in victim decision-making. Skogan concludes that hardly anywhere is this an important consideration once a crime has occurred, "especially if it was by any measure a serious one" (1987:122).

The Canadian Urban Victimization Survey (1987:7) also indicates that sometimes crime is unreported because of fear on behalf of the victim. In 17 percent of unreported crime events, the respondent expressed a fear of revenge as one reason for not informing the police. Another 31 percent of incidents are not reported because they are defined as personal matters, and in 19 percent of victimizations, a wish to protect the offender is a factor in nonreporting.

The past behaviour of victims may also affect their willingness to contact the police, particularly if they have contributed to their own victimization through negligent behaviour. Biderman et al. (1967) report that 35 percent of victims indicated they had acted foolishly and were loathe to report trouble they "got themselves into." Similarly, Sparks et al. (1977) found that persons involved in criminal activities themselves were less likely to report offences to the police. Mugging victims may not report the offence if they too are involved in discreditable activities. For example, men searching for sex with male or female prostitutes make themselves vulnerable to robbery yet may fear reporting the incident for fear of revealing their own involvement in illicit activities. Similarly, drug users and drug dealers who are robbed may also refrain from reporting the offence to the police. In a study of robbery in London, England, McClintock and Gibson (1961:16) found that one robbery in eight involved a preliminary association of short duration between victim and offender mainly for sexual purposes. The extent to which such robberies occur is difficult to assess because persons engaged in such behaviour are less likely to report their victimization. They may fear damage to their reputation or criminal prosecution, or they expect little sympathy or assistance from the police.

Most survey research defines robbery as occurring if something is taken and the offender has a weapon and threatens or attacks the victim. Attempted robberies are also included in this offence category (e.g., Canadian Urban Victimization Survey, 1987). Katz argues that when we define robbery loosely as the taking of something of value by force or threat of force, then the offence is found quite commonly in childhood.

> Much of the "bully's" behavior might be seen as robbery, as might much of the unkindness that gives sibling rivalry its bad reputation... These mean and predatory actions do not seem to warrant the archetype of "robbery," perhaps because they are more clearly expressive than economic projects: intimidating a classmate to "give" pocket change; using a tough posture to deflect requests by a friend that he be repaid money that was, some time before, handed over as a "loan"; seizing an item of clothing from another youth because it represents membership in an enemy group; approaching strangers in public spaces with a humble monetary "request" that subtly but quickly becomes recognized as an arrogant and inexorable demand (1991:277–78).

However it is measured, the seriousness of the crime strongly influences the victim's decision to report it. The principal effect of nonreporting is to ensure that the criminal justice system deals with the most serious crimes. Survey research tells that the pool of crimes unknown to the police is disproportionately likely to feature less injury, smaller financial losses, and less use of weapons, especially guns. It is possible that many of the offences categorized as robberies in self-report survey research studies are not robberies at all. For example, the police routinely receive complaints from citizens who have been "robbed," when in fact they have been the victim of another offence such as a theft or break and enter. Thus the term "robbery" is often mistakenly used by the public to refer to crimes in which they have suffered a financial loss. A discussion in one of my university criminology classes illustrates this point. I had defined the term "robbery" and discussed a number of robbery incidents. One student exclaimed that her family's pharmacy had been robbed five times in the past year. It became clear from her description of events that the store had been the target of five break and enters but had not been robbed. Even after clarifying the definition of "robbery," the student continued to describe these burglaries as robberies.

The analysis of robbery in this book will focus primarily on incidents in which victims and offenders are strangers. These events include the vast majority of holdups reported to the police; and the most serious incidents of robbery including those that are likely to lead to financial loss, personal injury, and the use of a firearm during an offence. Unfortunately, there are insufficient data on the dark figure of crime to comment in detail on robberies that victims fail to report. Most victimization surveys indicate that some robberies are not reported to the police but these studies usually provide little information on such holdups except that most are muggings rather than commercial robberies.

LAWS RELATED TO ROBBERY

Conceptualizations of crime from a sociological perspective frequently differ from legal definitions. Nonetheless, sociologists often use legal definitions for research purposes because laws reflect prohibitions that generate an official response from the criminal justice system. In addition, legal definitions are used to generate statistics that sociologists and others use for conducting research and testing hypotheses. Sutherland and Cressey (1978) assert that legal definitions of crime are marked by four ideals: politicality, specificity, uniformity, and penal sanction. Politicality means that laws are passed by the government and in the case of Canadian criminal law, by the Federal Government of Canada; specificity means that laws should be precise in defining what is prohibited; uniformity means that the laws apply equally to everyone; and penal sanction is the punishment threatened to violators of the law.

The majority of Canadian criminal law can be found in the Criminal Code, a legal document that applies throughout Canada. American criminal law, on the other hand, is state legislation and consequently varies across state boundaries. Certain offences such as bank robbery, however, have split jurisdiction because they are defined as crimes at both the federal and state level. Even in Canada where the Criminal Code is the major source of Canadian criminal law, numerous federal and provincial statutes create criminal and quasi-criminal offences.

A crime, then, is any act or omission that violates the Criminal Code of Canada and other federal statutes such as the Narcotics Control Act. The crime of robbery is defined in the Criminal Code under sections 343 and 344 as follows:

343. Every one commits robbery who

(a) steals, and for the purpose of extorting whatever is stolen or to prevent or overcome resistance to the stealing, uses violence or threats of violence to a person or property;

(b) steals from any person and, at the time he steals or immediately before or immediately thereafter, wounds, beats, strikes, or uses any personal violence to that person;

(c) assaults any person with intent to steal from him; or

(d) steals from any person while armed with an offensive weapon or imitation thereof.

344. Every one who commits robbery is guilty of an indictable offence and liable to imprisonment for life.

There are two types of offences in the Criminal Code—summary conviction and indictable offences. Summary conviction offences are less serious and allow for a sentence of no more than $2,000 or imprisonment for six months or both [s. 787 (2)]. Indictable offences are more serious and fall into five categories that allow for maximum sentences of two, five, ten, or fourteen years, and life imprisonment. Robbery is regarded as a serious offence and, like murder, carries a possible sentence of life imprisonment. This means that judges may sentence a convicted robber to life imprisonment or to no time in prison, depending on the circumstances surrounding the offence.

Is Robbery a Property Offence or a Crime of Violence?

Although robbery involves theft, it also entails a personal confrontation and a threat of violence to or an assault on another person. In the United States, some state penal codes define robbery as a property offence while other states define it as an offence against the person. In Canada, robbery (s. 343), like theft (s. 334), is found in the Criminal Code under the section dealing with offences against rights of property. But unlike theft, which either proceeds by indictment (theft over $1,000) and is punishable by a term of imprisonment not exceeding ten years or as a summary conviction offence (theft under $1,000) punishable by no more than six months in prison (s. 334), robbery is punishable by life imprisonment because of the threat or use of violence.

Yet despite being classified as a property offence in the Criminal Code, other government agencies categorize robbery as a crime against the person. For example, the National Parole Board of Canada defines robbery as a violent offence in its designation of violent offenders. Similarly, Statistics Canada defines violent incidents as offences that may result in physical injury to a person and includes the following offences: homicide; attempted murder; various forms of sexual and nonsexual assault; abduction; and robbery. Property incidents are defined as unlawful acts that are committed with the intent of gaining property but that do not involve the use or threat of violence against an individual. Theft, breaking and entering, fraud, and possession of stolen goods are examples of property crimes (Statistics Canada, 1992:7). Many criminologists also regard robbery as a crime of violence because there is victim confrontation, threats, and occasionally physical assault. Robbery is more serious than a simple theft because it requires the threat or use of force during the theft.

It can be argued that robbery should be viewed as a property offence since the intent of the crime is theft. The present study of 80 Canadian bank robbers indicates that bandits are motivated by money and do not intend to harm their victims. Offenders subjectively minimize the seriousness of the crime by diminishing the assaultive nature of robbery and emphasizing the property motive. Similarly, in his study of robbery in Philadelphia, Andre Normandeau (1968) applied the "subculture of violence" hypothesis (Wolfgang and Ferracuti, 1967) and found it to be inappropriate since robbers do not appear to be motivated toward violent confrontations, seldom use force, and avoid the use of violence whenever possible. Instead he suggests that a "subculture of theft" is a more theoretically sound way of viewing robbery since the offender's motive is theft and not violence. Factors related to motivation and the manner in which robbers perceive and justify their behaviour are discussed further in Chapter Three.

The definitional issue is clouded even further by the fact that robberies differ in the degree of force threatened or used and by the outcome and potential outcome of different robberies. Statistics Canada, for instance, recognizes that there are degrees of violence and classifies robberies into three categories: robberies involving the use of firearms, holdups committed with the use of other offensive weapons, and robberies committed without weapons. In addition, robbers differ in their use of force. For example, some people rob ranks by simply passing a note to a teller (a typology of "beggar bandits," as they are called, is presented in Chapter Four). Many of these offenders are unarmed, have no intent to harm anyone, act politely, use minimal threats, and simply walk away if the teller refuses their demand.

But why should we accept a subjective, self-serving definition of robbery presented by the perpetrators of the crime? Their views may be simply an attempt to justify their criminal conduct and minimize the seriousness of the offence. A robber's perspective also conveniently ignores the trauma inflicted on victims. Although society may reject the robber's view of robbery as a property offence, sociologists must seriously consider the bandit's perspective since it has theoretical and explanatory value. Sociology has long recognized that the definitions of reality constructed by actors in their everyday lives significantly influence their behaviours.

The debate over whether to classify robbery as a property crime or as a violent offence creates a conceptual dilemma that is usually resolved by one's purpose in dealing with the crime. For example, a sociologist who wishes to explain criminal behaviour is likely to portray robbery as a property offence motivated by money. A criminal court judge or a member of the National Parole Board of Canada, however, whose position requires him or her to consider the protection of society, is justified in treating robbery as a violent act. From a social control perspective, it is reasonable and defensible to consider the physical harm and emotional trauma suffered by victims of holdups and to treat offenders accordingly. It can be argued that society is correct in defining robbery as a violent offence because violence is threatened or used; it has the potential to harm persons; and even when victims are not physically hurt, they are frequently traumatized by the experience. Consequently, criminal court judges sentence robbers to lengthy prison terms to deter potential offenders and to incapacitate convicted offenders. Similarly, the National Parole Services of Canada is restrictive and cautious in granting robbery offenders early release from custody on parole.

Besides the conceptual issue in defining robbery, the courts may also deal with criminal incidents that represent a different type of definitional problem. The seizure of a woman's purse, for instance, clearly involves theft but the decision to classify the crime as robbery depends on whether force is used. Canadian courts have decided that a purse-snatching is not robbery if the accused takes the purse before the victim can offer any resistance and the offender uses no other violence to the victim [R. v. Picard (1976), 39 C.C.C. (2d) 57 (Que. Sess. Ct.)]. Where the victim's arms are held to prevent resistance while the money is taken, however, the offence of robbery occurs [R. v. Trudel (1984), 12 C.C.C. (3d) 342 (Que. C.A.)].

A threat of violence, even if it is implied, will also lead the court to define theft as robbery. Several bank robbers in the present study deliberately worded their notes to minimize the threat. One man's note was carefully worded, "I'm armed. Give me the money," because he did not wish to use an explicit threat.

> It's an implicit threat. They have to read into it what they want to read into it. Sometimes when they read the note, they'll hesitate and think about it. I'll take control and follow up with a verbal demand like, "Start with the large bills." This puts them in the frame of mind where they're not think-ing beyond what's happening in that situation and they give me the money. I never verbally threatened tellers at any time. In fact, I've never had anyone deny me. When I worded my note, I wanted the impression brought onto them that they weren't going to get hurt. I was always polite and pleas-ant and that reflects my nature because I am totally opposed to violence.

PUt tHE MONEY IN tHE BAG
I HAVE A GUN!
SomEONE iS WATCHING YOU
DoNt BE StuPID!
HuRRY.

This bandit's note contains a number of explicit instructions and implicit threats. *Courtesy Metro Toronto Police Hold-Up Squad.*

Even though the threat may be implicit, the law defines the act as a robbery that is subject to severe penalties. Although judges may consider aggressive versus polite behaviour and explicit versus implicit threats as aggravating or mitigating factors when they determine the offender's sentence, the accused will be convicted of robbery nonetheless. For example, a bandit who merely handed a bank teller a note stating, "Empty your till," was convicted of robbery because of the implicit threat. The court ruled that for the crime to constitute a threat of violence, the victim must feel threatened and have reasonable and probable grounds for this fear. The implied threat of violence from the note was judged sufficient to convict the offender of robbery

[*R. v. Katrensky* (1975), 24 C.C.C. (2d) 350, [1975] 5 W.W.R. 732 (B.C. Prov. Ct.)].

OTHER OFFENCES RELATED TO ROBBERY

Assault may also be included in the act of robbery since victims are occasionally attacked physically. Assault is a dual-procedure offence that can be tried through indictment with possible imprisonment for five years or as a summary conviction offence (s. 266). Assault with a weapon or assault causing bodily harm (s. 267) and aggravated assault (s. 269) are punishable by up to ten years' imprisonment.

The use of a firearm in a robbery can lead to additional charges under section 85 of the Criminal Code, is punishable by imprisonment of up to 14 years and, in the case of a first offence, of not less than one year. In second or subsequent firearms convictions, the term is still no more than 14 years but not less than three years. Moreover, the law stipulates that the firearms sentence must be served consecutively to any other sentence imposed for the original offence. That is, a person who is armed while committing a robbery will be charged with robbery but may also be charged with separate weapons offences. The Criminal Code does not distinguish between types of robberies such as the robbery of financial institutions, individuals, or businesses, nor does it distinguish between "armed" and "unarmed" robbery. Furthermore, the Criminal Code does not differentiate between a real or loaded gun and a fake or unloaded one. All guns are regarded as firearms and offenders with fake or unloaded guns may still be charged with the use of a firearm in the commission of an indictable offence. Using a loaded weapon, however, may lead the judge to impose a harsher sentence.

Pointing a firearm at another person is an offence punishable by up to five years in prison (s. 86). Carrying a real or imitation weapon in one's possession for the purpose of committing an offence is also a crime (s. 87), which is punishable by imprisonment of up to ten years. Carrying a concealed weapon (s. 89) and possession of a prohibited weapon (s. 90) or an unregistered restricted weapon (s. 91) are dual-procedure offences punishable by six months by summary conviction and up to five years by indictment. Section 244 states that discharging a firearm with (a) intent to wound, maim or disfigure any person, (b) to endanger the life of any person, or (c) to prevent the arrest or detention of any person is a criminal offence punishable by imprisonment of up to fourteen years.

The Criminal Code also includes the attempt to commit robbery [s. 24 (1)], which is punishable by a term of imprisonment that is one-half that of robbery [s. 463 (b)]. A person is a party to an offence (accessory before or during the act) if he or she commits or aids or abets a person in committing robbery and is liable to the same term of imprisonment as the person who commits it (s. 21). Someone who is an accessory after the act and knowingly "receives, comforts, or assists that person for the purpose of enabling that person to escape" is liable to one-half the prison term. Married persons are exempted from this provision (s. 463). On rare occasions, offenders may be charged with conspiracy to commit the offence of robbery [s. 465 (c)] and are subject to the same penalty as if they had committed the crime.

Wearing a disguise in a robbery is also a separate offence:

> Every one who, with intent to commit an indictable offence, has his face masked or coloured or is otherwise disguised is guilty of an indictable offence and liable to imprisonment for a term not exceeding ten years [Section 351 (2)].

Robbery creates the possibility that someone may be killed during the act, which would lead to murder charges. First-degree murder is defined in section 231 of the Criminal Code and includes murders that are planned and deliberate [s. 231 (1), (2), & (3)], the murder of certain law-enforcement personnel and peace officers [s. 231 (4)], and the killing of a person in the commission of certain listed offences [s. 231 (5)], of which robbery is not included. Any murder that is not first-degree murder is second-degree murder [s. 231 (7)]. First-degree murder carries with it a minimum sentence of life imprisonment with a parole eligibility of 25 years [s. 235 (1) and s. 742 (a)]. Second-degree murder also carries a minimum sentence of life imprisonment but the parole eligibility comes sooner and may range from between ten and 25 years as determined by the sentencing judge [s. 742 (b)].

One of the inmates interviewed for this study shot and killed a female teller in 1981 during a botched bank robbery in Montreal. He was convicted of second-degree murder and sentenced to life imprisonment with no parole eligibility for fifteen years [See case example, "The Death of a Teller" in Chapter Five]. The conviction was based on section 230 (d) of the Criminal Code, which has since been repealed. Section 230 is entitled, Murder in the Commission of Offences, and states that a person commits murder when he causes the death of a human being while committing or attempting to commit certain offences including treason, sexual assault, kidnapping and forcible confinement, arson, and robbery. The culprit is guilty of murder and liable to a sentence of life imprisonment regardless of whether he or she means to cause death and whether he or she knows death is likely to be caused to any human being. This section applies only if:

    (a) he means to cause bodily harm for the purpose of

        (i) facilitating the commission of the offence, or

        (ii) facilitating his flight after committing or attempting to commit the offence, and the death ensues from the bodily harm;

    (b) he administers a stupefying or overpowering thing for a purpose mentioned in paragraph (a), and death ensues therefrom; or

    (c) he wilfully stops, by any means, the breath of a human being for a purpose mentioned in paragraph (a), and the death ensues therefrom.

Section 230 (d) used to include the following:

    (d) he uses a weapon or has it upon his person

        (i) during or at the time he commits or attempts to commit the offence, or

        (ii) during or at the time of his flight after committing or attempting to commit the offence, and the death ensues as a consequence [Repealed 1991].

Section 230 (d) was repealed after the Supreme Court of Canada declared this section unconstitutional in *Regina v. Martineau*. Martineau had been convicted of murder in the death of James and Ann McLean during a robbery. He and his accomplice, Tremblay, broke into the McLean's home and robbed the couple. After the robbery, Tremblay shot and killed the couple, explaining to Martineau that they had seen his face. The Supreme Court argued that a murder conviction should be reserved for those who choose to intentionally cause death or who inflict bodily harm that they know is likely to cause death. Since Martineau had not caused or meant to cause death, the Court overturned the conviction and ordered a new trial [*R. v. Martineau* (1990), 58 C.C.C. (3rd) 353, (Fed. C.A.)].

As the law now stands, a robbery that results in death would generate a murder conviction only if the the killing was deliberate, resulted in the death of a law-enforcement official (s. 231), and/or resulted from an act meant to cause harm for the purpose of committing or attempting to commit the offence or to escape (s. 230). If these criteria were not met and a bandit did kill someone in the act of robbery, the offender could still be charged and convicted of manslaughter, which is punishable by a maximum sentence of life imprisonment. Manslaughter is defined by specific provisions (s. 232) and by declaring the residual category of acts of culpable homicide to be manslaughter. The mental component of manslaughter ranges from the intention to commit an unlawful act to the intention to kill, which is mitigated by provocation by the victim. There is no minimum sentence, however, and parole eligibility occurs after the inmate has served one-third of the prison term. The Criminal Code provides that all culpable homicide that is not murder (s. 229 and 230) or infanticide (s. 233) is manslaughter.

Critics of this recent change in law argue that it undermines any potential deterrence to serious offenders involved in robbery from using extreme force in the course of committing the act. Today, the offender who killed the teller (Case Example—Death of a Teller is discussed in Chapter Five) would likely be convicted of manslaughter and not murder because the death was not premeditated or deliberate. In all likelihood, he would receive a lesser sentence than the life term imposed.

CRIME AS LAW-BREAKING

For sociological purposes, crime is subsumed under the broader heading of deviant behaviour and involves a violation of social rules that regulate our conduct. A focus on deviance, however, ignores the structural and legal processes that transform rule-breaking into crime and authorize intervention by formal agents of social control, such as the police and courts. Crime and criminals cannot exist without the existence of criminal law. Although crime is typically viewed as behaviour that violates the law, this definition is incomplete because questions about who makes the law, which laws get passed, and the substance of these laws are theoretically problematic. In some studies of crime, the prohibited behaviour is accepted as a given and investigators concentrate on why and how crime occurs. This approach is not fully adequate since the definition of criminal offences can vary over time and across cultures.

Boyd (1995:25–26) argues that competing theoretical models of law can be simplistically condensed into two opposing camps: those who view law and its transactions as morally neutral exercises of logic and interpretation; and those who argue that law and legal practice must be viewed in a moral, political, and economic context. The former perspective accepts unquestionably and uncritically legal definitions of crime, criminals, and criminal events as the basic units or elements of criminal inquiry and examines them in a detached and clinical way. Most sociologists, on the other hand, do not accept definitions of criminal behaviour as given, normal, or natural prohibitions. Instead they attempt to understand the underlying value choices and conflicts of interests and power to appreciate how laws evolve and change. Sociology approaches the study of law with the assumption that deviance is a matter of social definition and behaviour becomes defined as criminal only if society passes laws to prohibit it. Law itself is a social product influenced by religious, political, and economic conditions. Two main theoretical models are used by sociologists to explain law: consensus and conflict theories of social order.

LAW AND VALUE CONSENSUS THEORY

Consensus theory of social order argues that crime is a violation of widely held values and norms. Crime is perceived as an act that attacks the collective conscience of a society and outrages the population. If left uncontrolled, criminal conduct becomes a threat to society because it undermines social order. Laws that define criminal conduct are commonly believed to have the support of citizens because the prohibited behaviour violates certain widely held values and principles. This view of crime and criminal law is based on the assumption that a common or cultural morality exists. Emile Durkheim (1933) suggested that even complex societies require a degree of consensus about right and wrong to maintain cohesion and social integration. For Durkheim, crime was functional in the sense that it brought people together in moral outrage to condemn the despicable act and punish the offender. From this perspective, law is based on the assumption that society is characterized by a consensus of values and that law reflects this common morality.

Although this theoretical model has been heavily criticized for overemphasizing the degree of consensus that exists in heterogeneous societies and for ignoring the significance of interest groups in the evolution of specific forms of law, research indicates that there exists a high degree of moral consensus behind laws that prohibit criminal conduct. A pioneering study by Sellin and Wolfgang (1964) attempted to measure value consensus in relation to criminal acts by sampling judges, police officers, and college students in Philadelphia. The authors found that there was considerable agreement among the subgroups about the relative ordering of criminal acts and the scale scores given on subject evaluation of seriousness. Two Canadian studies replicating this research (Normandeau, 1966; Akman et al., 1967) using students, judges, police, and white-collar workers found substantial agreement with the Sellin-Wolfgang findings on the ranking of offences and the designation of seriousness. Overall, research in criminology strongly supports the view that laws prohibiting criminal conduct are based upon normative consensus.

Conflict theory is thus faced with the difficult problem of explaining widespread and consistent agreement in the research literature about the manner in which the public judges crime seriousness and supports laws prohibiting and punishing such behaviours. Most studies have found consistently high levels of agreement among various groups in their evaluation of specific criminal behaviours and these high correlations are commonly interpreted to reflect normative agreement regarding the public's evaluation of the seriousness of various criminal acts (Hansel, 1987; Rossi et al., 1974; Goff and Nason-Clark, 1989; Miethe, 1982; Warr, 1991). Studies by Shrager and Short (1980) and Parton and Stratton (1984) also show that people evaluate the seriousness of criminal behaviour based on the physical, psychological, and economic harm that the act represents. Robbery incorporates all three and is typically rated near the top of criminal offences as judged by their potential to do harm (Hansel, 1987; Rossi et al., 1974).

Boyd (1995:10) argues that a theory that demands a linkage between law and morality must specify the moral premises that will be operative at any specific time and place. What, then, are the values underlying society's support of laws that prohibit and punish robbery in Canada? The defining components of robbery include theft and injury or the threat of violence against other persons. Laws that prohibit robbery and define it as evil, harmful, and disruptive of social order are based on strong societal values that are protective of private property and human life. It can reasonably be argued that most Canadians support the values that protect people against the theft, psychological trauma, and violence that robbery represents. In this sense, the law prohibiting this behaviour is based on a high degree of value consensus within our society.

It can be assumed that one measure of how strongly a society feels about its norms is the punishment applied to those who violate them. One problem with this argument, Durkheim (1969:72) contends, is that even when a criminal act is regarded as harmful to society, the amount of harm that it does is not regularly related to the intensity of the punishment that it metes out. Factors other than the objective harm that a behaviour represents influence the societal definition of the act as criminal. In addition, there are disagreements on how to deal with people who commit robbery and what type of sentence is appropriate. Even if value consensus exists about the evilness of this crime, there will be disagreements concerning the threat or harm that specific incidents of robbery represent or cause. This will lead to disagreements concerning punishment that in turn will result in sentencing disparities. For example, one bank robber from this study received six life sentences for his third robbery conviction while another bank robber was placed on probation. Both had committed their latest robbery unarmed. In complaining about his sentence, the inmate who was serving life asked: "Six life sentences! For what? For what?" The latter offender, however, robbed only one bank; committed his holdup spontaneously and under the influence of alcohol; turned himself into the police the following day; and cooperated with the investigation. His remorse and lack of a criminal record persuaded the judge that a prison sentence was unwarranted.

Conflict Theories of Law and Criminality

Through the 1970s and 1980s, conflict theorists critically examined traditional approaches to criminology, offered alternative explanations of crime, law, and social control, and produced significant research studies. Conflict theorists reject the assumption that societies are based upon a shared consensus about important norms and values. Instead, they assume that the most noteworthy feature of any complex society is the presence of conflict between segments of society that differ in terms of social power and other resources. The important task for criminological theory, therefore, is to understand processes of law-making and law-breaking within the context of the conflict-oriented nature of society.

Several writers have classified conflict theory into two broad categories: (a) liberal conflict (pluralistic or interest group) theories, and (b) radical (or Marxist) theories (Williams and McShane, 1988; Bernard, 1981; Gibbons, 1979 and 1992; Turk, 1986; Silverman et al., 1991; Gomme, 1993). Both theories highlight the roles of social conflict and power in producing deviance and crime. Liberal conflict theorists tend to view social conflict as involving a wide variety of groups in society. They conceptualize conflicts as emerging when various interests groups compete for social or economic advantage. Society is composed of a variety of competing groups with different and fluctuating sources of power. In contrast, radical theories of social conflict, which derive from the writings of Karl Marx, conceptualize social conflict primarily in terms of a struggle between social classes based on the inequalities of capitalistic societies.

Whereas conventional theories of crime have focused on the offender and attempted to explain motivational factors, a conflict perspective takes a very different view of crime, law, and social control. As a theory of crime, the conflict perspective—particularly the Marxist view—argues that capitalistic society benefits an elite class and is structured so that a huge underclass is deprived of material wealth. In other words, people are driven to law-breaking by economic oppression. As a theory of law, conflict models argue that laws are not based on consensus but on the power of the ruling classes. Law serves the interests of the elite and legitimizes the rights of the more powerful interest groups. As a theory of social control, conflict theories argue that law and the criminal justice system are used to maintain the status quo and punish those who threaten the wellbeing of the elite. Law results from the ability of more powerful members of society to impose their definition of behaviour upon those who are less powerful. The ruling class controls the political system and has the power to define any behaviour that threatens its own interests as illegal. Instead of arising from consensus and providing justice for all, in reality the law is a weapon of oppression and the police are servants of the ruling elite. Marxist criminologists argue that capitalists use criminal law to maintain their dominance through intimidation. Austin Turk (1976) argues that it is useful to think of the law as a "weapon in social conflict" and as a resource that more powerful groups may be able to secure to resolve conflicts in their favour.

If we apply a Marxist perspective to robbery, criminologists would argue that capitalism exploits workers by paying wages that do not reflect the true value of their labour. This creates poverty and an underclass, some of whom are motivated to steal or rob to survive. Criminals recognize the inequities in society and their illegal conduct is an unsophisticated attempt to restore economic balance. According to conflict theorists, for society to blame the offender who is both poor and oppressed is tantamount to blaming the victim. Even so, the ruling class creates crimes of theft and robbery to protect private property and have arrested those who would threaten their wealth and privileged position. From this perspective, acts that are prohibited by the Criminal Code are often not crimes at all, but instead are expressions of the will of the ruling class. "Real crime" stems from the actions of the political and economic ruling elite and from their power over law-making, policing, and the dispensation of justice. Thus although many of the behaviours of the capitalistic classes may be harmful to society, they have not been defined as criminal because their victims do not control the law. The causes of elite deviance, Marxist theorists maintain, rest in the single-minded pursuit of profit and power (Gomme, 1993:134). This leads to the creation of unsafe working conditions, the pollution of the environment, the manufacture of poor-quality goods and dangerous consumer products, monopolistic prices, low wages, worker exploitation, unfair tax laws, and other behaviours that cause great harm to society. Street crimes such as drug-dealing, petty theft, and minor acts of violence have comparatively little impact on society, whereas corporate and state wrongdoings have serious detrimental effects on many persons. For conflict theorists, the behaviours that should be defined as crimes are the harmful acts of the ruling class.

The claim by some Marxist theorists that violent and predatory criminal activity is a political response to oppression, marginalization, and exploitation is scoffed at by critics who see this as an overly romantic caricature. Killers, robbers, and thieves, Toby argues (1980) are not Robin Hoods and freedom-fighters involved in class warfare. A more moderate position taken by other conflict theorists, known as left realists, makes no claim regarding the political nature of street crime but nonetheless regards it as at least partly a response to deprivation. Left realists criticize the romantic portrayals of ordinary offenders by conflict theorists and argue that earlier versions of radical thought overemphasized the crimes of the socially powerful. Left realism takes into account victimization studies that demonstrate why street crime is a serious problem and how it affects society's disadvantaged more so than its privileged. Left realism thus attempts to retain the conflict orientation, while at the same time recognizing the exploitive nature of street crime and its harmful effect on its victims (Gibbons, 1992:132; Gomme, 1993:123). Although conflict theorists may disagree among themselves on whether the capitalist class alone or in concert with other power groups control the enactment of law, they agree that it is mainly conflict and power that determine the law.

Robbery Legislation— Conflict or Consensus?

Where does this discussion lead us in relation to the crime of robbery and the law that defines it as a serious criminal offence? Critics dispute claims by conflict theorists that laws serve only the interests of the ruling elite. Research by Rossi et al. (1974), for instance, indicates that laws prohibiting murder, sexual assault, robbery, and theft are viewed as serving all citizens and have broad value consensus. Similarly, Gomme (1993:123) argues that not only do such statutes reflect the interests of all citizens, but they also protect the weak and the powerless. No doubt there exists a strong societal consensus in Canada and widespread support for laws prohibiting theft with violence. Moreover, the very existence of a legal system in a democratic society presupposes a certain degree of consensus concerning the moral and social legitimacy of our laws, police, courts, and political institutions. Canadians clearly demonstrate a respect for law and order, recognize the right to protect private property, and condemn violence against innocent victims. It is therefore reasonable to apply a value consensus model to an understanding of the laws that prohibit the crime of robbery.

In addition, there is little validity to the assertion that criminals in Canadian society, although they may come from a socially disadvantaged group, are striking out against a ruling and exploitive tyranny. On the contrary, their victims are frequently ordinary citizens who may be socially disadvantaged and in need of protection from these predatory criminals who make their life conditions worse. In addition, Canadian society offers support programs such as free health care, welfare, and unemployment insurance to meet the basic needs of its citizens. It is unlikely that offenders rob because they need money to survive.

Despite the fact that there exists widespread moral support for laws against robbery, the conflict/pluralistic model still has theoretical applicability in ways that will be discussed in later chapters. In particular, the conflict perspective helps to explain the over-representation of offenders from disadvantaged groups, gives insight into the disparities in sentencing, and helps to explain the greater investment by law-enforcement agencies in the investigation and prosecution of crimes against financial institutions as opposed to muggings or the robbery of small retail businesses. Conflict theory is clearly appropriate in analyzing the development of many laws, but laws that prohibit theft with violence benefit everyone and have widespread support in all societies. Thus consensus theory best explains the prohibition against this behaviour.

SUMMARY

Robbery is an offence in which force or the threat of force is used to deprive a person of his or her money and/or valuables. It is a crime that often traumatizes and/or physically injures the victim. Typically the offender and victim are strangers and the confrontation requires that the robber control the victim to complete the crime. Theory and research on this crime must examine the interaction between both parties and consider the techniques used in victim management. Types of robberies include (a) the mugging or robbery of individuals in public but discrete settings; (b) the robbery of small retail stores and other commercial businesses; and (c) holdups of financial institutions and armoured vehicles. Most robbers choose a modus operandi that focuses on one type of target over another and repeat their crimes in a similar manner.

In Canada, robbery is defined under section 343 of the Criminal Code and includes acts of theft or extortion in which violence or the threat of violence is used to overcome resistance. Robbery is a serious offence with a maximum penalty of life imprisonment. In addition, there are a variety of laws that relate to robbery offences including assault; wearing a disguise in the commission of an indictable offence; using, pointing, carrying a firearm; carrying a concealed weapon; and discharging a weapon with intent to wound, endanger, or escape. The Criminal Code also makes it an offence to attempt or to conspire to commit robbery. Furthermore, robbery creates the possibility that someone may be killed during the act, which could result in a charge of murder or manslaughter.

Depending on one's perspective, robbery can be conceptualized as an offence against the person and a crime of violence or as a property offence motivated by a desire for money. Criminologists are not only interested in studying criminal conduct, motivation, or the characteristics of individuals who violate the law, but are also interested in the process by which laws are constructed, certain acts are defined as criminal, and social control mechanisms are imposed to deal with prohibited conduct. From a sociological perspective, the laws that define behaviour as criminal are social products created in a social, political, and economic context. Two main theoretical models have been developed to explain how law evolves. Consensus theory suggests that laws reflect a common morality supported by the population at large. Conflict theories, on the other hand, see laws as resulting from conflict among competing groups in a heterogeneous society. Robbery is an offence that violates fundamental values that protect persons and their property. It is defined as theft with violence and laws that prohibit robbery appear to have broad value consensus in Canada and other countries.

CHAPTER 2

An Overview of Robbery

Dog Day Afternoon

They called it a hostage-taking situation. I don't really call it that. The police came and had the bank surrounded before we could get out. We were amateurs. Our plan was to go in there, grab the money, and take off. Never really thought of all the complications. Everything was messing up from the start. We had masks but I neglected to put mine on. A teller was talking on the telephone, saw the play, and said to her friend "Oh my God, we're being robbed! Call the cops." When we got in there, they all froze! They just sat there and everybody looked at us. Nobody was moving and I had to yell again. Then they snapped and started moving. You should have seen the fear on these people's faces. I told this old lady to open the tills but she had the wrong keys. I yelled at her a bit—tough-guy syndrome—and she started shaking. "Come on lady, you're stalling me here." You expect her to get the keys and open the drawers because you've got a gun and you're a bank robber.

You see, my vision of robbing a bank was what I had seen on T.V.—very naive. I never did this type of thing before. I never hung out with that kind of crowd that you could sit down with and say, "How's it done?" I never got coached. Most of the ideas, if you can call them that, are stuff that you can see on movies and T.V. And just stuff me and my partner put together. It sort of stemmed from my partner having some guns. We were talking about what we could do with them and the idea just popped into our heads. Rob a bank! I don't know how long we were in the bank before the police came.

3 IN BANK SURRENDER, FREE HOLD-UP HOSTAGES

TORONTO (CP)—A hostage-taking at a suburban bank ended peacefully Monday afternoon when three people surrendered to police about 80 minutes after an attempted robbery.

No shots were fired and the seven employees of the Canadian Imperial Bank of Commerce taken hostage were not harmed.

The drama began shortly after 3 p.m. when the would-be robbers entered the bank just as it was closing and produced three handguns. No customers were in the bank at the time.

A bank employee tripped a silent alarm shortly before the staff was ordered to lie on the floor. Two policemen responded to the alarm and called for reinforcements.

When the robbers tried to escape through the rear door of the bank, they saw the waiting police and ran back inside, where they forced the employees into the safe.

Police established contact with the three on the telephone and eventually talked them into surrendering.

"They said that if we stormed the bank they would start shooting hostages," said Insp. Roy Soplet of the Metropolitan Toronto Police. "But after a while they started to worry about what would happen if we came in.

"They realized that the only way out was to blast their way out," he continued. "The guy we were talking with kept his cool. Eventually, he said they didn't want to get shot."

Police have charged three persons with robbery and use of firearms in the commission of an indictable offence.

Source: Kitchener-Waterloo Record (*9 February 1982*). *Reprinted by permission of The Canadian Press.*

CHARACTERISTICS OF ROBBERY

AN UNSOPHISTICATED CRIME

> "I always picked them spontaneously just walking down the street."
>
> *—Heroin-addicted bank robber*

Early studies of robbery have presented an image of professional individuals or crews of armed men planning their crime in detail and executing it with speed and skill (DeBaun, 1950; Roebuck, 1967; Einstadter, 1969; Letkemann, 1973). Recent studies dispute this view and portray robbery as an unsophisticated crime committed by unskilled young men (Camp, 1968; Feeney and Weir, 1975; Petersilia, Greenwood, and Lavin, 1977; Gabor et al., 1987). The case example presented describes a holdup that goes wrong and illustrates a number of characteristics of robbers and robbery; the offenders are men in their early twenties; each has a criminal record but is criminally unsophisticated; they do little planning; they fail to consider the risks; and they are caught and sentenced to prison for several years. Although the robbers in this case are similar to most offenders, their robbery is somewhat atypical since it results in a hostage-taking incident and a woman is involved in the crime.

Camp (1968) notes that because of the increased risk and smaller profits, the role of professionals in robbery, particularly bank robbery, has declined dramatically since 1945. Gabor et al. (1987:48) argue that the classic studies depicting armed robbery as a vocation undertaken by fairly large gangs who meticulously plan and execute their crimes is probably outdated, if this "Hollywood image" ever applied at all to more than a very small fraction of armed robbers. What is astonishing about the new breed of armed robbers, they suggest, is the apparent absence of planning and the seemingly nonchalant attitudes about the consequences of their crimes (1987:28). Current research indicates that robbery is an unsophisticated crime committed by unsophisticated criminals. Most offenders are young men between 16 and 25 years of age, have less than a secondary-school education, come from a lower socioeconomic or blue-collar background, often have a drug or alcohol problem, and even commit offences while under their influence. The targets are usually convenience stores and other small businesses. Most report far more criminal activity than is indicated by their records and have committed a variety of offences before attempting robbery. As discussed in detail in Chapter Four, robbers rarely plan their crimes, they wear minimal or no disguise, steal small sums of cash, and seem unconcerned about the consequences of getting caught. Most are apprehended, convicted, and serve lengthy prison terms.

Gabor et al.'s (1987) study of 1,266 cases of armed robbery in Quebec, for instance, found that the suspect's age was usually under 22 years; no disguises were worn in three-quarters of the incidents; and half the subjects either did no planning whatsoever or only undertook about an hour of preparation. Feeney and Weir's (1975, 1986) study of 113 offenders describes the casual attitude that most robbers take toward their crimes. Not only were many robberies an impulsive act, but over one-half of the offenders reported not planning their offences and about two-thirds did not consider being apprehended by the police. Another

17 percent said that they had thought about the possibility but did not believe it to be a problem (Feeney, 1986:60–61).

Street robberies or muggings are considered to be the most crude type of holdup and are often opportunistic events. But even bank and commercial robberies commonly develop out of quickly made plans and involve minimal preparation or "casing" of the target. As a result, the amount of money obtained in all types of robbery is largely a matter of chance. Research also indicates that older, more experienced robbers are not necessarily more sophisticated in planning robberies. Katz (1988:172) suggests that the appropriate metaphor for "casing" is not that of the prudent investor assessing whether to take a calculated risk, but that of the sports player, evaluating the opposition's defensive setup before determining how to execute a play that will probably, but not inevitably, be successful.

THE FINANCIAL GAINS ARE SMALL

Research data and official statistics indicate that robbery usually provides small sums of money. How much cash can a robber expect from a holdup? The answer depends, of course, on the target selected since individuals, retail outlets, and other businesses vary in the amount of money they handle and leave vulnerable to robbery. For example, commercial robberies in the United States paid only a median amount of $35 in 1964 and $46 in 1968. Cab holdups and purse snatchings were even less profitable. By 1975, the average loss per robbery for retail stores was $154 nationally. The average take in 1986 was $303 for service-station robberies; only 15 percent of noncommercial victims reported losses of $500 or more in 1987; and in 1988, convenience-store robberies averaged a loss of $344. In approximately 40 to 50 percent of all retail robberies in these years, the victims reported theft losses of less than $100. In fact, dollar loss from robbery is a small percentage of the total retail-sales volume and is also small compared to losses from shoplifting and employee theft (Crow and Bull, 1975:16; Federal Bureau of Investigation, 1986–89; United States Bureau of Justice Statistics, 1989). Ethnographic evidence also indicates that burglary and robbery bring in small cash rewards of under $100 (Katz, 1988:164). Similarly, Gabor et al. (1987:105) found that over a quarter of the robberies in their Canadian study yielded $100 or less; more than half yielded under $200; less than a quarter brought in $500 or more for the perpetrator(s); and the average loss amounted to slightly over $300. Yet even these very modest profits often had to be divided among partners.

Bank robbers do much better financially than muggers or convenience-store robbers but they fare worse at getting away. Hold-Up Squads report clearance rates for bank robbery of 70 to 80 percent and this compares with a clearance rate of 33 percent for all robberies in Canada in 1992 (Statistics Canada, 1992:33). Data on bank robberies in Canada indicate that the net dollar loss for 1991 was $4.4 million in 1,609 holdups; $4.2 million in 1,530 robberies in 1992; and $4.0 million in 1,641 bank holdups in 1993. The average net loss per offence was approximately $2 800 in 1991; $2,925 in 1992, and $2,510 in 1993. The averages are partially misleading since less than $1,500 was stolen in 60 percent of bank robberies in 1991, 47 percent in 1992, and 48 percent in 1993. The median in all three years was approximately $1,500 and the percentage of robberies in which bandits walked out with less than $1,000 totalled 47 percent of 1991 holdups, 47 percent in 1992, and 48 percent in 1993. These amounts are also diminished in 20 to 25 percent of bank robberies since the proceeds must be shared with a partner(s). These data show that in the vast majority of cases, bank robbery provides small rewards for an offence that entails great risk.

Haran and Martin's study of 500 New York City bank robbers (1984:51) found that twelve percent of robbers received less than $500; 25 percent less than $1,500; 50 percent less than $3,500; and 75 percent received less than $8,000. Sixteen robbers received $10,000 each and 14 (less than three percent) achieved a big score of $40,000 each. Although these sums are not insignificant, the risks are high. The authors note that a new breed of bank robbers has emerged in the United States. In the 1960s in New York, most bank robbers were white males in their late twenties or early thirties who carefully planned their offences to maximize gain and minimize risk. "He was a 'pro' with a certain maturity and pride in his criminal activity and prestige among his peers" (1977:29). Currently, however, bank robbers are usually black, in their mid-twenties, often addicted to opiates, unskilled and unsophisticated, do little planning, choose their accomplices casually, and form loose groups thrown together for the job. The robberies are amateurishly conceived and executed. Professional criminals seldom rob banks anymore because the crime simply doesn't pay enough for the risks involved. Haran and Martin (1977:29–30) conclude that bank robbery is a crime for which most people are caught and imprisoned for years, with little chance of early parole. The amateur robbers, however, appear to be unaware of the enormous risks and penalties attached to their crime.

Since robbery pays so little, the proceeds are spent quickly and the offenders soon return for more. Robbery, therefore, is a crime that is usually repeated until the culprits are arrested. As will be seen in Chapter Four, offenders also use the same modus operandi time and again.

STRANGER AND VICTIM

The Canadian Urban Victimization telephone survey (Solicitor General of Canada, 1984) of 61,000 persons age 15 and over found that 82 percent of robberies against individuals were committed by strangers, 16 percent by acquaintances, and only two percent by relatives, spouses, or ex-spouses. Nearly half of the incidents involving strangers were reported to police but only 29 percent of those involving acquaintances led to official complaints being made. Statistics Canada's Uniform Crime Reporting (UCR) survey for 1992 indicates that the relationship of the accused to the victim was coded by the police as strangers in 69 percent of incidents of robbery and as unknown in 19 percent of robbery offences. Most of the "unknowns" are likely strangers as well (Statistics Canada, 1992:62). The General Social Survey (Sacco and Johnson, 1990) of 9,870 Canadians age 15 and over found a much lower percentage (45 percent) of the incidents classified as robbery were committed by strangers. In one-third of the cases, the offender was an acquaintance of the victim while in the remaining instances, offenders were relatives or unspecified persons. Most robberies occurred away from the victim's residence whereas other crimes such as assault typically occurred at or near the victim's home (Sacco and Johnson, 1990:91).

On occasion, culprits may target persons or businesses known to them but they are likely to disguise themselves to avoid being identified. The insider-offender will have the advantage that he or she is more familiar with the setting, the victim's habits, and the potential gain than if he or she were a stranger. An unknown proportion of robberies by "acquaintances" appear to evolve out of illicit sexual or drug activities where a brief relationship may have existed between the offender and the victim. In these cases, the victim may fail to report the holdup because of his or her own discrediting/criminal conduct.

Crimes such as assault, sexual assault, and homicide typically involve victims and offenders who know one another. Robbery, on the other hand, is usually committed by a stranger in a surprising and highly threatening manner. Although some robberies of individuals occur between persons who know one another, most holdups, particularly those of commercial and financial outlets, are committed by strangers. It can be concluded based on the victimization research on unreported robberies and official reports of holdups known to the police, that robbery is typically a stranger-to-stranger criminal event. Since the motive is to obtain money and then escape, maintaining one's anonymity helps to prevent apprehension and conviction in a criminal trial.

VICTIM CONFRONTATION

Robbery was one of the first types of behaviour codified into law and it is prohibited and controlled in all modern cultures. Robbery is generally classified as an offence against the person because the offender confronts a victim and uses violence to steal money or other valuables. Besides the loss of property, there is always a possibility of bodily injury. In addition, the courts have recently considered the psychological or emotional trauma that victims experience, which has resulted in increasing the seriousness of the crime in sentencing. It is the suddenness, the threat, the confrontation with a stranger, and the unknown response that gives robbery its potential for violence. Despite the threat to the person that a holdup represents, some researchers define robbery as a property crime because many holdups are accomplished without physical force or violence. Gibbons (1992:229), for example, argues that although robbers sometimes threaten or use force, it is essentially incidental to the real purpose of the crime—namely, to relieve the victim of money or other personal property. Haran and Martin (1984:51–52) similarly refer to bank robbery fundamentally as a property crime, and suggest that the range of penalties in U.S. courts should be reduced from the life sentences that many states allow. Normandeau (1972:15), on the other hand, points out that robbery is also an assault and differs from other property offences in that the perpetrator physically confronts and dominates the victim. Subterfuge is not usually part of this "heavy" crime.

Luckenbill (1980:365) defines the core element of robbery as the transformation of interaction between the offender and target from some routine frame, such as that between a customer and clerk, to the robbery frame. The robbery frame consists of two basic elements: (1) to avoid death or serious injury, the target should suppress opposition and permit the offender to take his or her goods or otherwise assist in the transfer; (2) the offender should control the target's conduct by means of force. Similarly, Letkemann (1973) differentiates between offences committed surreptitiously (e.g., burglary) and overt crimes such as robbery, which involve direct confrontation with the victim. Clearly, theory and research on robbery must consider the confrontational and violent nature of the interaction that occurs between the offender and the victim.

VICTIM MANAGEMENT

Whereas surreptitious criminals avoid their victims, robbery requires that the offender interact with his or her target. Letkemann (1973) uses the term "management" to differentiate this process from what might be termed "victim manipulation," which is used by fraud artists. To this end, robbers employ a number of techniques: (1) they choose victims who are vulnerable; (2) they use speed and surprise to control victims; and (3) they use a weapon and/or threats and violence to gain compliance. In addition to controlling the victim, robbers must also handle their own fears and deal with the danger that offender-victim confrontations create. Letkemann (1973) argues that the skills associated with robbery include those necessary for the management and manipulation of people. Although there are some mechanical or technical skills needed to commit robbery, the fact that the victim is present and must be controlled adds a significant dimension to the offence. Victim management is a skill that the robber must develop to be successful in this type of crime.

Since robbery is an overt crime in which the robber must confront and control the victim to achieve his or her goal, robbers must be willing to face the possibility of resistance. In fact, they must be aware of a number of risks: they may be hurt or they may harm the victim because of victim resistance; they may be identified by the victim who is now a witness; the police or other witnesses may intervene; and they are likely to receive a lengthy prison sentence if they are apprehended and convicted. Like other offenders, the robber must learn to avoid identification, apprehension, and conviction. Letkemann notes that from an objective and rational perspective, the probability of a prison sentence should deter the criminal. It does not deter him or her, he argues, because the culprit cannot afford to consider this possibility (in particular, just before a holdup) because he or she will lose confidence. "At that stage, it is rational not to consider failure, since by so doing you will bring it upon yourself all the more surely" (1973:112).

TYPES OF ROBBERIES

Robberies can be classified into three distinct types based on victims/target characteristics: (a) muggings of individuals; (b) commercial robberies; (c) and bank and other financial institution holdups.

MUGGINGS

The term "mugging" as used by offenders and the police refers to acts of robbery committed in public and semi-public places against individuals involved in their everyday activities. The attack is immediately threatening because the victim fears for his or her safety and life if the transaction does not proceed smoothly. Typically, the victim is accosted by a stranger who uses force and/ or produces a weapon to gain compliance. Furthermore, the mugging usually takes place in a secluded area in which the victim is vulnerable and isolated—at night in a park, a stairwell, parking garage, or in an alleyway.

Robbers may use stealth and surprise to overcome their victims. This type of attack, referred to as "blind-side mugging" (Katz, 1988:170), relies not only on bulk or strength but also on physical speed and agility. Another technique is to choose victims who are particularly vulnerable, such as people who are intoxicated. Once known as "jackrolling" (Shaw, 1930), the selection of drunk victims is especially attractive to young robbers. Like blind-side muggings, the robber feels secure that he or she will not be well identified.

Robbers may use a certain degree of trickery to lure victims to an appropriate place to be robbed. The classic strategy, known as "the Murphy," takes advantage of a moral weakness built on the victim's physical desires. For example, a prostitute may lure a customer to a private place, where he is assaulted by a stickup man while she mysteriously vanishes. His prospects of pleasure abruptly fold up and disappear, like a Murphy bed (Katz, 1988:171; Brown, 1965:154). The victim is doubly disabled, by the isolation he sought and by the illicit nature of the scene, which will often inhibit his complaint. The stickup artist simultaneously rips off and ridicules the victim. A variation on the Murphy uses the lure of drug sales instead of sex. Sometimes stickups emerge only over the course of an evening, after several indications of the victim's weakness have materialized.

COMMERCIAL ROBBERIES

Commercial robberies include holdups of persons in the process of conducting business. These include robberies of retail businesses such as grocery stores, liquor outlets, gas stations, and convenience and drug stores. Taxi holdups have characteristics of both commercial and noncommercial robberies because the driver is engaged in business but is victimized in a manner similar to a mugging. These holdups are usually treated as commercial robberies, however, since their business activities, like convenience stores, make them an attractive and easily approachable target. In addition, like other commercial ventures, taxi drivers have adopted strategies to deter robbers and minimize their financial loss if a robbery occurs.

THE ROBBERY OF FINANCIAL INSTITUTIONS

The robbery of an individual or a convenience store results in small sums of money. Banks, however, represent a more profitable score. But financial institutions such as trust companies, credit unions, banks, and armoured vehicles have characteristics and policies that make them difficult targets. Unlike convenience stores, banks are not isolated, do not operate in the late evening, nor are they staffed by a single person. They are generally located in busy commercial areas, employ a large number of staff, and use security measures such as cameras, silent alarms, locked safes, and time-locks. Some also have controlled entrances and armed guards to deter potential bank robbers. Thus, financial institutions are better prepared to deal with robbery and represent an intimidating target to robbers. It is not surprising, therefore, that offenders who rob banks are generally older and more experienced than those who commit muggings and commercial robberies. The average age of bank robbers in the present study, for example, was 31 at the time of interview and 24.6 at the time of their first bank holdup.

In fact, bank robbers tend to view muggers as "punks," who "make it hot for everybody." Small neighbourhood grocery stores and gas stations are the domain of these punks. The cost-benefit tradeoff of ease in getting away versus the likelihood of getting away without much, makes muggings especially appealing to the young and disdained by the experienced career robbers (Einstadter, 1969:80; Katz, 1988:169).

THE ROBBERY RATE

Recent Canadian crime statistics (Statistics Canada, 1991 & 1992) indicate that 33,225 and 33,186 robbery offences were reported to police in 1991 and 1992. This translates into a 1991 and 1992 robbery rate for Canada of 123 and 121 incidents per 100,000 population respectively. The 1991 rate was the highest recorded since 1982 and marked the fourth consecutive year in which an increase was registered. It was also an increase of 16 percent over 1990 and 14 percent above the 1981 rate of 108. The 16 percent increase in the robbery rate over 1990 was the largest yearly increase recorded during the 1981–91 period. The 1992 rate is down slightly from 1991 but Statistics Canada cautions that this decrease may be due to a change in reporting practices in Metropolitan Toronto (Statistics Canada, 1992:32).

The 1991 and 1992 national rate for robbery with firearms was 33 and 32 offences per 100,000 population respectively. In the 15 years between 1977 and 1992, the rate of robbery incidents involving firearms has remained relatively stable. In 1977, the rate was 33 per 100,000, peaked at 36 in 1982, returned to 33 in 1991, and dropped slightly to 32 in 1992. In contrast, the rate for robbery with other offensive weapons has risen sharply from 14 incidents per 100,000 population in 1977 to 39 in 1992. The 1992 rate marked the fifth consecutive year in which this rate increased. The fact that gun usage has not increased in robberies but the use of other offensive weapons has increased significantly may be due in part to the gun-control provisions of the 1977 Bill C-51 Criminal Law Amendment Act, which provides an additional one year to the sentence of anyone convicted of using a firearm during a robbery.

Regionally, Quebec, with a rate of 59 and British Columbia with a rate of 33, were the only provinces to record a robbery with a firearm rate in 1992 that was higher than the national average of 32 per 100 000 population. Alberta, Manitoba, and Ontario recorded the next highest rates of 27, 25, and 23 per 100,000 population respectively. For the fifth consecutive year, the rate for robbery with other offensive weapons (39 per 100,000) was higher than the robbery with firearm rate (32 per 100,000). Only Quebec recorded rates of robbery with offensive weapons (55 per 100,000) that were higher than the national average.

Robbery rates in the United States (1962–91) have typically been two to three times higher than those found in Canada. Overall robbery rates in the U.S. range from a low of 59.4 per 100,000 population in 1962 to a high of 250.6 in 1981. Canada similarly had a low of 26.6 robberies per 100,000 in 1962, reached a high of 108.6 in 1981 and declined steadily until 1990, peaking again at 123 in 1991. Blau and Blau (1982) suggest that the higher U.S. robbery rate may be due to the higher level of income inequality and economic disparity in the United States, which create potentially violent situations.

Since 1974, when national data on armed robbery became available in Canada, official statistics show that American rates have been between two-and-a-half to three times those of Canada. The gap between the two countries has narrowed as the Canadian rate has increased during 1974–85 from 38.6 to 49 incidents per 100,000 population while the American rate has declined from 137.9 to 120.5 over the same period. Both countries

FIGURE 2.1

ROBBERY INCIDENTS, 1977 TO 1992

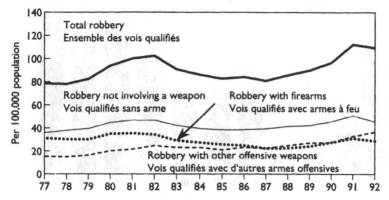

Reproduced by authority of the Minister of Industry, 1994, Statistics Canada, Cat. No. 85-205 (1992:32).

experienced a peak in their armed robbery rates in the early 1980s and have shown rather steady declines since then. Despite these fluctuations, the American rate has consistently been about two to three times greater than that of Canada. Within each country, however, major regional differences exist.

Bank robbery in Canada has increased throughout the 1980s and into the 1990s, from 1,160 annual holdups in 1984 to 1,641 in 1993. Most of the increase has occurred in Ontario and the western provinces, with the four Atlantic provinces averaging only eleven bank robberies per year from 1984 to 1993. The Quebec rate has fluctuated somewhat over the past ten years, ranging from a low of 480 in 1984 to a high of 626 in 1991. Bank robberies in Ontario have increased over the past ten years with a low figure of 246 holdups in 1986 to a high of 581 in 1993 (Ballard, 1994:28–30). Most of the increase in bank robberies in the 1980s and 1990s reflects the emergence of the so-called "beggar bandit"—the robber who works alone, enters the bank, and passes a note to the teller demanding ("begging for") money. The beggar bandit's modus operandi and the influence that the media have on motivation are discussed in later sections of this book.

Since the rapid increase in the rate of robbery in the 1960s and 1970s parallels the increase in violent and property crimes in both countries, many of the explanations for the overall increase in crime rates no doubt also apply to robbery. Both Canadian and American rates of violence have tripled between 1964 and 1985

FIGURE 2.2

CANADIAN BANK ROBBERIES 1984-1993

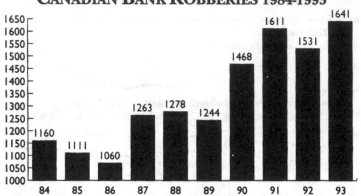

Source: Canadian Banker *(Ballard, 1994). Reprinted with permission.*

TABLE 2.1

Canadian Bank Robberies by Province
1984–1993

YEAR	B.C.	ALTA	SASK	MAN	ONT	QUE	NB	NS	PEI	NFLD	NWT	YKN	TOTAL
1984	225	103	11	26	303	480	2	7	2	1	0	0	1,160
1985	179	61	14	41	249	561	1	5	0	0	0	0	1,111
1986	147	107	33	37	246	496	3	1	0	0	0	0	1,070
1987	191	118	18	43	299	585	1	8	0	0	0	0	1,263
1988	212	91	12	71	364	511	6	10	0	1	0	0	1,278
1989	264	94	7	39	308	518	5	9	0	0	0	0	1,244
1990	304	87	11	79	460	512	2	13	0	0	0	0	1,468
1991	300	122	5	36	511	626	1	10	0	0	0	0	1,611
1992	227	130	14	60	463	619	5	10	1	0	1	1	1,531
1993	290	90	21	46	581	618	2	1	0	2	0	0	1,641
TOTAL	2,576	1,098	152	499	4,125	6,114	28	78	3	4	1	1	14,677

Source: Canadian Banker *(Ballard, 1994). Reprinted with permission.*

(Statistics Canada, 1986; Federal Bureau of Investigation, 1985; Brantingham and Brantingham, 1984). Thus, the rates of violence in general have increased at about the same pace as those of robbery and armed robbery since the 1960s. The trends in armed and unarmed robbery in both countries must be understood against this background of an overall increase in crime.

One explanation forwarded to explain increasing crime rates is the demographic hypothesis. The "baby boom" of the postwar years led to a large increase of the teenage population in the 1960s and 1970s and this demographic trend coincided with a rise in the crime rate in Canada and the United States. Since most robbery offenders are young adults, the increase in crime is attributed to the growing number of persons in this crime-prone age group. The slowdown in the crime rate during the 1980s may be explained in part by the fact that the proportion of the population in prime crime ages has declined in that time period.

The increased use of hard drugs is also suggested as a reason for the increasing crime rate (Inciardi, 1981). The rise in crime during the 1960s and 1970s parallels the great increase in drug usage, particularly among young persons. Drug usage is strongly associated with crime as many drug users turn to crime to support their addiction. Although the crime/drug association is complex, research on the link between crime and drug usage has shown that some addicts admit to having committed thousands of predatory street crimes to support their habit (Ball, 1981). The relationship between drug usage and crime is discussed in Chapter Four, which deals with motivation.

Conklin (1972:181) suggests that the increased availability and ownership of firearms may also affect the rising crime rate. Two young men in my study, for example, indicated that they had moved from break and enter to robbery after finding a handgun in one of the homes that they had burgled. The gun provided the means to commit robbery. The greater availability of guns in the United States might explain in part why the U.S. robbery rate is consistently higher than the Canadian rate.

URBANIZATION AND ROBBERY

Increases in crime since World War II, and particularly in the 1960s, have occurred virtually worldwide. Some theorists explain this phenomenon by pointing to the trend towards increased urbanization and the social dislocation that this entails (Radzinowicz and King, 1977). Philip Cook (1983) calls robbery the "quintessential urban crime" due to the anonymity of city life and the virtually unlimited number of targets in an urban centre. Research and official crime statistics consistently show that robberies are overwhelmingly committed in large urban areas (Conklin, 1972; Crow and Bull, 1975; Hartnagel and Lee, 1990).

An overview of bank robbery in Canada reveals the urban nature of this crime. Almost 90 percent of bank holdups occur in the three most populous provinces: British Columbia, Ontario, and Quebec. In 1993, 70 percent of Canadian bank robberies took place in our seven largest urban areas and most of the remaining 30 percent also occurred in relatively large cities. Major cities account for most bank holdups within their respective province in 1993 with Montreal having 73 percent; Toronto 51 percent; Winnipeg 93 percent; Edmonton 47 percent; Calgary 43 percent; Vancouver 58 percent; and Ottawa 17 percent. Looking at overall robbery statistics for Canadian cities, Montreal is the robbery capital of Canada, with a rate of 459.6 offences per 100,000 population while Toronto is at the other end of the scale with a rate of 96.8 per 100,000—about one-fifth the Montreal rate. Calgary is also at the low end of the scale with a rate of 99.5, while Vancouver and Edmonton fall in between with rates of 214.2 and 200.6 per 100,000 population, respectively. In absolute numbers, Montreal retains the title of bank robbery capital of Canada with 454 robberies in 1993. Expressed as a ratio of holdups to branches, Montreal, with one robbery for every 1.2 branches ranks second to Vancouver, which experienced a rate of one robbery for every 1.1 branches, almost one robbery on average for every bank branch in the city. The ratio for other cities are Toronto, 1:2.7; Ottawa, 1:1.5; Winnipeg, 1:4.2; Edmonton 1:4.5; Calgary 1:5.3; and the combined ratio for other Canadian cities 1:10.4 (Ballard, 1994). Although bank robbery rates and patterns may be fairly consistent over time, across provinces, and from city to city, the figures do fluctuate annually. The arrest of a small number of prolific bandits can dramatically reduce the robbery rate overnight. Similarly, the success of a few bandits over an extended period will dramatically increase the robbery rate in the cities in which they operate.

The extent to which robbery in the United States is an urban crime can be appreciated by looking at the FBI's Uniform Crime Reports. There is a positive, linear relationship between the size of American cities and their robbery rates. For example, cities of over one million people collectively have the highest rates, cities between 250,000 and one million people have the next highest rates, and this pattern continues through to the smallest cities and rural communities, which have the lowest rates (FBI, 1985). Several theoretical perspectives have tried to explain the connection between urban centres and crime including (a) social disorganization theory, (b) inequality theory, (c) demographic hypotheses, and (d) opportunity, routine activity, and social control theory.

According to social disorganization theory, urbanization is equated with a heterogenous population, anonymity, lack of common values, lack of family controls, and a weakening of interpersonal ties, primary relations, and normative consensus.

TABLE 2.2

Robberies by Major Cities 1992 & 1993

# 1993 RANK	CITY	# HOLDUPS 1992	# HOLDUPS 1993	1992 RANK	% OF CHANGE	# BRANCHES 1993	RATIO: HOLDUPS /BRANCH 1993	RATIO RANK 1993
1	MONTREAL (MUC)	446	454	1	+ 2	556	1: 1.2	2
2	TORONTO (METRO)	231	299	2	+23	802	1: 2.7	4
3	VANCOUVER	111	169	3	+34	196	1: 1.1	1
4	OTTAWA	55	98	7	+44	145	1: 1.5	3
5	WINNIPEG	58	43	6	−35	182	1: 4.2	5
6	EDMONTON	67	38	4	−76	172	1: 4.5	6
7	CALGARY	60	32	5	−87	171	1: 5.3	7
X	ELSEWHERE	503	508	X	X	5,294	1: 10.4	X
X	TOTAL	1,531	1,641	X	+7	7,518	1: 4.6	X

Source: Canadian Banker *(Ballard, 1994). Reprinted with permission.*

These factors result in increased crime because the informal mechanisms of social control break down. Radzinowicz and King (1977) argue that city life offers increased criminal opportunities and fewer controls (particularly informal social controls) over behaviour. Modernization brings rising expectations and undermines family cohesion as parents spend more time at work and less time at home. Social disorganization theory argues that fewer persons in urban areas are effectively controlled by internalized value systems and informal social control mechanisms. However, the theory does not explain motivation to crime. Critics also challenge social disorganization theory by positing the existence of small and effective primary groups in large urban environments.

Demographic characteristics of urban versus rural populations have also been used to account for differing crime rates. Because of migration to the city, greater proportions of young, unattached, crime-prone males in the city help account for the crime/urban phenomenon. The demographic explanation and social disorganization theory are not mutually exclusive, however, since it can be argued that young, unattached males may be less socially integrated and therefore less subject to the restraining influence of social groups (Hartnagel and Lee, 1990:174).

A number of theories account for the urban/crime association by pointing to the social and economic inequality in large urban areas. A study by Carroll and Jackson (1983) looked at rates for robbery, burglary, and crimes against persons in a sample of ninety-three U.S. cities and found that levels of income inequality were directly related to crime. The researchers concluded that increased opportunities to engage in crime do not themselves result in higher crime rates; there must also be factors that motivate potential offenders to break the law. Theories that implicate income inequality in higher crime rates presume a degree of awareness on the part of those who are economically deprived and that this awareness provides the motivation for their lawbreaking. These theories suggest that crime results from poverty either through absolute or relative deprivation. Absolute deprivation explanations focus on the criminogenic conditions of life experienced by the poor and oppressed in the slums of our cities. Conflict theory, for example, associates crime with exploitation and alienation of the working class. From this perspective, people commit crime because they desperately need the money.

The concept of relative deprivation emphasizes poverty in the midst of wealth. Merton's anomie theory suggests that the important motivational component for certain crimes is deprivation or inequality in the face of plenty. While others have an abundance of wealth, some have very little. Blau and Blau (1982) argue that relative deprivation engenders a sense of injustice and hostility that is criminogenic. Conklin (1972:86) notes that since few bank robbers in his study are starving when they commit their holdups, the concept of relative deprivation offers a better explanation of their reasons for stealing.

While these theories focus on factors that motivate offenders and the social structural variables that allegedly generate higher crime rates, opportunity theory emphasizes the crime-eliciting potential of immediate circumstances or situations. Opportunity theory suggests that certain features of the urban environment increase opportunity for crime. Robbers prefer urban areas because there are large numbers of potential targets, many opportunities to escape anonymously into the crowd, and easy access to transportation.

Routine activities theory argues that crime rates are affected not only by the absolute size of the supply of offenders, targets, or guardianship, but also by the factors affecting the frequency of their convergence in space and time. Cohen and Felson (1979) suggest that changes in North American society since the end of World War II have increased the likelihood of victimization. The world beyond the household, rather than the household itself, has increasingly become the locus of routine activities. Because modern metropolitan life separates people from family and household itself settings, it draws strangers together, assembles adolescents without parents or other adults who know them, and otherwise weakens informal social control. A tight community—where people know people, property, and their linkages—offers little opportunity for predatory exploitative crime. The dispersion of families and friends in large cities and the increased use of cars make it more difficult to supervise young people. Such changes have important implications for the levels of victimization. The dispersion of routine activities away from the home increases the probability that people will come into contact with strangers who might threaten them with criminal harm.

> As daily activity patterns disperse people away from family and household situations, it is more likely that criminogenic conditions will apply. Not only will offenders find targets with guardians absent, but they will be able to get away from their handlers and be fairly sure that their handlers will not recognize the loot or compare notes with the guardians. It is not that urbanities lack friends or family ties, or that they are unhandled, but merely that their handlers are scattered and segregated from the suitable targets and capable guardians (Felson, 1986:123–24).

Cohen and Felson's analysis implies that these changes will increase victimization levels even if the number of motivated offenders does not increase. Crime is not simply the product of an offender's intention but also of the spatial and temporal combination of this intention with other elements. Routine activities theory also argues that a proliferation of consumer goods accounts for increasing crime rates in the 1960s and 1970s. Felson (1987:911) argues that modern society invites high crime rates by offering temptations with many illegal opportunities. Predatory crime rate increases in North America since World War II can be explained in large part by expanded crime opportunities.

CHARACTERISTICS OF OFFENDERS

AGE OF OFFENDERS

Research and official statistics on robbery indicate that most offenders are relatively young. Statistics Canada (1992) reports that one out of four (27.22 percent) robbers charged by Canadian police in 1991 was under 18 years of age. A New York City study indicates that the majority of bank robbers (71 percent) were in the 16- to 30-year-old age bracket, with 35 percent between the ages of 21 and 25, and 48 percent within the relatively young age bracket of 16 to 25 years of age (Haran and Martin, 1984); Ottawa robbers averaged 24 years of age (Ciale and Leroux, 1983); and Camp's (1968) sample of bank robbers similarly fell within the 20 to 30 age bracket. In a study of 28 muggers, the ages ranged from 14 to 32, and the median age was 21 (Lejeune and Alex, 1973). Crow and Bull (1975) found in their study of convenience-store robberies that the estimated age of robbers included 22 percent below the age of 20 and 68 percent between 20 to 30 years old. In an examination of 1,266 cases of armed robbery in Montreal and Quebec City using police files, Gabor et al., (1987:38) similarly found that 85 percent of suspects were estimated by victims and witnesses to be under 25 years of age, with the most active category (44 percent) between 18 to 21 years. U.S. statistics similarly indicate that robbery arrests peak at ages 17 and 18 (Federal Bureau of Investigation, 1987 and 1988).

Data indicate that muggings are more likely to be committed by youthful or teenage offenders, and bank robberies by men in their twenties. This may be due to the fact that young persons have less experience with banks on a day-to-day basis and thus find them more intimidating than retail outlets as potential targets. Robbery is also more often a group activity for young offenders (Reiss, 1988). In recent U.S. crime surveys, victims report that they were attacked by multiple offenders in about 25 percent of the robberies in which the offenders appeared to be between the ages of 12 and 20, compared to about eight percent of robberies in which the offenders seemed to be 30 or over (Bureau of Justice Statistics, 1989). According to the reports of robbers themselves, bank robbery is pursued at more advanced ages because robbing banks is easier than robbing convenience stores, individuals, or committing other financial crimes. Research on other conventional crimes reveals similar patterns to robbery. A U.S. study indicates that the median age of persons arrested for burglary is 17. Burglars are described as having limited skills at gaining entrance to buildings, as doing little scouting or planning, and as reaping modest profits for their efforts (Reppetto, 1976).

Arrest statistics and research data typically do not differentiate between first and repeat offenders nor do they differentiate between the age at arrest (or interview) and the age at which offenders commit their first robbery. When such data are available, it appears that offenders often commit their first robberies at a very young age. Even though the median age for muggers in Lejeune's and Alex's (1973) study, for example, is 21 years, the median age at the time of their first offence is only 14 years. Similarly, Gabor et al. (1987) found that the criminality of chronic offenders in their sample began at 12 or 13 years of age while that of occasional offenders started, on the average, at 15 years.

THE AGE-CRIME CURVE

The relation between age and crime, as seen in official criminal statistics for any given year, is well known. Typically, the crime rate increases from the minimum age of criminal responsibility to reach a peak in the teenage years; it then declines rapidly throughout life (Farrington, 1986; Blumstein et al., 1988). Gottfredson and Hirschi point out that this sudden rise and rapid decline in criminality characterizes the age-crime relation regardless of sex, race, country, time, or offence. "Indeed, the persistence of this relation across time and culture is phenomenal. As long as records have been kept, in all societies in which such records are available, it appears that crime is an activity highly concentrated among the young" (1986:219–20).

Persons under 25 are disproportionally involved in criminality compared with the rest of the population and it is clear that robbery, like other conventional crimes, is a young person's offence. Farrington (1986:230–35) has suggested that the age-crime relationship can be explained by familiar theoretical constructs, including variations with age in the strength and sources of social control, mechanisms for behavioural reinforcement, and variations in ease of access to legitimate means of obtaining economic resources. Social control theory points out that although young children are influenced by their parents, teenagers gradually break away and become influenced instead by peers, who may encourage offending. The rate of offending declines in the twenties as peer influences give way to family influence, except that now the family influence originates in spouses rather than parents. People desist from offending as adult reinforcers, such as employment, income, spouses, and children, become available. Research supports the notion that poor parental control and delinquent peers are both important correlates of delinquent conduct (Loeber and Dishion, 1983; Elliott, Huizinga, and Ageton, 1985).

Also consistent with social control theory, Gabor et al. (1987) found that young robbers are less deterred or fearful of prison sentences than older men who have already served time. Older offenders admit that they too were less worried about apprehension and imprisonment when they were younger. The researchers surmise that young men are more likely to take risks than older men, who are more deterred and feel that they have more to lose, such as their jobs and families.

Greenberg (1979a, 1983) emphasizes the role of economic factors in explaining the age-crime curve. He argues that juveniles have financial needs but are excluded from the labour market or limited to part-time, poorly paid jobs. Because they have insufficient funds from legitimate sources to finance their social needs, they use illegitimate means. When they become adults, leaving school, employment, military enlistment, and marriage eliminate major sources of criminogenic frustration and at the same time supply informal social controls that are lacking in their teenage years. Blumstein et al. (1986) suggest that offending decreases with age partly because of incapacitating sentences. Offenders who maintain a high level of activity are removed from the game. "In the criminal justice system as it now operates, superstars have the shortest rather than the longest careers" (1986:224).

MALE VERSUS FEMALE CRIMINALITY

Data from Statistics Canada indicate that 93 percent of robbers charged by Canadian police in 1992 were men. Other studies reveal the same pattern: of 500 convicted armed bank robbers from the New York City area, 96 percent of the offenders were male (Haran and Martin, 1984); 102 of 108 offenders charged with armed robbery in Ottawa were males (Ciale and Leroux, 1983); a sample of 28 persons involved in muggings included 24 males and four females (Lejeune and Alex, 1973); and over 97 percent of bank robberies committed across Canada in 1991 were committed by men (Ballard, 1992:30). Research also indicates that when women are involved in robbery, they usually act with men. Of the 18 convicted female bank robbers in the New York City study, only two assumed a principal role in the crime and only one was known to be armed. The others drove getaway cars or provided ancillary services (Haran and Martin, 1984).

Sociologists frequently express concerns about arrest data because they suspect or presume the existence of gender, class, and racial biases. Whereas it is argued that the system is biased against racial minorities, the arguments about gender tend to emphasize biases in favour of women. Women's involvement in crime is assumed to be under-represented compared with men's involvement because women are less likely to be arrested, prosecuted, and convicted. Research indicates, however, that this is not necessarily true. For example, Michael Hindelang's (1979) analysis of victimization data in the United States reveals that both self-reports of victimization and arrest data show clearly that male involvement in crimes such as rape, robbery, assault, and burglary is proportionately much greater than that of females. He notes that official arrest data and victimization data agree regarding the relative frequency of women's involvement in specific crimes: female offenders infrequently use force against a person (robbery) or enter a structure illegally (burglary) in crimes of theft. They are most likely to be involved in theft crimes that do not require force. Results strongly suggest that gender is a central correlate of involvement in the crimes examined and cannot be dismissed as simply an artifact of biases reflected in arrest statistics (Hindelang, 1979:153).

With reference to gender, the statistical description of the relationship generally cites a ratio of 10 to 15 robberies by men for each robbery by a woman. Gender is clearly an important correlate of involvement in criminal behaviour and gender differences in criminal conduct need to be incorporated into theoretical explanations. To many commentators, the contemporary problem of robbery can be viewed as a way in which people with unusually limited means obtain what the commercial culture encourages everyone to need. If poverty and the lack of economic opportunity do not themselves direct men toward robbery, they are often thought to create a range of associated social problems, such as drug addiction, which regularly do (Katz, 1988:165). Anomie theory as presented by Merton suggests that differential male involvement in crime occurs because monetary success goals are more acutely applied to men than women. Critics point out, however, that as women have progressively moved into the business world over the past two decades—and presumably sought financial success—their involvement in crime, and in robbery in particular, has not increased. It can be argued that the suffering that poverty brings is the same or perhaps even greater for women and that materialistic and utilitarian explanations of gender differences in robbery rates are therefore inadequate.

A version of control theory formulated by Hagan, Simpson, and Gillis (1979, 1985, 1987, 1988) offers another explanation of male/female differential involvement in criminal and delinquent activity. By integrating control theory with insights offered by Marxist and feminist criminologists, "power-control theory" maintains that gender differences in criminal conduct are rooted in historical changes that have assigned men and women to different social realms and created differences in the kinds of social control to which each gender group is subjected. Specifically, as modern industrial economies developed, spheres of consumption and production emerged. The growth of the criminal justice system, which coincided with these economic changes, was largely concerned with the regulation of behaviour in the public sphere. As a result, criminal justice has had more to do with controlling the behaviour of men than women. By contrast, the household has become characterized by informal, rather than formal, control processes in which women are more actively involved than men. Hagan and his colleagues argued that these changes have stratified social control so that men more than women have become both the "instruments" and "objects" of formal control, while women have become more the "instruments" and "objects" of informal control.

They also argue that the family, because it is the social agency primarily responsible for early socialization, provides the means by which these differences are maintained from one generation to the next. Mothers are primarily assigned the responsibility for the control of children, and daughters more than sons are subjected to these control processes. The authors argue that these differences are maintained through patterns of social control of offsprings' attitudes toward risk-taking. The socialization of girls may encourage passivity and in so doing, prepare females for "the cult of domesticity." The socialization of boys, however, frees males from many of the controls that might discourage risk-taking and thus prepares them for activities within the production sphere. Since much crime and delinquency may be understood as risk-taking activity, gender differences in delinquent conduct follow logically from these more general differences in socialization processes.

Perhaps the most common explanation of male/female involvement in robbery relates to physical and gender role differences. For instance, women are often portrayed as less practised in or capable of enacting the physical aggression that is an integral part of robbery. In addition, males are socialized to be more aggressive; cultural role models promote male violence and risk-taking; and childhood and adolescent socialization allow males to engage in physical combat. These differences lead to disproportionately higher male involvement in aggressive crimes such as robbery.

Some critics argue, however, that the much lower male/female ratio for assault (about 3 or 4 to 1) than for robbery (about 10 or 15 to 1) raises doubts about how much work this argument can be asked to perform. Reports also show the same enormous over-representation of males in nonviolent offences such as auto theft and burglary as they do for robbery. Thus, it is not clear that positing a female incompetence or distaste for violence is necessary to explain the over-representation of males in robbery. In addition, the "aversion to risk" argument is undermined by the fact that female involvement in prostitution exposes women to substantial physical risks (Katz, 1988:241).

Katz explains the relationship between robbery and gender by focusing on the act itself and asking, "What are people trying to do when they do a stickup?" He argues that robbery enacts and extends a particular version of being male. On a rational level, street robbery makes little sense as a means of making money.

> Unless it is given sense as a way of elaborating, perhaps celebrating, distinctively male forms of action and ways of being, such as collective drinking and gambling on street corners, interpersonal physical challenges and moral tests, cocky posturing and arrogant claims to back up "tough" fronts, stickup has almost no appeal at all (Katz, 1988:247).

Katz argues that the stickup represents for men, and black men in particular, a distinctive form of masculinity—the "hardman" or "badass." In an oblique reference to differential association theory, he further suggests that it is not uncommon for robberies to emerge casually out of corner-group drinking situations. Women are less likely to become involved in robbery because they are not commonly found in ghetto poolrooms or in crap games held in alleys and hallways where such crimes are discussed (Katz, 1988:242). Katz's explanation is specific to robbery and does not account for disproportionately higher rates for men in other street crimes such as auto theft and burglary.

Differential male involvement in robbery appears to be more complex than might be suggested by ideas of male superiority in physical combat, male socialization into violence and risk-taking, or differential interactional experiences. Although these explanations give some insight into this phenomenon, they do not provide a full explanation.

SOCIOECONOMIC STATUS, RACE, AND ETHNICITY

In Canada and the United States, police reports, arrests, and convictions, surveys of victims, and self-report studies of offenders all indicate that robberies are overwhelmingly committed by men in the lower socioeconomic class. In recent U.S. history, black ethnic identity has been strongly correlated with robbery, whereas in Canada, French Canadians have the highest rates for holdups. Gabor et al. (1987:12–13) point out that the predominantly French province of Quebec accounts for 60 percent of all armed robberies in Canada. while accounting for only one-quarter of Canada's population. Similarly, the black minority in the U.S. comprise only 12 percent of the population but represent two-thirds of all robbery suspects. A number of theories offer insight into the disproportionate involvement of American blacks and French Canadians in crimes of robbery. Anomie and opportunity theory explain the financial need among the lower socioeconomic class; conflict theory focuses on discrimination, racism, and the relatively hopeless position that some minorities face; social control theory attributes higher crime rates to the social disorganization of poor urban neighbourhoods; and differential association theory explains how a tradition of robbery within urban neighbourhoods can be passed on to younger generations.

Despite the centrality of the relationship between race and robbery in modern criminology, the academic community has been reluctant to address the matter. Katz (1988:239) suggests that this reluctance is due to the fact that theorizing about blacks who are involved in crime inevitably leads to the imputation of general racial tendencies and to highly offensive ideas about what blacks or black men "tend" or "are likely" to do. He argues that in an attempt to avoid acknowledging a true empirical relationship between robbery and the contemporary black identity, two lines of argument have often been pressed. One argument is that when police statistics on arrests for robberies are compared to population percentages, the enormous over-representation of black versus white arrests reflects the police bias in making arrests. That is, the police arrest blacks for offences that would be handled informally or ignored if they had been committed by whites. Studies indicate, however, that differential law enforcement does not account for the higher rates of involvement of blacks in many kinds of crimes. Hindelang (1978), for instance, shows that the arrest ratio of black offenders is virtually identical to the percentage of black offenders identified by robbery victims.

The second argument is to attribute the relationship between race and robbery to underlying economic differences. Socioeconomic data reveal that robbers have less education and income, and fewer occupational skills (Camp, 1967; Haran and Martin, 1984; Gabor et al., 1987; Katz, 1988). Using anomie and conflict theory, many criminologists view social and economic discrimination in American society as the indirect but root cause of black criminality. Green (1970), for example, accounts for higher crime rates among blacks in terms of their economically disadvantaged position, including high unemployment and unskilled jobs, and in terms of handicaps stemming from black migration from the rural South.

Gabor et al. (1987) similarly evoke anomie and conflict theory to suggest that the over-representation of both French Canadians and black Americans can be understood in terms of their historic underprivileged position in their respective countries. They describe how the province of Quebec has undergone an extraordinarily rapid transformation from the early 1960s to the present day. Through the 1950s, Quebec was a parochial society, fraught with corruption, economic under-development, high fertility rates, and illiteracy. It was also a primarily rural society based largely on agriculture and even life in the cities revolved around the local parish. Much of the labour force in Quebec was poorly educated and engaged in unskilled work for business interests that were often controlled by people living outside the province or by the English-speaking minority. In the 1960s, Quebec rapidly became an urbanized, industrialized, and cosmopolitan society, in which social institutions and values were constantly undergoing change. A formerly conservative society had become liberal and pluralistic. Rising opportunities and expectations led to a struggle for power and privilege among special interest groups (Gabor et al., 1987:15–17).

Gabor et al. (1987:15–17) argue that both American blacks and French Canadians have faced political oppression and disenfranchisement; experienced the humiliations accorded those considered inferior in status; and recently migrated en masse from repressive and parochial communities to large, competitive urban centres. In Quebec and the United States, both groups have seen some of their members rise into the spheres of business, education, politics, and other professions. Although many of the social and economic barriers have been removed, a large underclass has remained. These groups suffer from high rates of unemployment, low wages, poor educational opportunities, poverty, and hopelessness. They live in the city slums that are characterized by crime and drug problems. The slums leave few alternatives to youth to move ahead and it is from this underclass that young male robbers emerge.

Other sociologists argue that conditions of racism and exploitation justify speaking of criminogenic influences within black society because these conditions exert massive pressures on blacks to engage in lawbreaking. Using anomie, conflict, and social control theory, Gibbons (1992:119) argues that among blacks, economic pressures cause property crimes; disordered neighbourhoods and weak social ties lead to crimes of violence; and black crime is a consequence of white racism and other defects of the society in which American blacks live.

The heavy proportions of American blacks and French Canadians involved in robbery cannot be explained solely by their over-representation in low-income groups. Comparisons between the rates of blacks with those of other low-income groups using U.S. national crime statistics indicates that poverty and the lack of economic opportunity do not in themselves account for the higher black involvement. The over-representation of blacks is much greater with respect to robbery than to either violent nonproperty offences (simple assaults and aggravated assaults) or nonviolent property offences (burglary) (Katz, 1988:240). Similarly, although Quebec has far higher levels of robbery than the rest of Canada, it has noticeably lower rates on other violent crimes. In 1985, Canada had a violent crime rate of 749 incidents per 100,000 people, whereas Quebec's rate was 514 per 100,000 (Gabor et al., 1987:15). Why is robbery more prevalent in Quebec than embezzlement, break and enter, or other forms of theft? Katz (1988:240) asks a similar question: "Why should the over-representation of blacks be so much greater in robbery than in violent offenses without property-acquisition objectives and in property-acquisition offenses without violence (burglary)?" Anomie theory helps to explain higher rates of property crime among the poor but it does not explain why robbery is preferred by certain groups.

Conflict theory has been used to explain how racial oppression leads to crime and how discrimination affects oppressed persons. Conflict theory portrays black crime as the product of endemic racism and oppression in American society. Because of low incomes and systematic discrimination in employment and housing, blacks have received inferior education that affects their chances for success and upward mobility. As a result of racism, American blacks have been, and continue to be, "the truly disadvantaged" (Wilson, 1987). This oppression breeds resentment, hostility, and crime.

Silberman (1978) suggests that the robber is an admired folk hero in America's underclass because robbery has become a symbolic act of contempt against the norms of the dominant white community. After enduring years of oppression, many blacks experience quiet satisfaction from defiant acts against their oppressors. Society's norms become inverted and even symbolic acts are considered victories, since legitimate victories may be unattainable. As a result, among large segments of the black community, there may be some underlying support for violent acts committed against members of the dominant group. The moral inhibitions against serious crime that one would ordinarily expect to find are weak or absent. For young urban black males raised in the ghettos, robbers are role models and represent the anti-hero who challenges the establishment.

Similarly, Katz argues that to explain the relationship between race and robbery, we have to appreciate that for some urban, black, ghetto-located young men, the stickup is particularly attractive as a way of being black. Being black, being male, and being "bad" merge into one social type—the holdup artist—as a distinct black ethnic identity:

> The black version of the hardman, the bad nigger, has long had an appeal far beyond the ghetto... On the emotional level, within the modern poor black urban community, the seduction is provoked by the existential attractions of being "bad" as a collectively celebrated way of being that transcends good and evil (1988:233 and 241).

Gabor et al. (1987:ix) use conflict theory to make a similar argument about French Canadians. They contend that robbery constitutes the ultimate means by which unskilled and unconnected persons from the lower rungs of society can meet their financial needs quickly and, at the same time, achieve a feeling of potency. The oppressed often suffer from feelings of fatalism, hopelessness, and impotency. Robbery is attractive to young offenders because it allows them to experience a sense of power.

> For the person who is at the bottom of the social ladder, both along economic and racial or ethnic lines, and with little hope of achieving success through other means, robbery might be the quintessential way of resolving, simultaneously and dramatically, their economic woes, as well as the frustration stemming from their low social status. For a few brief moments, a person who may have experienced rejection in many different situations (family, employment, etc.) and who may feel socially incompetent (school, work, interpersonally, etc.) commands center stage and holds the major cards relating to the fate of victims and witnesses. At the same time, he may be able to vent his anger at symbols or representatives of those he feels are responsible for his situation (Gabor et al., 1987:21).

A French Canadian from Quebec who robbed 49 banks and was interviewed for this study, stated proudly that he had never struck any of the province's "caisses populaires" because these were the "people's banks." Robbing from English-controlled financial institutions, however, was justifiable according to his own ethics. A careful examination of his offences reveals, however, that he did indeed rob two "caisses populaires"— indicating perhaps that his personal morality was breached for reasons of expediency and opportunity.

Gabor et al. use opportunity theory to suggest that a lack of professionally organized criminal syndicates provide few criminal alternatives for those interested in pursuing crime as a way of life. Robbery is open to most because crude robberies require no collaborators, no contacts to unload stolen merchandise, and few skills to execute. Armed robbery, because of its potential simplicity, can be an ideal crime for unskilled and unconnected persons who need cash quickly.

> Robbery (both armed and unarmed) is a primitive crime. Most robberies require little sophistication. They involve the application of fear and sometimes brute force to achieve their principal end: the acquisition of cash. The pursuit of cash is another feature of robberies that indicates the lack of sophistication entailed. Fraud requires planning and deception. Burglary and other property crimes often require the conversion of stolen goods into cash through criminal associates or contacts. Robbery can provide immediate access to cash for those urgently needing it (perhaps due to drug dependency) or for those unwilling to wait. It just so happens that a young French Canadian male or young black male in the United States is more likely to find himself in dire financial straits than, perhaps, persons of other social groups. He may also have fewer illicit, let alone legitimate, options available than those of other ethnic or racial groups (Gabor et al., 1987:20–21).

Gabor et al. further suggest that if robbery becomes a solution to social, political, and economic impotence and is adopted by a sufficient number of people in an area or a social group, it can become entrenched as a means of survival and develop its own momentum. With implicit reference to differential association theory, they argue that robbery can become a traditional means of adaptation in which values and skills in support of it are transmitted to younger generations. Thus people continue to commit this crime with frequency even after it has outlived its original purpose.

DRUG USAGE AND ROBBERY

The great upsurge in the use of drugs that occurred in the late 1960s and continued through to the 1990s has paralleled increasing crime rates. Both the public and the police commonly believe that drug addiction is the leading cause of crime. Most Hold-Up Squad officers interviewed for this study mention drug usage as a significant factor in robberies. Similarly, Conklin (1972:50) found that police officers typically refer to drug use when asked about rising robbery rates. Although this "drug addiction causes crime" hypothesis may explain higher crime rates, it does not account for factors contributing to the increased use of addictive drugs. In fact, it is probable that other societal changes are partially responsible for both the increased crime rate and increased drug addiction.

The drug addiction hypothesis typically makes the following assumptions: the drug is addictive and produces withdrawal symptoms if usage stops; increased usage results in increased tolerance, which means that greater quantities must be used to achieve the same effect; increased tolerance leads to increased usage and higher costs; and the higher costs force the addict to commit crimes to pay for the drugs. According to these assumptions, rational utilitarian crimes such as burglary and robbery should rise as the addict attempts to support his or her habit. Not all increases in crime rates can be attributed to the need to get money to purchase drugs, however, since rates of other crimes that produce no profit have increased at the same time as robbery rates have soared.

The exact contribution of increased drug use to rising rates of robbery is difficult to determine. Conklin (1972:57) found that a minority of robbers (18 percent) in his study report using drugs at the time of their robberies and that the vast majority of offenders (90 percent) who robbed had never been arrested or convicted of a drug-law violation. He concludes that although addicts may be partly responsible for rising robbery rates, this argument has been overdone and factors other than increasing drug addiction have contributed significantly to the rise in robbery rates.

An alternative to the "drug addiction causes crime" hypothesis is the "criminalization" explanation of the drugs/crime connection (Faupel and Klockars, 1987:54–55). In this view, criminal associations precede and give rise to drug usage. The social world of drug users becomes intertwined with the criminal world because of the illegal nature of the drug. Through criminal associations (cultural transmission, differential association, and illegitimate opportunity theory), the individual is introduced to illegal drugs and both crime and drug use are facilitated and maintained. The criminal subculture then encourages criminal solutions to the problem of financing drug addiction. This second hypothesis predicts increases in drug usage following or coinciding with periods of criminal association and activity.

Many studies have found a high probability of criminality preceding drug addiction (Ball and Chambers, 1970; Chambers, 1974; Jacoby et al., 1973; Inciardi, 1979; O'Donnell, 1966; Robins and Murphy, 1967) and some have noted that criminal and drug careers may begin independently of one another yet become intimately interconnected as each evolves (Fields and Walters, 1985; Morris, 1985; Faupel and Klockars, 1987:56).

Faupel and Klockars' study of heroin addiction notes that drug usage changes over time and different stages of drug usage influence the drug/crime connection. During the "occasional user" phase, drug use can be sustained with a legitimate income, and any criminal activity is often quite spurious to drug use. In the "stabilized junkie" and "free-wheeling junkie" periods, the level of drug use is related to availability, which is typically enhanced through criminal income. Rather than drug use causing crime, it seems more accurate to suggest that crime facilitates drug use during these periods. Quite the reverse is true during the "street junkie" phase where availability through normal channels is lacking and the addict lacks the necessary structure to regulate his or her drug needs. Under these conditions, the drug habit does indeed appear to "cause" crime in the manner commonly depicted.

UNEMPLOYMENT AND ROBBERY

Since the late 1970s, many social scientists have concluded that the unemployment-crime (U-C) relationship, measured at the aggregate level, is both inconsistent and insignificant (Fox, 1978:29; Long and Witte, 1981:126; Orsagh, 1980:183; Cantor and Land, 1985:318; Chiricos, 1987:188). This "consensus of doubt" questions the strength and the significance, and even the direction, of the U-C relationship (i.e., whether it is positive or negative) (Chiricos, 1987:188).

While some studies indicate little or no relationship between unemployment and crime, others have found a positive relationship. Sviridoff and Thompson (1983) conclude from interviews with offenders released from prison that a simple "unemployment leads to crime" thesis is inconsistent with the releasees' experiences. Cantor and Land (1985) argue that unemployment can have both a positive and negative impact on crime rates, by simultaneously increasing the motivation and decreasing the opportunity for criminal activity.

The consistent characteristics of persons involved in robbery are employment instability, low educational level, and high rates of unemployment. In Haran and Martin's sample (1984:48), 18 percent had a eighth-grade education or less; 67 percent were high-school dropouts; and 66 percent were unemployed at the time of robbery. Work histories reveal that most changed jobs frequently, 71 percent were unskilled, and when they did work, they were employed at menial, low-paying, seasonal jobs. The lack of education and employment skills clearly affected legitimate employment opportunities by limiting them to the most menial and low-paying jobs available. Camp reports that only 11 percent of the robbers in his study explored legitimate solutions to their financial situation. Some had poor credit ratings, and others had borrowed all they could from their families or friends or these people did not have the quantity of money they wanted. The fact that so few bank robbers even consider legitimate sources indicates the extent of their involvement in the illegitimate world (Camp, 1968:87). Feeney (1986:62) notes that many offenders mentioned the inability to find work as a factor in their general situation prior to robbery. None of the juveniles and only 20 percent of the adults who robbed for money had jobs at the time of the robbery, and most of them were in low-paying or part-time jobs. No systematic information was available as to how many offenders considered satisfying their needs through legitimate channels.

To what extent is unemployment correlated with predatory property offences such as robbery? It seems reasonable to assume—and consistent with anomie and conflict theory—that persons who suffer long periods of unemployment may be driven to steal to get by. In addition, social control theory suggests that high unemployment may attentuate a community's social bonds and social controls, with the result that those who are motivated to steal are less subject to legitimate social controls. That is, unemployment may directly affect specific individuals and may also result in pervasive alterations in community organization (Gibbons, 1992:233).

Although studies of the unemployment-crime (U-C) relationship conducted in the 1960s or earlier often reported little or no relationship between unemployment and crime, more recent studies tend to show positive U-C relationships. A review of 63 largely post-1970 studies of predatory crime and unemployment by Chiricos (1987) outlines a consistent, positive, and statistically significant U-C relationship in these investigations. Chiricos also found, however, that the U-C relationship is a conditional one. His analysis shows that estimates for property crimes using data from the 1970s are essentially positive and very often significant, yet other conditions produce "inconsistent" and "insignificant" U-C relationships. The relationship between unemployment and crime, therefore, appears to be complex and is not a simple causal connection stating that unemployment causes crime.

Kohfeld and Sprague (1988) similarly found that high levels of unemployment were strongly associated with burglary and robbery rates in St. Louis. Thornberry and Christenson (1984) not only found that unemployment led to lawbreaking, but also that involvement in persistent criminality had negative effects upon employment experiences. Their study suggests that the unemployment-crime connection may be reciprocal—unemployment may sometimes lead persons to engage in crime at the same time that involvement in lawbreaking may affect the subsequent employment experiences of individuals. Cantor and Land (1985) argue that unemployment can have both a positive and negative impact on crime rates by simultaneously increasing the motivation and decreasing the opportunity for criminal activity.

FAMILY BACKGROUND

There are few studies that examine the family background of robbers in depth. Research on the social background of robbers and the available life-history data indicates that their families are characterized by disorganization; lack of parental supervision; broken homes; poverty; alcoholism; promiscuity; a preponderance of one-parent, female-headed family structures; and a history of crime, arrests, and convictions among male family members. Most robbery offenders are unmarried and unattached at the time of their offence. Unattached male robbers—single, separated, or divorced—comprised 80 percent in one study (Haran and Martin, 1984:49) and two-thirds of bank robbers in another sample (Camp, 1968). Robbery offenders represent a normless and drifting group of relatively young men with weak family relationships, commitment, and little investment in the social order. Katz (1988:219) argues that most mundane criminals succumb to chaos, moving from addiction to petty hustle to abused status in prison, and being identified as some subtype of "loser" by the law-enforcement, street, and prison communities alike. Robbery, he suggests, is sufficiently attractive to make sense as a sustained commitment only when it is part of a larger lifestyle of deviance.

OFFENDER TYPOLOGIES

Typologies are ideal-type constructs based on and abstracted from the real world. Offender typologies are derived from an analysis of research on specific offenders and aim to simplify reality by highlighting the criminal's defining characteristics. Over the past several decades, criminologists have attempted to profile diverse types of criminals such as "the professional thief" and "organized and disorganized murderers." Typologies can be based on criminal activities or on characteristics of the offenders or a combination of both; they are constructed to assist in the understanding of criminal behaviour and the development of theoretical explanations; and they are sometimes used to assist criminal investigations.

Many researchers on robbery have developed offender typologies. Gabor et al. (1987) classify robbers into four types: (1) the chronic offender has a long career, commits many other offences, is poorly prepared, and gains moderate amounts from this crime; (2) the professional also has a long career and commits other offences, but is better prepared and makes larger profits; (3) the intensive has a very short career, commits poorly planned robberies in quick succession, and brings in modest sums of money; and, (4) the occasional offender also has a fairly short career in armed robbery, commits only a small number of robberies relative to other crimes, puts little planning into his or her crime, and receives minimal profits.

Haran and Martin (1984) have constructed a typology based on the career patterns of 500 bank robbers and their degree of involvement in crime as a way of life: (1) the heavy-career typology (29 percent) consists of bank robbers with four or more convictions for property crimes including bank robbery; (2) the casual group consists of robbers with two or three property convictions and makes up 25 percent of the sample; (3) the compulsive typology (24 percent) includes heroin and alcohol addicts whose thefts are related to their drug abuse; and (4) the amateurs (22 percent) have no more than one property-crime conviction.

Using an index combining the source of income and types of associates, Camp (1968) differentiates three criminal life situations of bank robbers: (1) individuals who derive their income from legitimate sources are classified as noncriminal (18 percent); (2) quasi-criminals (27 percent) combine legitimate and illegitimate income; and (3) the criminal group (55 percent) earn a living through illegitimate means and associate primarily with other criminals.

Conklin's (1972) typology of robbers is based on motivational factors, modes of operation, and degree of involvement in criminal activity: (1) the professional views criminal activities as work or a trade, belongs to a gang, and carefully plans his or her crimes; (2) the opportunist or amateur—either a juvenile or young adult—selects the most vulnerable targets; (3) the drug addict is marginally involved in robbery but will commit a holdup to support his or her drug habit; and (4) the alcoholic steals to continue drinking.

TYPOLOGIES AND THE REAL WORLD—CRIME SPECIALIZATION

Kempf (1987) addresses the issue of specialization within the criminal career and focuses particularly on the measurement of specialization. He suggests that the rejection of specialization has been premature and misguided by the conclusions of previous studies that have been inconclusive. While research studies fail to support the specialist career pattern, some studies indicate that the phenomenon is more likely to be observed within unique crime categories, during certain career stages, and among some demographic subgroups. Kempf's own research on criminal specialization indicates a low level of specialization amid more random, general, or versatile behaviour. He argues that criminal careers follow a variety of paths, including some minimal specialization; that careers may co-exist simultaneously; and that the stage of career involvement should be considered when criminal careers are investigated. While general, random, or "cafeteria style" offending may prevail as a career type, the widely accepted rejection of specialization is premature and has been misled by the measurement techniques used in previous research (1987:416).

Criminologists have commonly assumed that lawbreakers are crime specialists such as "robbers," "rapists," and "burglars." Research indicates, however, that few criminals concentrate on a single kind of criminality. It is therefore difficult to classify criminals into career types since most exhibit diversity rather than specialization in their offences. Critics argue that typologies oversimplify reality and attempt to abstract types that do not exist by assuming an unrealistic degree of offender specialization. In the real world, criminal careers seem to be far more complex than a typology is capable of capturing (Koenig, 1992:380). Most robbery offenders, for example, have previous criminal convictions for other crimes. In Ciale and Leroux's (1983) study, 84 percent had either been convicted of a prior offence (70 percent) or charged (14 percent) for one or more offences. Similarly, 81 percent of the 500 bank robbers in Haran and Martin's (1984) sample had prior criminal records and averaged seven arrests each before being convicted of bank robbery. Only 19 percent in their group and 16 percent in Ciale and Leroux's sample had no prior adult record—although juvenile records were not included in the analysis. Gabor et al. similarly find that most subjects began their careers in crime by committing burglaries, auto thefts, and drug trafficking before moving into armed robbery. The criminal careers of their subjects spanned anywhere from a few weeks to several years. Most of the offenders in Gabor et al.'s typology of "robbers" commit a variety of other crimes. Similarly, in Conklin's typology, the opportunist robber commits other forms of theft but robs infrequently, and addict and alcoholic robbers engage in criminal acts other than robbery. Besides engaging in illegal substance abuse, robbery offenders also commit a variety of other crimes including break and enters, theft, fraud, and assault (Petersilia, Greenwood, and Lavin 1977; Chaiken and Chaiken 1982; Gabor et al. 1987). Given such variability in their selection of offences, the criminal-type "robber" may be more fiction than fact. It appears that the path leading to robbery is not a direct one for most robbers, and offenders who rob typically commit other crimes as well.

CRIMINAL RECIDIVISTS

About 20 to 25 years ago, research began reshaping the image of serious criminals. Several studies identified small groups of persistent lawbreakers variously labelled "chronic," "intensive," and "repeat" offenders, "professionals," "violent predators," "heavies," "habitual criminals," and "career criminals." These terms describe criminal recidivists who are committed to crime as a way of life and who are responsible for a disproportionate number of the most serious crimes including robbery. "Heavy" criminals, in the argot of offenders, are those who use violence and threats of violence in the commission of their offences. From a corrections perspective, they represent a grave danger to the community and an enormous expenditure of criminal justice system resources.

Two famous and provocative Rand Corporation studies used an occupational perspective to classify offender types. The first Rand study (Petersilia et al., 1977) was based on the self-reports and official records of 49 "habitual" armed robbers serving time in California prisons. They averaged 39 years of age; had lengthy criminal records spanning many years; and admitted to committing an average of 214 offences in nine categories of crime including robbery. These men were not specialists in armed robbery or any other crime; rather they committed a variety of offences throughout their careers. The second Rand study (Chaiken and Chaiken, 1982) surveyed over 2,200 prison inmates. The majority of offenders were occasional criminals who dabbled in crime and had been employed prior to being imprisoned. The researchers identified 15 percent of the prisoners as "violent predators" who had committed robbery, assault, and drug deals in the year or two prior to incarceration. These men also admitted to other previous offences including burglary and/or theft. The "violent predator" was found to begin his criminal career before age 16; frequently committed violent and property crimes before age 18; and was involved in robbery, drug dealing, and assault. Chaiken and Chaiken found that, in the period preceding confinement, 10 percent of the violent predators reported committing robberies at the rate of 135 per year. Since the offenders were unmarried, with few family obligations, not employed steadily or for long stretches, and frequently using hard drugs, these violent predators became entrenched in a highly deviant lifestyle while they were very young. Very few offenders could be classified as criminal specialists since they admitted to a variety of offences.

Wright and Rossi's (1986) questionnaire survey of 1,874 inmates identified a small group of intensive offenders whom they dubbed "handgun predators" and who committed "more than a few" drug deals, robberies, and assaults. These men were not criminal specialists but "omnibus felons"—criminal opportunists prone to commit virtually any kind of crime. In an earlier study that examined the records of 400 offenders, Roebuck (1967) similarly found that the most common pattern was a "mixed" or "jack-of-all-trades" offender followed by a double pattern of burglary and larceny. Petersilia's (1980) review of research on criminal careers indicates that serious criminals commonly begin their careers between the ages of 14 and 17; engage in a variety of crimes; realize a small amount of income, averaging a few thousand dollars a year, from crime; and their income does not increase substantially as their criminal career progresses. The earlier the criminal activities begin, the more likely it is that sustained serious criminal conduct will ensue in the adult years. Nevertheless, relatively few juvenile delinquents become career criminals. Offenders commit a variety of offence types rather than specialize. The mixture may shift from one stage to the next, often increasing in seriousness, but not as a consistent rule. Crime targets are more likely to be opportunistic than as a result of methodical planning. In commenting about research findings on the careers of persistent offenders, Travis Hirschi concludes: "The criminal career does not appear to be a career of increasing skill and sophistication but the reverse, a career that starts with little of either and goes downhill from there (1986:115–16)."

"GARDEN-VARIETY" OFFENDERS

The term "garden-variety" or "cafeteria-style" offender is meant to reflect the fact that most criminals have committed a variety of offences. These offenders engage frequently, but perhaps sporadically, in property crimes. Different labels have been used to describe these relatively unskilled criminals: "occasional," "compulsive," "casual," "opportunists," "amateurs," "addicts/alcoholics," and "semi-professionals." Their crimes are usually crude, lack planning, and result in small profits. Many of these persons have average intelligence, come from socially and economically deprived neighbourhoods, and have had numerous contacts with the police, juvenile authorities, and custodial institutions.

Not all predatory crime is committed by full- or part-time criminals who are recidivists. As Gibbons (1992:239) points out, many "one-time losers"—novices in lawbreaking—are found in probation caseloads, diversion programs, and other places to which amateur offenders are sent. Predatory crime is common in North America, and most of it is committed by amateur criminals, who are relatively uncommitted to lawbreaking or pro-crime sentiments, and who live amid law-abiding citizens. Gibbons suggests that for many predatory offenders, involvement in crime unfolds in ways that parallel the drift of many young adults into occupational niches. For example, there is much blundering about, experimentation, and short-term employment in an array of relatively low-paying jobs before new recruits to the labour pool finally settle on an occupation to be pursued over a longer period. In much the same way, many violators experiment with criminality without committing themselves to crime as a way of life. They are drawn into misconduct for a variety of reasons, but they also manage to withdraw from crime. Despite using a career perspective himself, Gibbons warns that occupational concepts should be used cautiously.

> Many predatory crimes are one-time acts by individuals who lead law-abiding lives. It makes little sense to speak of crime as an occupation in such instances. Even more important, offenders who become involved in repetitive acts of criminality also work at least intermittently at conventional jobs. For these individuals, crime is a form of "moonlighting," not a career (Gibbons, 1992:236).

CRIME SPECIALIZATION

Kimberly Kempf (1986; 1987) argues that while some research studies fail to support the specialist career pattern, some results indicate that specialization occurs within unique crime categories, during certain career stages, and among some demographic subgroups. She argues that the rejection of specialization has been premature and misguided by the conclusions of studies whose methodology can be questioned, particularly in the areas of crime-category specification, portion of career examined, and method of measurement. Kempf points to the fact that researchers have examined the entire career span of offenders, discovered a variety of crimes, and concluded that most offenders are generalists and not specialists. She suggests, however, that if we consider the complete range of crime types in which offenders could have become involved and contrast this with the limited number of types actually committed at particular points in their careers, one could equally well make the case for a form of "serial special-ization." Kempf's own research on criminal careers indicates a low level of specialization amid more random, general, or versatile behaviour. While general, random, or "cafeteria-style" offending may prevail as a career type, she argues that criminal careers may follow one of a number of paths, including some specialization. Careers may co-exist and the stage of career involvement should be considered when criminal careers are investigated. Kempf concludes that a closer examination of previous research concerned with crime specialization reveals that the issue has not yet been investigated thoroughly and is by no means resolved.

CRIMINAL CAREERS AND CAREER CRIMINALS

Traditionally, the term "career" has been reserved for persons within a respectable profession and implies a course or progress through life and a way of earning a living. In his book, *Social Pathology* (1951), Edwin Lemert broadened the use of the term by introducing the concept "deviant career" to describe a nonoccupational life history. Erving Goffman (1961) later coined the term "moral career" to refer to any social strand of a person's course through life. Goffman's conceptualization of the term emphasized self-concept, sequential stages of the career, and the ability to pursue simultaneous careers. Thus, one could have an unsuccessful career or desist from deviance rather than continue. The term has been broadened even further to include two different but related concepts—criminal careers and career criminals.

THE CRIMINAL CAREERS CONTROVERSY

The term "criminal career" is used to describe a course or progress through life, whereas the "career criminal" concept focuses on serious offenders who are committed to crime as a way of life. The notion of a career criminal is derived from the more general concept of a criminal career. The construct of the criminal career is not a theory of crime because it leaves unspecified the various causal factors that may be at work in generating crimes. Rather, it is a way of structuring and organizing knowledge about certain key features of offending for observation and measurement. Blumstein, Cohen, and Farrington (1988) have studied the temporal properties of criminal careers in the context of an ongoing program of longitudinal research on crime. They argue that it is useful to conceptualize individual criminal activity in terms of a criminal career with entry into a career at or before the first crime committed. Criminal careers are characterized during a lifetime by a beginning (onset or initiation), a duration (career length), and an end (dropout or termination). At one extreme, a criminal career could consist of a single offence. During the interval between onset and termination, research examines such features as the rate of offending, the pattern of offence types, and any discernible trends in offending patterns. A career perspective does not assume that criminal careers have any particular tendency or direction in seriousness or that offenders necessarily specialize in particular types of offences.

While not a theory itself, the construct of the criminal career should be of value in the development of theory. The criminal-career approach distinguishes the individuals who commit crime from the crimes that they commit. Such distinctions allow for the possibility that different causal factors and processes may account for each element. Blumstein et al. (1988) argue, for example, that different sets of "causes" may influence individuals' initiation to criminal activity, the frequency with which they commit crimes, the types of crimes they commit, and their termination of criminal activity. Basic knowledge about these separate aspects of criminal careers may be fundamental to understanding how various causal factors work to encourage, to intensify, or to inhibit criminal activity.

The concept of a career criminal has been coined to describe persons who commit serious offences at high rates and over extended periods. Most definitions of career criminals emphasize a combination of a high frequency of offending, a long duration of the criminal career, and high seriousness of offences committed. Although the concept of "criminal careers" is a reasonably neutral one, the concept of "career criminals" has proved highly controversial and has attracted considerable discussion and criticism. Two rival positions dominate recent discussions of the temporal properties of criminality. Alfred Blumstein and his collaborators have found the career concept useful in their longitudinal research on crime. Gottfredson and Hirschi (1986), however, argue that the concepts of criminal careers, career criminals, selective incapacitation, prevalence and incidence, and longitudinal studies all have little value for criminology. In particular, they object to the "career criminal" concept:

> Whatever else it has come to mean, the idea of a career criminal suggests that some people pursue crime over an extended period of time, that the intention to pursue such activities may be determined in advance of their pursuit, and

that the acts intended can be prevented by timely intervention by the state... One currently popular policy option suggested by the career criminal notion is a sentencing strategy that seeks to imprison the career offender... Discovery of the career criminal by criminologists stimulated the idea of selective incapacitation... It turns out that the particular career criminals identified in criminological research are no longer active and their replacements cannot be identified until they too are on the verge of "retirement." The 20-20 hindsight of career criminal research turns out to have been misleading. When asked to identify career criminals in advance of their criminal careers, the research community requests additional funding (Gottfredson and Hirschi, 1986:216–17).

Gottfredson and Hirschi also object to the concept of a criminal career. If crime represents a career, they argue, then it must have a beginning and an end, a determinable length, and a certain tendency or direction (for example, increasing skill, increasing seriousness, or increasing profitability). It also follows that those who embark on a criminal career may tend to specialize in certain crimes or to advance from one crime to another in predictable ways.

There is virtually no evidence of offense specialization anywhere in the life cycle of ordinary offenders (rape and assault are intermixed with crimes for pecuniary profit); most offenses do not require any particular skill (doors are simply smashed open), knowledge (little training is required to snatch a purse), or even expectation of great gain ("hand over all your big bills," the career criminal says to the cabbie); there is no evidence of escalation of any sort as the offender moves from adolescence to adulthood; and the crimes that occur most frequently are the crimes most frequently committed by "career" criminals (Gottfredson and Hirschi, 1986: 218).

A defining feature of most offenders, they argue, is a short-term orientation—a tendency to pursue immediate pleasure despite the consequences. Another feature is what Short and Strodbeck (1965) call social disability, a tendency to experience difficulty in managing the ordinary tasks of life. Such offenders, according to Gottfredson and Hirschi, are incapable of pursuing a career in its conventional sense.

Blumstein et al. (1988) argue, on the other hand, that existing knowledge favours the criminal career approach, which has demonstrated, for example, that influences on onset (e.g., inadequate parenting techniques) are different from influences on termination (e.g., marriage). The use of a criminal-career perspective allows for the possibility that the factors at work in explaining such features as participation and frequency may be quite different. Even if most offenders are highly versatile, that is, they engage in many different crime types, the factors that influence the commission of one offence type might well be different from those that influence another. In addition, the factors that influence early involvement in crime might become unimportant in later stages of a career.

Blumstein et al. (1988) argue that Gottfredson and Hirschi confuse the construct of a "criminal career" by repeatedly referring to "career criminals" where the context clearly calls instead for the very different construct of "criminal careers." Kempf (1987:402) further suggests that when Hirschi (1985:16) argues that the notion of a criminal career is implausible because "career involves a capacity for long term commitment denied by criminality," he has accepted a definition for "career" that differs from the generally accepted definition.

Blumstein et al. (1988:23) argue that much of Gottfredson and Hirschi's criticism against the construct of "career criminals" is associated with the degree to which "career criminals" (defined by any reasonable criteria) can be identified, and especially identified early enough in their criminal careers to be useful for policy purposes. They suggest that whatever difficulties there may be in prospectively identifying career criminals for policy purposes, they do not invalidate career criminals as legitimate objects of scientific inquiry.

> Contrary to Gottfredson and Hirschi's claims, career criminals are neither elusive nor nonexistent. Such claims belie common sense and deny the ample empirical evidence of wide variations in individual offending, i.e., some offenders display considerably more criminal activity than others. Career criminals, by any reasonable definition, are evident within offending populations, and particularly among incarcerated offenders... Whether or not career criminals can be identified in advance of their criminal careers has no bearing on the theoretical validity of the concept of career criminals, which rests on well-established differences in offending patterns (Blumstein et al., 1988:23–24).

SUMMARY

Research examined in this chapter indicates that the characteristics of persons involved in street crimes such as robbery include racial and ethnic minority status, low educational level, and high rates of unemployment. The majority of robbers are young men from low socioeconomic backgrounds, frequent drug users, generally unmarried with few family obligations, and are entrenched in a highly deviant lifestyle from a very young age. In addition, robbery rates are highest in urban areas characterized by poverty and social disorganization. In examining the behavioural dimensions of predatory crime, research shows that very few career criminals are crime specialists since they admit to a variety of offences. The typical robber also engages in a variety of mundane criminal activities with modest returns. Robbery itself is a low-skill, high-risk crime that usually brings small gain. Evidence of planning and personal discipline is uncommon and professional robbers are rare. Rather than being romantic adventurers and rebels, most robbers can be characterized as losers participating in a losers' game.

The Motivation to Robbery

A Commitment to Crime

Age 23, this solo gunman escaped from a halfway house while on parole and is suspected of 14 bank robberies. He operated alone, wore a balaclava, and kept the staff and customers at bay with a loaded pistol. His values, motivations, beliefs, rationalizations, attitudes, and self-concept depict a person who is confident, calculating, boastful, and committed to crime as a way of life. He has few regrets and indicates a desire to continue in crime when he leaves prison.

I was doing banks long before this. It's a matter of having the courage to do it. The principle applies to other things. If somebody does something legal or illegal and they gain a little ground, they'll do it again. Once you get away, it gives you incentive and you begin to feel as though you're good at it. I wasn't even a suspect for a lot of bank jobs. I was pretty good at it there for awhile. I'd do one, get on a plane, fly back, party, and have a good time. I did most of them out of town. You've got to have discipline and in my case, I was pretty heavily into drugs. I

dropped my guard or I wouldn't be here. I've got five years for this but I was lucky. I'm well aware of the fact that if I had been caught for the rest, it would be a lot more time. I've never liked it in here but I like the things that life has to offer. It's not money that buys you happiness but it can make you comfortable.

I wasn't thinking of the future when I was doing these banks, just the present. Travelling, partying, and having a good time. These are phases you go through. When you're on the run, you do it and you realize you could get caught. But you go out and have a good time and don't really consider it. You're partying and you're partying out of control which is your downfall. I'm not a strong believer in working. I respect people who can work but on the other hand I see so many people who work years just to survive. I see a lot of people work their entire lives and have nothing to show for it. When I was in the paddy wagon and being taken to court, I could see people going to work on a bus with long faces. It don't make sense.

You only live once. You can't have a good time every day but as far as I'm concerned, you can sure as hell try. Why should you toil all your life just to be thrown in an old age home? Forget that! I'm not lazy but there is more money to be made in other ways than working nine to five. I just find crime easier.

I was talking to this lady who used to come to prison for group discussions. She started telling me how she was on welfare and how she had two kids and she had one dollar left in her purse and only a carton of milk in her fridge. She says to me, "But I get by. I don't go out and commit crimes." I said to her, "That's good for you. I'm glad you can do that. I respect you for that but if you think I'm going to sit in my house with absolutely nothing in it and continue living that way, that's out of the question. I want to live comfortably and I know I'm going to do just about anything to reach those goals."

The first time I did a bank, it was hard to do it. Afterwards, one minute you've got nothing and the next you have $15,000 and you can do what you want. So it's up to you. Once you're gone, you're gone. It's over and done with, you're safe. There is a risk factor all right but there is a risk factor in everything you do. There's a risk walking across the street. I've never had anybody bother me 'cause they know I'm serious. With a hood on your head and a gun in your hand, they know you're not playing games. I don't hesitate to point a gun and I don't hesitate to fire either. If a guy's going to come after you, then he's got to be a fool. I'm a mild-mannered guy and my philosophy is to do things with the least amount of trouble as possible. I don't think I'd ever shoot anybody when it comes down to it but the most saintly could kill if it meant their life. I'm not there to hurt anybody, but I'm going to get what I want and they best listen. Just because I'm a little bit crooked doesn't mean I'm a bad guy.

I don't go out and do crimes for my own entertainment. It's not something I get a thrill out of doing. I feel happy 'cause I got away. I rob banks for the money and I spent most of the money I had. I like to have a good time. I've got a few things to show for it but nothing really. I've got a car and a little bit of money in the bank but the majority is spent. I'd go out and buy a pair of $275 sunglasses, leather jackets with big fur collars, jewellery. If I walk into a night club and I'm wearing a pair of designer jeans, a cashmere sweater, a Rolex watch, and gold jewellry, people notice: "The guy's got a cashmere sweater." People will be impressed. It's a cut above. I see crime from the lower class to the upper-class. I go to the upper-class clubs and all the people around you look good, they're doing good, you're doing good, and you feel good. You've got this and they've got this, and nice women. Nobody can deny that they really enjoy it. Lots of glamour and the things people see on T.V.

I'm still young, I just turned 23. I'm not going to be here for the rest of my life. I figure I know as much or more than anybody that has finished high school. I have a good future ahead of me. So I spend a few years in jail. I don't like being here but I'm a lot better off than a lot of people. I'm ready to take risks because only a small amount of people get caught. I'm not ready to settle down, but I need to get a little more low-key. None of this Jesse James gun-slinging bullshit anymore. Bank robbery was a phase that I went through. Drugs are one of the things I'm considering. By the time I make some big money, I'll be banking it in another country.

There are so many people out there that never get nothing because they think small. If you think small, you are small and that's the way it is. I can't be one of these people. I'm good enough to be with the best. Some of the greatest leaders that ever existed spent time in jail.

PAIR PLEAD GUILTY TO ROBBERY SPREE

OTTAWA (CP)—A Modern-day Bonnie and Clyde pleaded guilty Monday to a robbery spree in March that included at least nine holdups in Peterborough and the Ottawa area.

In most of the robberies, [male offender], 28, wielded the gun, while [his female companion] drove the getaway car.

Both admitted to robbery, weapons and related offences.

Court heard [the male offender] has a criminal record including two- and four-year jail terms for past robberies, while [the female offender] has a record for prostitution and a history of drug abuse.

The pair's holdup spree lasted from March 17 to 26, when they were arrested in Peterborough.

[The male offender] managed to escape from an Ottawa jail in August. He then robbed a bank the following month in nearby Osgoode, Ont., but was captured after a final holdup in Nova Scotia.

Source: The Kitchener-Waterloo Record (27 October 1992). Reprinted by permission of The Canadian Press.

AUTHOR'S NOTE: Five years after the above interview, the offender escaped from prison and was re-arrested for additional bank robberies. He did not achieve his goal of moving into a lucrative criminal career and is now serving a 16-year sentence in a maximum security penitentiary.

RATIONAL CHOICE THEORY AND CRIME

This chapter focuses on the decision-making processes that lead offenders to commit robbery, to offend repeatedly, and to eventually desist from crime. Economists have generally believed that property offences are the result of rational decision-making reached by men or women who confront a problem faced by many others—a need or a desire for money. Implicit in the economic perspective is an actor who views theft as a rational and productive activity despite the fact that the consequences may include capture, imprisonment, and death. The expected utility model in economics (Becker, 1968) is based on the assumption that offenders rationally attempt to maximize the monetary and psychic rewards of crime. If crime has a higher utility than conforming behaviour—that is, an acceptable chance at not getting caught and a desirable amount to gain, then the individual should decide in favour of committing the crime. On the other hand, if the perceived risk of capture is high and the expected penalty is great, the potential criminal should be deterred.

Since robbery is an economic crime, it might be expected that potential robbers mentally calculate whether they need money and which legitimate or illegitimate opportunities are available. If legitimate means are blocked, presumably the offender considers illegitimate means, possible financial gain, potential risks, necessary actions, and his or her motivation. Because robbery is a serious crime with severe penalties and the possibility of personal injury, we might assume that would-be robbers might carefully choose their targets and develop plans to reduce the chances of apprehension.

Research on robbery, however, does not support an image of offenders as rational, careful economic planners. Fewer than 60 percent of Feeney's (1986:55) sample of 113 robbers, for example, cite money as the primary goal of their robbery; over half did no planning at all; and over 60 percent said that before the robbery, they had not even thought about being caught. The sample included both adult and juvenile offenders, offenders from different racial backgrounds, criminals involved in commercial robberies and individual muggings, and inmates serving both long and short prison sentences. Feeney expresses surprise that robbery, which is regarded as such a serious crime by society should frequently be embarked upon with such apparent lack of deliberation and that experienced robbers fail to demonstrate superior skills, planning, or cautiousness. As noted in Chapter Two, other researchers (Camp, 1967; Conklin, 1972; Ciale and Leroux, 1983; Haran and Martin, 1984; Gabor et al., 1987; Ballard, 1992) similarly find that robbers do little planning, use minimal disguise, fail to consider the possibility of getting caught, and generally approach robbery in a less than cautious way.

The offenders' behaviour does not appear rational when risk and reward are looked at objectively. Robbery is an irrational act when small potential rewards are weighed against risks. Holdups are high-risk crimes because victims may resist, attempt to capture the offender, call for assistance, or use weapons in self-defence. Alternatively, force used to subdue victims increases the seriousness of the offence and the risk of a long prison sentence. The victim is also a witness who may identify the offender and provide the police with information leading to his or her capture. In addition, businesses deploy security systems such as video cameras that aid identification and/or conviction. Forms that are available to bank employees and filled out by the teller or victim immediately after the crime assist the police in the investigation. Height indicators near the exit door in variety stores help store clerks to accurately estimate the bandit's height. The risk of identification, apprehension, and conviction increases with victims who are prepared and trained to respond quickly and appropriately.

Furthermore, robbery is frequently reported as the crime is in progress or immediately afterwards. Robbery alarms will send armed police officers racing towards the scene as the dispatcher informs them of the robber's description and direction of travel. The robber not only risks being captured, but he or she also risks being shot or killed. The robber may also endure rough treatment by the police, who are frequently accused of dealing harshly with armed bandits.

Yet with all these risks, robbers get away with very small amounts of money. In a credit-card economy, individuals cannot be counted on to carry much cash. Businesses or individuals who handle large sums of cash or other valuables use security measures that "harden" them as targets. Banks and stores keep small sums of cash in their drawers or cash registers. Large amounts of money are routinely dropped into night deposits or safes with time-locks. Opportunity theory suggests, therefore, that it is difficult to secure large sums of money through robbery because video cameras, armed guards, locked safes, locked doors, well-lit cash registers, and other security devices make it a high-risk crime with small rewards. Given the unpredictability of robbery, it is clear that rational persons would not elect to pursue it as a career after carefully weighing potential costs and benefits.

Robbery, therefore, may be undertaken with little consideration of, or in spite of, the risk. Katz (1991:289) argues that, in fact, this attitude is sometimes necessary to commit robbery. To persist as a robber, he argues, it is necessary to steel oneself against utilitarian thinking, becoming impervious to attacks of reason.

> The study of interaction within robbery events indicates that,
> in order to conduct robbery persistently, one must commit

oneself spiritually and emotionally beyond what material and mundane calculation can recommend. "Nonrational" violence makes sense as a way of committing oneself to persist in robbery in the face of the risks and chaos inherent in the criminal event (Katz, 1991:289).

RATIONAL CHOICE THEORY

In contrast to the economic or "normative" rationality underlying the expected utility model, rational choice theory (Clark and Cornish, 1985) suggests that criminal decision-making is characterized by a very rudimentary cost-benefit analysis. The theory analyzes the decision-making process as it relates to the various stages of criminal involvement including initial motivation, the motivation to continue, and the decision to cease criminal involvement. Choice theory also analyzes decisions of a more tactical nature relating to the criminal event itself, including the selection of a specific type of crime and target, the getaway, or the decision whether to use a weapon. Choice theory adopts a crime-specific focus not only because different crimes may meet different needs, but also because the situational context of decision-making and the information being handled will vary greatly among offences. Although the rational choice perspective on crime is best suited to utilitarian offences such as theft, burglary, and robbery, its proponents argue that even behaviours that appear to be pathologically motivated or impulsively executed have rational components.

Rational choice theory portrays criminal behaviour as the outcome of choices and assumes that decisions made by offenders exhibit limited or bounded (Simon, 1957), rather than normative, rationality. The bounded rationality hypothesis assumes that human information-processing limitations place constraints on decision processes and that people make simplifications and shortcuts that are reasonable but that may produce inferior outcomes (Carroll and Weaver, 1986). Criminal behaviour may be planned and premeditated but not fully rational in the strict sense that the expected utility model assumes. The picture that emerges from research on criminal decision-making is that of a limited information processor, often working under time constraints who uses many different strategies to simplify the task of evaluating choice alternatives in the complex environment of everyday life. In his analysis of how burglars and robbers select victims, for example, Walsh (1986:50) concludes that a partial and limited rationality characterizes criminal behaviour. Even though the gains may be small, they still meet the offender's immediate requirements and can subjectively appear much larger than they are. The planning and rationality used may subsequently be viewed as flawed, but at the time, the offender feels that he or she has taken enough precautions. Feeney argues that although robbers' behaviour would seem more rational if there was greater evidence of planning and concern about the possibility of apprehension, their decisions nonetheless meet the standards of minimum rationality.

> There is clearly a thinking process involved. It is not Benthamite, but it is not much different from what people do in their everyday lives. This is particularly true for the decisions made by highly experienced robbers. Although these robbers frequently say that they undertake no planning, their experience is in a sense a substitute. Many of these robbers seem to feel that they can handle any situation that rises without specific planning (Feeney, 1986:66–67).

Rational choice theory considers the offender's perspective to understand which factors he or she considers when planning a crime. The characteristics of offences that render them differentially attractive to individuals have been termed "choice-structuring properties" (Cornish and Clarke, 1987:935). Such properties provide a basis for selecting among alternative courses of action and, hence, effectively structure the offender's choice.

In this chapter, we will apply rational choice theory to examine robbery from the offender's perspective. What are the motives for robbery and to what extent are they based on rational choice? Why would anyone choose to commit a crime that has such high risk and low reward? In the following sections, we present a summary of research findings on the motives for robbery. This is followed by an in-depth analysis of the responses of 80 Canadian convicted bank robbers concerning their motivation.

THE MOTIVATION TO ROBBERY

MONEY, SPENDING, AND LIFESTYLE

Interview research indicates that robbers often define themselves as rational actors whose principal motive for committing crime is the need and/or desire for money. Robbery is appealing because it is perceived as a crime that is straightforward, easy to execute, involves low risk, and requires little planning or time commitment (Gabor et al., 1987:62). Conklin (1972:85) notes that robbers steal to support themselves and for the symbolic value of the money. He found that most of the 67 robbers interviewed sought money for its utilitarian and symbolic value, not because they were psychologically disturbed, wished to control others, or prove their masculinity. Feeney and Weir (1975) note that about two-thirds of the 113 robbers interviewed sought money for everyday expenses such as clothing, transportation, food, and shelter. Nearly one-quarter of the adult offenders committed robberies to obtain money for drugs. Those who robbed to pay for necessities were generally not destitute but they may have been in low-paying jobs or were unemployed. Camp (1968:83/106) reports that bank robbery is a means to provide for short-term needs. He found that 58 percent of the men in his sample have been able to cope financially, 10 percent are in a good financial position, and 32 percent report excessive debt. Most offenders who owed money did not indicate that pressures from unpaid debts led them to rob banks.

Research on robbery tells us little about the spending habits and lifestyle of offenders other than that they admit to spending the money quickly and foolishly. Einstadter (1969:82) reports that career robbers reveal that they "blow it" and remain true to the "easy come, easy go" style of their social surroundings. The primary motive for robbery is financial gain, and offenders, like most people, seek money for a variety of mundane purposes. An additional illicit motive for robbers, however, is the desire to pursue or maintain an unconventional lifestyle characterized by leisure as opposed to work, and hedonistic pleasures including alcohol, drugs, sex, and partying. Haran and Martin (1984:51) report that almost all robbers quickly squander the money on wine, women, and drugs. Few report that they steal to pay bills. Katz (1991:290–91) argues that to understand the robbers' motivation, one must consider the larger context of criminal involvement. Offenders, he says, do not shape the rest of their lives to facilitate their commitment to robbery; they shape their involvement in robbery to fit in with the deviant character of their social life. For example, the habitual use of some form of intoxicating substance, whether legal or illegal and whether physically addictive or not, influences the active criminal life phases of virtually all persistent robbers. He points out that self-report studies and biographies of serious criminals often contain remarks that scoff at conventional lifestyles with an attitude of presumptive sensual superiority.

> Indeed, rhetorical flourishes with which offenders dub crime their "business" and robberies as "getting paid" should be appreciated for their mocking undertones... Through property crimes, sexual adventures and partying, and illicit drug use and gambling, the persistent offender embeds his criminality

in a lifestyle that operates in parallel to sensual processes of the body and in juxtaposition to the image of the constricted conventional self that he mocks (Katz, 1991:291–92).

The decision to engage in robbery, Katz argues, must be examined in the context of offenders' life situations. The lifestyle itself is frequently nonconforming and motives to crime are woven into a variety of deviant pursuits. There may be no single or clear decision to commit robbery or continue in this activity, rather, the pursuit of illicit pleasures exposes persons to behavioural patterns, values, and associates that combine with biography, need, opportunity, and chaos to create a drift into crime.

POWER, EXCITEMENT, AND OTHER MOTIVES TO ROBBERY

Robbery obviously does not have to be motivated primarily or exclusively by money for it to be rational since other motives can be regarded as sensible and utilitarian. The search for thrills and excitement, power, retribution, status, and acceptance by their peers are sometimes mentioned as factors that motivate offenders to crime. Feeney (1986:56–57) found that over 40 percent of the robbers in his sample (one-quarter of the adult offenders) indicated that money was not the real purpose of the robbery. A sizable group wanted excitement or a change of some kind in their lives. Risk-taking, danger, excitement, and the desire for new experiences are frequently cited by young offenders as motivational components to robbery (Gabor and Normandeau, 1989:201; Gabor et al., 1987:63). Even adults report being stimulated by the excitement generated in a holdup. The Rand Corporation survey (Chaiken and Chaiken, 1982) of 2,200 prison inmates found that 40 percent of "violent predators" agreed with the statement that "committing crime against an armed victim is an exciting challenge." For a significant proportion of serious criminals, the thrill of confrontation with victims appears to be part of the motivation to crime.

Lejeune (1977:124–25) reports that the motivation in muggings includes money, status, and excitement or thrill-seeking. Petersilia et al. (1978) similarly report that the main reasons given by their armed robbers for crimes in the juvenile years were thrills and peer influence. During adulthood, the main motivation for crime was to obtain money, most commonly for drugs, alcohol, self-support, or family support. West and Farrington (1977) also report that a significant proportion of juveniles mention excitement or enjoyment as a motive to crime while older offenders stress economic reasons and material gain.

Similarly, several subjects in the present study report that they find bank robbery exciting, like taking risks, enjoy living life in the fast lane, and "get off" on their criminal lifestyle.

> I have to admit, I was on a trip. I saw myself as a bank robber and I guess I thought it was glamorous. I was living it up. It was the whole scene.

A man who had been previously employed as a male stripper draws a connection between dancing and robbing banks:

> I've always been a wild and crazy guy. I was always the kid who would take the dare. I like excitement and challenges. Take the dancing. That requires a lot of courage to get up in front of 300 rabid women and show them your talent. When you're on stage, you control the audience and when you're in the bank, you control the people in there... When I went into the bank, I owned that bank. It was my bank. That was my state of mind. I was going to get that money.

Younger robbers, and men in particular, who have spent little or no time in prison enjoy the excitement, status, and feelings of power and control afforded by the crime. Whereas the young, naive, and over-confident bank robber is thrilled by the danger, the older convict finds no pleasure in committing the crime. An offender typifies the changing attitudes of aging criminals:

> I've changed. I used to have this idea of myself as a bandit. This time, it was just surviving. This time around, I hated doing banks. I didn't get any kicks out of it no more. Didn't get any kicks out of it. I was scared. Dreading doing it. Glad to get it over with. I'd be flat broke before I'd do it. No guns this time round. I'd go a couple of days broke and then finally have to go do it. Force myself.

Even the few younger men who report some enjoyment from the holdup experience emphasize that this was not their primary motive. They commit the robbery for the money and any other benefits are by-products or secondary gains. Gabor and Normandeau (1989:201) similarly note that young robbers appear to be less deterred or fearful of prison sentences than older men who have already done time.

Power-Tripping

This 25-year-old offender operated in a six-man crew that robbed downtown banks in a large city. The gang was heavily armed, occasionally struck tellers and customers, and discharged their weapons in the bank. Several of the gang members were shot by the Hold-Up Squad after they attempted to escape after a bank robbery.

It was all done very theatrically. To me, it was basically a big game. I remember the first time I did it, I was scared as hell. Afterwards I thought, "Hey, this is fun." It was a rush. It all left after we got shot up, the fun seemed to fall out of it. [Laughs.] I remember getting a big kick out of watching what was going on. I can remember everything. I wasn't scared. I was nervous the first time. I can't remember the first bank we held up, it was like a dream world. But after that, it was a game. I was absorbing this, everything that happened, every movement. It was so easy, so damn easy. Then, "Ouch," we were ambushed. [Laughs.] To me it was a new experience, a new thing, being part of a gang. Watching people's reactions. It's a power trip. It was kind of superior because you can tell them to shit and they would. [Laughs.] Yah, for sure it was a power trip. A lot of people would be right down on the floor so fast. I remember one woman who went underneath her desk and the desk went right up in the air. I was looking at her and one of the guys was looking at me and shaking his head. She was yelling, "Don't hurt me, don't hurt me." I thought to myself, "Holy shit, just leave that one alone. Better not crawl under there." [Laughs.] Another one wanted to scream but could only go, "Yip, yip, yip." It was a quick little beep. [Laughs.] Most men dove to the floor faster than any women did. That's the first thing they'd do. They see you come in and they're on the floor. I noticed that right off the bat. A lot of females would just stand there and look at you. They're just calm and cool and you tell them to get down on the floor and they get down. We never had anyone try to play hero. Why would a guy want to jump you anyway? Leave that to the cops. Let them play hero. They don't play hero anyway, they just shoot. [Laughs.] From behind a building. [Laughs.] Some people got paranoid or go into shock. It wouldn't connect. All they see is the barrel of that gun and they couldn't hear the words, "Get down on that floor." I can picture them too, just looking and staring at this gun. So what we would have to do is knock these people on the side of the head with the gun. Grab them and lay them on the floor. It never failed, in every bank people went into shock. I try to think back and say to myself, "Why did I do something like that?" I never thought it was all that serious at the time. I never even thought about the crime being serious. What happened was it ended up being fun. I think everyone dreams of being Jesse James or Billie the Kid. I guess you could say that we followed in their footsteps because we got shot up too.

Some researchers note that for a few subjects, the feeling of power that comes from using a weapon and/or from controlling and dominating a victim is an additional motive to robbery (Lejeune, 1977:131; Gabor et al., 1987:63). Peer influence and concerns with status are other motivational components. Adolescents often view robbery as a challenge through which they can prove themselves. Juveniles frequently cite the influence of friends for their involvement in robbery and many explain that they were just trying to prove they could do it. In some cases, their partners started something and they just went along (Feeney, 1986:58; Gabor et al., 1987:63). Another motive relates to feelings of being victimized by society and a desire for retribution for past injustices (Lejeune, 1977:131).

Sociologists must apply a healthy scepticism to the stated motivations of offenders. Some explanations of motives such as those based on a sense of injustice or peer influence may be no more than post-factum justifications for wrongdoing. In addition, stated motives may represent secondary gains that emerge in the course of the act and are by-products of, and not motives for, committing the crime. The thrill, danger, excitement, power, and control that robbery affords, likely emerge in the process of committing the crime and are not the reasons that propel many to initially commit robbery in the first place. If one gains pleasure from the exercise of power over victims of robbery, for example, this may become a significant motivation to reoffend. Lejeune (1977) argues that each time a mugging does not lead to negative consequences, it becomes easier to view it as free of major risks. Moreover, some bandits come to enjoy the activity itself, separate from the monetary rewards. Gabor et al. (1987:121–22) similarly suggest that the euphoric feeling following initial success increases confidence, is reinforcing, and may help to explain why offenders continue to rob. Camp (1986:126) reports that once offenders realize how easy it is to rob a bank, they also know that they can return if they need more money. To the extent that this occurs, it is difficult to tease out motivation to crime and determine whether power-tripping and excitement attract people into robbery or whether these pleasures emerge as one gains experience and proficiency in committing holdups.

Katz (1988:197–98; 1991:290) points out that a variety of motivational factors may be woven together to produce the act of robbery. Young offenders, for example, often combine many forms of illicit action with robbery: they engage in group attacks that gratuitously humiliate victims; they sometimes combine sex or sadistic pleasures with the property-acquisition purpose of the event; and they may engage in particular robberies as part of a "spree" conducted within a drug-induced mood.

ROBBERY, RISK, DETERRENCE, AND RATIONAL CHOICE

Understanding motivation requires that we consider more than the offender's need for money, the perception of robbery as a fast and easy crime, and any secondary pleasures that evolve from the act. Many persons may be attracted to robbery as a means of solving financial problems but fear the consequences. Even if one is inclined to commit a holdup, why doesn't the possibility of arrest and imprisonment act as a powerful deterrent? How do offenders consider and overcome the risks inherent in this crime? It appears that offenders do not objectively evaluate the risks associated with robbery; rather, they subjectively define it as a low-risk crime. The threat of arrest and imprisonment fails to deter potential robbers because they believe that they're unlikely to be caught. In addition, some offenders are not deterred because they view arrest and imprisonment as no worse than their current situation. From interviews with 132 bank robbers, Camp (1968:75) concludes that most view their life situation as one in which they have little to lose and a great deal to gain by robbing a bank. Camp argues that existing social control mechanisms collapse because their effectiveness depends on the individual's ability to perceive that arrest and imprisonment will remove the possibility of realizing aspirations through legitimate means. Since the bank robber is unable to see this possibility, the severe sanction does not deter.

MOTIVATIONAL COMPONENTS IN BANK ROBBERY

Motivation for both deviant and conforming behaviour can be influenced by a complex variety of factors. Some variables are significant and immediate while other components of motivation are distant and may even operate at an unconscious level. The following section is based on interviews with 80 convicted Canadian bank robbers and examines the criminal's decision-making process from a rational choice perspective. Rational choice theory suggests that offenders make a conscious decision to become involved in robbery after weighing the potential gains against the risks. The rationale behind the decision to rob a bank includes a need and/or desire for money; a belief that bank robbery provides fast, accessible, and sufficient amounts of cash; and a perception of this crime as easy, low-risk, and nonviolent. Variables examined include drug usage, unemployment, the role of others, the influence of the mass media, and techniques of neutralization.

The obvious reason for robbery is to obtain money but this does not completely explain why someone commits a crime. While the need or desire for money is common, most people choose legitimate paths to solve their financial problems. Even those who use illegitimate means may choose other avenues to obtain needed funds. In addition, people who are desperate for cash and who find either legitimate or illegitimate financial opportunities blocked may be deterred from robbery because of moral prohibitions, a lack of knowledge, or a fear of apprehension and punishment. Bank robbers in this study stated that they needed money quickly and that this was their main motive for initially robbing a bank. Offenders believe that bank robbery provides fast, plentiful, and easily accessible funds. They are also clear about something else—they need and/or want cash quickly. The specific reasons why money is needed are diverse: to meet debts; pay the rent; keep a business afloat; buy a retirement trailer; purchase Christmas gifts; maintain a drug, alcohol, or gambling habit; support oneself after a prison escape; and manage day-to-day expenses. Bank robbers need money for many of the same reasons we all do. It is very common for escaped prisoners to commit holdups to support themselves on the run because other crimes require criminal contacts that entail certain risks or start-up funds that escapees typically do not have. Bank robbery is a quick and easy way to obtain a cash "fix."

It is perhaps surprising that offenders are willing to risk the threat of severe penalties to achieve quite normal and modest goals. Very few commit robbery to accumulate large sums of money. Nonetheless, most bandits express the view that the quantity of money that can be obtained by robbing a bank exceeds that which can be obtained through other means, both legitimate or illegitimate. Camp (1968:88) similarly notes that over half of his sample considered other forms of criminal activity before deciding on bank robbery but dismissed them because they did not present as lucrative and as easy a target as a bank.

Bank robbery is an attractive means by which to solve financial problems because, unlike other crimes, successful bank robbery assures a financial payoff. Committing a break and enter or safecracking may be a fruitless endeavour if there is no money present. However, everyone knows that banks contain cash and therefore robbers do not have to deal with "fences" to sell stolen property. One inmate states:

> If you're going to be a criminal, it's the crime to be into. Let me put it that way. It's the only crime that you're guaranteed a payday.

Another says:

> With me it was the money. Plain and simple, the money. Right? If I rob this bank I can get a lot more than if I sold a dime of weed here and sold a dime of weed there.

Initially, bank robbers believe that the money justifies the risk. In prison, however, many reassess these beliefs and retrospectively conclude that the payoff does not justify the risk of arrest and imprisonment. Some even calculate the money obtained and divide it by the time they have to serve in prison and are unimpressed with their "annual income."

On average, the take for bank robbers operating alone and hitting one till amounts to approximately $1,500–$2,000. Robbers acting in pairs who jump the counter and rifle through two or more tills can generally count on $3,000–$4,000 each. A more lucrative modus operandi involves a solitary robber demanding or taking money from several different tellers, usually by displaying a weapon. Such robbers report receiving from $6,000–$20,000 per crime with an average of approximately $8,000–$10,000. Although these figures are not overly impressive, the amounts are judged adequate relative to the time involved. Most criminals view a $1,500–$2,000 payoff as an excellent return for 35 seconds or (more accurately) for an hour or a half-day of work. Comparisons are also made with regular employment and $2,000 is viewed as the equivalent of or better than an average working person's monthly take-home pay. Many robbers also view it as more money than they could expect to make through legitimate employment.

THE APPEAL OF BANK ROBBERY

Robbery is chosen as a means of obtaining money because it requires few technical skills or equipment and little or no financial investment. In addition, robbery need not involve violence and robbers assume that there is a slim chance of being caught. Robbery primarily relies on knowledge of banking procedures and a certain amount of courage and determination. Men who use weapons find them readily available through previous criminal contacts. Others simply bluff their way past potential resistance by claiming to have a gun or by displaying a replica gun or starter's pistol. One does not even need a partner to rob a bank.

Many robbers wear no disguise or use minimal disguises such as glasses, hats, make-up, a mask, or a nylon stocking. Most of the equipment and props are simple, inexpensive, and easily obtained. The modus operandi (M.O.) of most robbers similarly does not require the criminal contacts or complex skills that may be needed in other crimes such as selling drugs or safecracking. Bank robbery, in particular, is viewed as relatively safe and easy. The uniform nature of banks and bank operations reduces the amount of preparation needed to rob a bank. There are hundreds of banks in large urban areas, each with numerous possible getaway routes. Robbers gain access to banks by simply walking through the door and they expect little or no resistance from tellers or customers. Although respondents emphasize that bank employees are told not to resist, many bandits use weapons as precautions.

Bank robbers simply enter the bank and ask for or take the money. Since they expect and receive cooperation, their techniques require mainly the courage and confidence necessary to commit the crime. As one inmate stated:

> You just walk in and do it. There's no big plan. There's no big elaborate plan to do it. You just walk in and do it. You don't have to go through days and days of planning or anything. It's not that complicated.

The getaway is another component of bank robbery perceived as relatively easy to accomplish. Offenders typically escape by car, taxi, or on foot, bicycle, or public transportation such as the subway or bus. Those who use a stolen vehicle either know how to steal the car themselves, have a partner who can do so, or pay someone trustworthy to do it. Many robbers avoid using a stolen vehicle because of the problems and risks in both obtaining and driving one. Some also fear being informed on by the person hired to steal the vehicle. Although the getaways of bank robbers are relatively simple and straightforward, most offenders agree that caution and imagination are important.

Bank robbery is viewed as a low-risk crime that allows the perpetrator an excellent opportunity to escape if it is planned and carried out properly. Chances of getting caught for any one robbery are perceived as slim. Eluding arrest depends upon one's ability to obtain the money quickly, minimize and control resistance, exercise caution in planning the escape, and retain a minimum of good luck. Most bank robbers agree that escape from the bank should be relatively easy and assured unless something unexpected happens.

NOTHING TO LOSE—
A MOOD OF FATALISM

For some, the decision to take the risk is based on another reality—they are already in trouble with the law and expect to be imprisoned anyway. For example, men who have escaped from jail may decide to rob banks as a means of support. In part, the decision to escape is predicated on, and may be influenced by, the assumption/knowledge that they can support themselves by robbing banks.

A few men report experiencing emotional disturbances prior to becoming involved in bank robbery. These emotional states vary but can perhaps best be summarized as a fatalistic attitude. One man decided to rob a bank after his wife left him to move in with a wealthy businessman. Embittered by rejection, he wished to prove that he too could make money and was unconcerned about getting caught because: "She would have [to assume] the blame." Another man who was depressed because a love affair had ended, hoped to "buy" back his lost affection while a third offender lost his job and his girlfriend at the same time. Others report being depressed and financially frustrated after losing their jobs and subsequently pass the blame on to their bosses and the government. The emotional state of these men is one of dispiritedness but not despair—no one describes himself as suicidal. Frustrated but not angry, although a few harbour resentments, most accept responsibility for their crimes and imprisonment.

FROM NEED TO GREED—
THE MOTIVATION TO CONTINUE

The perception of bank robbery as a safe and easy crime is heightened by initial success. The ease with which they pull off their heist increases confidence and contributes to offenders engaging in a pattern of successive holdups that, for the men in this study, eventually result in arrest and imprisonment. Even after they have robbed several banks, most offenders intend to quit following the next robbery.

In his famous essay on marijuana usage, Howard Becker (1963) distinguishes between the motivation to try marijuana for the first time—initial motivation—and the motivation to continue. Similarly, the initial decision to commit a robbery to solve a pressing financial need is different from the decision to rob again once that need is met. Bank robbers in this study soon become hooked on a partying lifestyle that includes not working, hanging out in bars, staying up late, sleeping in, taking drugs, chasing women, and drinking to excess. They continue to rob banks in order to continue the deviant lifestyle. Becker's (1963:42) comment on marijuana usage also applies to bank robbery: "Instead of the deviant motives leading to the deviant behaviour, it is the other way around; the deviant behaviour in time produces the deviant motivation." If need convinces men to rob banks in the first place, then greed motivates them to continue. The small amounts of cash available from individual tellers combined with the lavish spending habits that robbers quickly acquire lead them to commit a series of robberies in rapid succession to support their escalating lifestyle. Conklin (1972:85) similarly notes that robbers often see themselves as greedy, stating that they never seemed to have as much money as they wished. Because of the ever-increasing probability of arrest, the career of most bank robbers normally ends after several weeks of robbing, spending, and partying.

ORIGINATING THE IDEA—THE ROLE OF THE MASS MEDIA

One of the striking findings of this research is the extent to which the idea to commit a bank robbery originates from the mass media. Approximately one-third (25/80) of the sample conceive of the idea from reading or viewing reports and/or portrayals of bank robbery in newspapers, television, and movies. The majority obtain the idea from ongoing newspaper reports but a few attribute specific media portrayals for having launched them on their careers as bank robbers. For some (8/25), the idea to rob a bank lay dormant for months or years until sudden financial problems developed and the notion presented itself as a the means of obtaining needed cash. For the majority (17/25), however, the process is reversed and they first experience financial problems, then conceive of bank robbery as a solution by reflecting upon day-to-day news reports of this crime.

CASE EXAMPLE

University Student

This 24-year-old university student supported himself through school for two-and-a-half years by robbing banks. He would patiently wait in line, pass the teller a note, display a replica handgun when *necessary, and make his getaway by foot or bicycle. He was arrested when a customer followed him out of the bank and flagged down a nearby police officer.*

I got all my ideas, the M.O., everything, from the media. In my city, the first guy to do the single solo play was the "Friday Afternoon Bandit" and he was eventually caught. He pulled off a whole bunch about five or six years ago. I was in high school at the time. There were write-ups in the paper for a couple of weeks. Full page! A reporter from the paper interviewed him. He was like the city's hero, so to speak, a real folk-hero type of image. The paper played it up. They don't do that anymore. But at that time they did. So he explained his whole M.O., exactly how he did it. I read about that and it sort of floated around in the old noggin for a number of years. So when the crisis came, I said, "Well that's what I should do. I'll just follow what he did." The first time was definitely a spontaneous irrationality. I played the customer waiting in the line and gave myself 30 to 45 seconds to get the money and be out the door walking down the street. One minute is the maximum you should spend inside a bank when they know what's going on. If you get out inside a minute you're generally scott-free, is the general conception from what I've read. The first time I was so nervous but it had to be done, and I figure: "Do it! You've got to do it." I went through with it and it was easy. The first time around I thought it would solve all the problems but all it did was reinforce them because you pay off the drug debt and you go out and you buy more and you keep doing that and it reinforces the wrong habits—bad habits basically. It also destroys monetary values. I was spending too much. I was smoking too much.

I had a major drug debt. The thing is, I was paying for part of my university and I liked to smoke marijuana. I was into a bit of trafficking. What happened is I got to a point where I was putting out a lot of money. I was smoking a lot of the profit and then the market went dry. There were a bunch of problems and I owed a guy about a grand and that's a lot of money when you're trying to go to university. It was enough stress, especially when you're halfway through your Christmas exams. And so a combination of the two propelled me to that bank that day. I mean, when you think about it, it's a very immature thing to do, to decide that there's no other alternative but to rob a bank. I could have gone home to the parents, explained everything, and taken my lumps.

I'd read the newspaper afterwards. I'd always have to see whether they connected anything. You're always interested in what they're willing to publish. Then I found something! The New Year's edition (in this other city) was just phenomenal. They used to give everything. They'd list every single bank robbery in the city and where and when they happened. They'd plot all the banks and other institutions that had been held up and you could see the parts of the city that were heat scores. So I'd go to those areas that weren't heat scores. I was graduating and planning a little trip and this was going to be my last bank.

It was a big thing with the cops that I didn't have a record at all, except for a possession thing. They couldn't understand how I could leap into it where 90 percent of the cases they dealt with, there was this definite progression. There was progression with me too. The thing with me without question is the fact that I was involved in the dope culture. For four years in university and then about two years in high school. That's a fairly lengthy period of time, and that colours one's perception of the world, the police, society, and institutions. And the fiscal need, that came from this involvement in drugs.

Media reports on bank robbery make it an attractive option for people with financial difficulties because it is portrayed as non-violent, impersonal, fast, easy, and a low-risk means of obtaining cash. Offenders believe that bank robbery is a low-risk crime because newspapers report many robberies in which offenders escape but few in which culprits are caught. In addition, those who are arrested appear to be unlucky, stupid, and/or have been tripped up by something beyond their control. Potential robbers fail to realize, however, that the number of reported arrests are small in comparison to the number of robberies because the same offenders frequently commit many crimes before they are arrested. Someone may be arrested for a dozen holdups but only one newspaper article appears—leaving the uninformed and imprudent reader with the impression that bank robbery is a low-risk crime.

The data in this study probably underestimate the importance of the media in originating the idea to commit a bank robbery because several respondents (11/80 13.75 percent) could not recall when or how the ideas originated. It is possible, therefore, they were consciously or subconsciously swayed by media presentations.

Using different research techniques, Clarke and McGrath (1992) examined the effect of newspaper reports of bank robberies on the bank robbery rate in Australia and New Zealand. Earlier research by Phillips (1983) in the United States reports that media publicity of suicide, homicide, and other violent acts results in a significant increase in suicide and homicide rates, with the rate peaking on the third day following the reports. Clarke and McGrath found no evidence that newspaper reports led to increased bank robberies in the week following media reports. In fact, their findings conflict with the results of this study in which one-third of bank robbers originate the idea from the media. However, the present study would not predict an immediate increase in bank robberies following newspaper reports. Some men are influenced instead by movies and/or television and many who originate the idea to rob a bank from the media indicate that the idea lay dormant for weeks or months until they developed financial problems and decided to act. Others report thinking about the idea for several weeks before acting on it—many taking days or weeks to get up the confidence to commit the robbery. Thus it is not surprising that Clarke and McGrath found no evidence of copycat holdups in the week following newspaper accounts of bank robbery. The present study suggests that any increase would be measurable only over a much longer period.

TECHNIQUES OF NEUTRALIZATION

> "A bank is a church of the capitalist society. When you rob a bank, you're stabbing them right in the heart."
>
> —*University-educated bank robber using a conflict theory justification for his crimes*

Media reports make bank robbery attractive when they portray the crime as non-violent and impersonal. This is also a technique of neutralization (Sykes and Matza, 1957) that is used by offenders to diminish the seriousness of the offence. Bank robbers often argue that no one is physically or financially hurt—banks are insured or can afford the loss—and that banks are deserving victims because they are powerful and insensitive bureaucracies that make immoral profits by exploiting the unfortunate. Criticisms of the banking establishment in the media and reports of high profits are used by offenders to legitimize their crimes. Men who rob banks regret being caught and incarcerated but few express remorse over their actions. By stressing the fact that no one is physically hurt, they minimize the seriousness of the offence. The emotional terror inflicted on tellers and customers is denied or dismissed as transient and harmless. Bank bandits emphasize that they are robbing from an institution that can easily afford the loss and not from individuals who have to work for their money.

CELEBRITY STATUS

The bank robber as a cunning, daring, anti-establishment individual is an image created and perpetuated in the media, particularly in film and fiction. Some robbers admit to enjoying this celebrity status and almost all express pride in their criminal accomplishments. Celebrity status may not be the motivation for robbing a bank but consciously or subconsciously, it appears to influence some offenders in their choice of crime. A tendency to romanticize their "exploits" is evident in statements made about themselves and their references to famous bandits:

I got her off the hook and she hasn't bothered writing. I really resent that. I should have had my eyes open but I was so hung up on being John Dillinger that I was blind to all the things going on.

You do it for the money first then it becomes a trip. It becomes a lifestyle, you could say. You're a bank robber. This is a romantic lifestyle. Like Jesse James.

You always read stories about the older legendary folk heroes. The colourful images of bank robbers that were portrayed, these were images implanted in my innocent mind.

I fell into that Bonnie and Clyde syndrome. I had my girlfriend drive the getaway car and that was a very sexual experience for us. We had to have sex right after getting back. It was a trippy moment.

The temptation to boast ultimately results in the downfall of some robbers. A group of men who returned to their local bar after having robbed a bank began watching the news:

Back at the hotel, we watched T.V. and saw how the police had set up roadblocks to catch the robbers. People in the hotel knew we had done it and were cheering because we got away with it. I knew then we were done.

Mr. Boffo

MR. BOFFO reprinted by permission of NEATLY CHISELED FEATURES.

The public's and the media's fascination with crime is illustrated by the fact that three men in the present study of bank robbery have published autobiographies on their criminal adventures.

CRIMINAL OPPORTUNITY—
THE ROLE OF OTHERS

In accordance with differential association and opportunity theory, almost one-half of the subjects in this study (39/80 48.75 percent) were initiated into bank robbery through associations with other criminals either in prison (11/39) or "on the street" (28/39). Typically, they learn their M.O. from experienced criminals who convince them that bank robbery is fast and easy. In most of these cases (32/39), offenders commit their first bank robbery with other criminals. Culprits report that they not only learn how to rob a bank, but they also learn to justify the act and view it as a low-risk offence.

The idea to rob a bank can also arise from legitimate sources and activities. Within this study, three men originated the idea after seeing large amounts of money being handled in the bank. Another attributes his interest in bank robbery to his youth, when he frequented the bank where his father worked. A fifth man conceived of the idea following a conversation with an acquaintance who was a police officer. The officer spoke about the many holdups occurring in the city and described how easily robbers were obtaining money from banks by simply passing a note.

Illegitimate opportunity theory suggests that physical opportunities are significant situational determinants of crime. Bennett and Wright (1984a:34), in their study of burglary, however, found that the majority of burglars are first motivated to offend, then to seek out physical opportunities to commit the crime. Similarly, bank robbers in this study are motivated to offend independently of the existence of a physical opportunity for crime. Since banks are situated on most city street corners, and since robbers typically search out suitable targets, physical opportunity influences the choice of target, not the decision to offend.

THE EMPLOYMENT HISTORY OF
BANK ROBBERS

Most bank robbers in this study report short employment histories. Institutionalized in youth and/or adult correctional facilities for years, many are lethargic, lack initiative, and do not enjoy working. Not surprisingly, some describe themselves as lazy while others blame a lack of education and employment skills for their inability to obtain well-paid, satisfying employment. Most report a general disdain for legitimate employment because of the long hours and low pay. Compared to work, bank robbery is an easy shortcut to solving financial problems. The money obtained from a single holdup is viewed as the equivalent or better than an average person's monthly take-home pay. Some bank robbers approach the crime in the same way that others approach legitimate employment, even referring to it as "my work," "my job," "my occupation," or "my profession." Their disdain for work and the lazy streak fostered in prison or elsewhere leads them to develop a lackadaisical attitude, take few precautions, and put little effort into their robberies—factors that lead to their quick demise.

Most offenders (64/80 80 percent) in this study were unemployed prior to committing their initial bank robbery—29 percent have recently lost their job, and another 51 percent were unemployed, with the majority released from prison only a short time before; only 20 percent were employed at the time of their first bank holdup; 9 percent continued to work afterwards; and 4 percent were arrested at the time of the offence. The men who continued working used stolen funds to increase their standard of living while those who quit their jobs lost interest in work because bank robbery was easier and provided more money. One man stated that his drug usage made his work hazardous since he was employed as a window-washer on high-rise apartment buildings. Only 19 percent of unemployed men were actively seeking work prior to robbing a bank—most having recently lost their jobs. Three who sought employment admit, however, that they expended little time or effort and one says that he would probably have robbed banks regardless of whether he had found a job. Only four men actively sought work for several months and believe that they would not have committed bank robbery if their job hunt had succeeded.

It can be concluded from these observations that an improved job market would have little influence on the incidence of bank robbery because few offenders actively seek employment. Crime is a predetermined path for most and legitimate employment is not seriously attempted or considered for several reasons:

1. Crime as a way of life: Most bank robbers in this study have a history of criminal involvement, criminal association, and imprisonment that spans many years. It is understandable, therefore, that crime is always a possible solution to financial problems. For some, it is far more difficult to change course and begin working than to continue in crime.

2. Indolence and institutionalization: Partly because they have become institutionalized, many offenders have little initiative or motivation. Because they are not accustomed to mak-

ing the effort to set and attain goals, crime represents a more attractive option than work because it is faster and easier. Lethargy partly accounts for (a) the fact that few bank robbers attempt "the big score" because this requires considerable planning and effort; and (b) their eventual arrest because many are so lazy and careless that they fail to take basic precautions in committing their crimes.

3. Crime as a shortcut: Besides requiring less effort than working at a job, bank robbery entices because it provides instant financial gain. The desire for immediate gratification is particularly evident in the complaints of men released from prison. Their wish to have what others have—spending money, clothes, a place to live—leads to crime as a "quick fix" solution that puts them back on their feet: "I want everything the Joneses' have—only faster." A man recently returned to prison explains the feelings of released inmates:

> Guys who get out of the joint are completely on their own for the first time in many years. They've lost their girlfriend and their contact with family. They have joint clothes on. Everything they want, everything that is important to them in society is not available if they don't have money. Even a girl, you can't pick up a girl if you're dressed like you've just got out of jail. You can't even buy her a cup of coffee. And if you're going to look and wait for a job and hang around a halfway house, it's going to take you forever.

4. Unattractive working conditions and poor pay: Because they have spent so much time in prison, offenders often have an unimpressive employment history. Most have minimal education, job training, or marketable skills. This creates problems in obtaining work and limits them to low-paid, low-status, tedious, manual employment that offers little chance of advancement or job satisfaction. Aware of their limited opportunities, many are discouraged before they begin. The résumé of an inmate about to be released from prison illustrates the obstacles that ex-prisoners confront. His only work experiences and references come from prison workshops— hardly the background that inspires confidence and enthusiasm for potential employers. It is not surprising, therefore, that men released from prison return to crime without attempting to find employment.

5. Partying is more fun: Complaints about the "humdrum 9 to 5 routine" or the "lunch-bucket brigade" indicate a desire to

remain free from the constraints of work. Several offenders say that they prefer leisure to work and choose bank robbery over employment to secure money and freedom. In most cases, this means the freedom to party constantly. A married man with two children who drifted into crime through drug usage and criminal associations explains his reasons for not seeking employment after having been fired from his job:

> My wife worked and paid the bills. I was out all the time hanging around this bar frequented by bikers, hookers, and other bums. I didn't want to work. It cut into my free time for what I regarded as fun—hanging around the bar and getting stoned.

CHOOSING TO OFFEND— THE WISH TO BE INDEPENDENT

The perception of the bank robber as financially desperate and driven to robbing banks as a last-resort source of income is not borne out in this study. Most admit wanting, rather than needing, money and few describe themselves as financially desperate since they could either do without the funds or could receive assistance from friends or family. Pride and a desire to remain or become independent eliminate this option and lead them to investigate means to solve their financial problems on their own. Also, because of pride, offenders reject the idea of turning to others and/or refuse to consider welfare as an alternative: "I ain't going on welfare. I'm a capable person. I'm young, I can work, and I can steal." Surprisingly, four men in this study robbed banks because they wished to pay for their upcoming wedding and honeymoon. A young man who had been unemployed for months and had been supported by his fiancée summarized his feelings.

> Here I was living off my girlfriend and I was getting tired of it. We were getting married and her parents were paying for everything. They wanted to pay for our honeymoon but I wouldn't let them. She didn't mind that I wasn't working but I did.

He was arrested the day before his wedding while robbing a bank. His brother was arrested at the wedding rehearsal that same evening and was charged as an accomplice for driving the getaway vehicle.

Seeking Independence

This 25-year-old man was interviewed two years earlier and had subsequently been released on parole. He robbed another bank with three partners and received seven years for the robbery and an additional three years for the use of a firearm. Since he described his first robbery as a "mistake" and swore that he would never rob again, this interview focused on his motivation to re-offend.

I was on the street exactly eleven months three weeks and I got re-arrested for another bank robbery. I had served 16 months of a four-year bit and got out on parole. I was doing all right. I wasn't involved in crime and I was seeing my parole officer every two weeks. The circumstances just prior to my release is that I had all my things in storage at a friend's house and it burned down. It was exactly ten days before I got out. All my possessions were there, my colour T.V., my stereo, all my clothing, all my jewellery, everything I owned. I got out of jail with $200 in my pocket and no clothes. I had nothing, nothing at all. My parents are trying to help me out but they're going through a tough time and I don't need to be a burden. I was staying with my girlfriend at her apartment, looking for a job, and bumming a few bucks off my brothers and my parents. My parents are building their house so I start to help my father and he was shooting me whatever he could afford.

Now the old lady and me, we'd been going out for over five years and she wanted to get married, "Come on, let's get married." I wanted to but I didn't have any money. She really wanted, she was like—every intimate moment—like women know the moments to ask. So eventually I said, "Yah, we'll do it, but we're gonna have to wait." She said, "Well look, my parents are going to lend me the money so we can go on a honeymoon. Oh come on, come on, they don't mind. They know that when you're on your feet, you'll pay them back. They're happy for me." She was all happy.

What it comes down to is that it started to get to me. I was being supported by this woman. I was not working. I wasn't doing much of anything. I was bored, depressed. I wanted to get married but I wanted to have my own money and I wanted to be able to help pay. I know that my father would give his left arm for me except that I don't want to ask. I had been dependent for too long. It was getting to me, more and more so. Every day it was getting to me and I know I shouldn't have done it, I knew what I was doing was wrong, but I wanted to be independent. I wanted this, I wanted that, and I wanted it now. I could have made do on what I had but things were getting me down. I wasn't desperate. I wasn't sleeping on a park bench. I could have made ends meet in other ways. But it was things I wanted and I saw a way of getting it. I had only four or five pair of pants and six shirts and I wanted to get myself some nice clothes. I wanted to have money to pay for the wedding. I wanted to have my own money to take my wife on a honeymoon. I didn't want to borrow off her parents for that. My girlfriend began to get suspicious and said, "Don't you be doing something stupid for that money. You've already been to jail once." "No, no, I won't be doing nothing like that." "I know you better," she says, "You're lying to me." "No, I'm not lying to you." The day I was arrested, she and her mom had gone down to put a deposit on her wedding dress and buy cards for the invitations.

An analysis of offenders' account of their rationale for bank robbery shows that they choose to offend. Very few blame others, society, alcohol, or drugs for their decisions. Rather than deny responsibility, most acknowledge that they chose to commit bank robbery and are primarily to blame for their actions. Consistent with rational choice theory, bank robbers admit to deliberately and consciously taking a chance and acknowledge that they could have made other decisions. Although they were not financially desperate, slightly more than one-third of these men report a degree of emotional and/or situational impetus that includes elements of dispiritedness or gloom in some cases, and fatalism or indifference in other cases. Some offenders believe that they have nothing to lose in robbing a bank and proceed with a degree of reckless abandon.

THE BANK ROBBER'S ASSESSMENT OF RISK

Bank robbery is defined as low risk because most offenders intend to rob only one bank. Afterwards, however, they repeat the offence, each time telling themselves: "This is the last one." A travelling salesman convicted of 49 bank robberies explains, "Each bank robbery was going to be the last. The first was supposed to be the last." This man and other robbers promise themselves that they will retire before they are caught. Implicit in this view is the prevalent belief that the risk of getting caught for a single robbery is low. Indeed, few men in this sample were captured during their first robbery, but most continue until they are caught. Retrospectively, bank robbers admit to engaging in self-deception in believing they were only going to rob one more bank.

Bank robbers who are career criminals frequently deny the inevitability of arrest. They believe that the risk attached to each robbery is low and that the commission of previous bank robberies has little or no influence on their chances of successfully committing future scores. The next holdup is just as likely to succeed as the last. A compulsive gambler assesses the risk in the following way:

> Bank robbery is like rolling the dice. Each roll is independent of the next. But you're working with pretty good odds in doing any one bank. In any case, I enjoy taking risks.

Like most bank robbers, this man believes that once he is out of the immediate vicinity of the bank, the danger of arrest has passed.

Offenders tend to evaluate risk situationally and within immediate time frames. Each target is assessed individually and the long-term risk of committing successive criminal acts is not considered. Bank robbers evaluate the risk associated with a particular target and proceed if the risk is acceptable. If the risk is high, they choose another target. Many offenders choose to dismiss the threat of capture and other risks involved in robbery in order to commit their crimes. Even after they have been arrested, robbers continue to believe that the chances of getting caught are relatively small.

Their self-concept as highly competent criminals is another reason why some bank robbers deny the inevitability of arrest. This cockiness is accurately summarized by one young robber who states:

> I got away with all these, why shouldn't I be able to get away with more? The thing is at that time, I was young, right? I was like 19–20. I thought that they'll never get me, I'm too smart.

Ironically, confidence increases after culprits experience a "close call." Bank robbers who commit a series of holdups, not surprisingly, experience situations from which they narrowly escape. These include walking or driving past the police; being stopped in a roadblock; being pursued by bank employees or customers; being involved in car chases; or being shot at. Although they may re-evaluate their actions, postpone the next robbery, and/or take more precautions, robbers in this study were never intimidated enough to quit. On the contrary, their safe escape from a dangerous situation reinforces their self-concepts as intelligent and skilled criminals. It proves to them that they can maintain composure under stressful conditions, which in turn encourages further holdups.

THE VARIABLES ARE KNOWN

Bank robbers target banks because they believe that most of the variables are known and/or can be controlled. This is a somewhat surprising view since they are committing a dramatic and overt crime in broad daylight, in the middle of a crowd, and in a bank equipped with surveillance cameras and alarm systems. They know, however, that bank policy requires tellers to cooperate and not to press the alarm until it is safe to do so—usually only after the offender has left the premises. Bandits assume tellers will not call out for assistance and that others will not be aware of what is happening. Robbers also believe that anyone who does witness the act will either be reluctant to interfere or can be controlled.

> You go in there, you give them a note, they are not going to
> yell or scream, no one is going to notice or interfere, you get
> the money, and you get out. Away you go and nobody follows.

Furthermore, even if the alarm is activated immediately, robbers spend so little time in the bank—15 to 60 seconds—that they have plenty of time to escape before the police arrive. The factor emphasized the most—and which bandits can control—is speed. Since the police usually need several minutes to reach the scene, escape is easy and assured unless the robbers spend too much time in the bank. Bandits believe that if they're not caught at or near the bank, they're home-free. Most offenders breathe a sigh of relief, ten minutes after the escape, when they are far removed from the scene of the crime.

Offenders also believe that arrest results from bad luck or a "fluke." Bank robbers almost unanimously fail to attribute innovative or skilled police work as an important variable in leading to their arrest. As one robber says, "It's not true that it's great detective work that solves crime. Like 90 percent of their arrests are made by somebody informing." Few give credit to the police for their capture:

> It was a fluke chance. The police arrest people on fluke
> chances and informers. But you have to know when to quit or
> the odds are against you. I didn't know when to quit.

All bank robbers acknowledge that some contingencies are beyond their control and that luck is a variable. Some eventually realize—often only retrospectively—that to continue robbing banks means that arrest is inevitable, since bad luck will eventually occur. "Something can always trip you up. You might fall down a manhole cover. It happens." "The police can make all kinds of mistakes and you only have to make one." However, even acknowledging the possibility or inevitability of a chance occurrence does not deter most bank robbers. They continue to view it as a low-risk crime, are confident in their abilities, and/or intend to stop robbing banks shortly. Many claim that their most recent robbery was definitely supposed to be their last. Most bank robbers also swear that they are now retired and will never rob again.

THE SPENDING HABITS OF BANK ROBBERS

"I always liked nice things and once I had them, I wanted more."

—A hairdresser turned bank robber

"I'm just a regular guy who leads a regular life but who happens to rob banks."

—Solo gunman with a lengthy record of convictions

The lifestyle and spending habits of the 80 convicted Canadian bank robbers interviewed in the present study follow a distinct pattern: the vast majority rob several banks, spend the money quickly and foolishly, rob repeatedly, and get caught. Approximately two-thirds wish to increase their standard of living and purchase goods and services they could not afford. The remaining one-third wish to protect what they have: "My standard of living stays the same all the time. If I have to rob a bank to do it, then that's what I'll do." In some cases, robbers report that the threat to their financial wellbeing comes from the loss of illegal income, particularly from selling drugs. In only a few instances does the threat come from the loss of legitimate employment. A 28-year-old ex-inmate who was employed for two years and supporting his wife and daughter before losing his job, reports that as the bills began to pile up, he became increasingly frustrated in his inability to find work. A series of articles in the local newspaper detailing the increase in bank robberies in the city convinced him to rob a bank.

I was married and had a daughter and things were going well as far as trying to get into a normal life. Being as close to good as I possibly could—smoke a little dope once in awhile— nothing really bad. Things began piling up and then one day I just thought, "I need some money." I've never owed money before and I didn't like it. Five to six thousand dollars is not a lot. Like there are people who owe hundred of thousands. I've never owed hardly anything before. I bought a car and I was working hard to pay it off. I didn't want to lose what I had. Finally I just said, "Fuck it. Let's do something." I thought there's got to be a way to get a few bucks that's not dangerous. I intended to do just one—like all thieves, just one. Greed controls man—if you got one, you want two.

This man injected the earnings from his five bank robberies into his family's day-to-day living in such a way that his wife would not notice. At the time of his arrest, he no longer had any debts. Other men (13/80 16 percent) in this study indicate that their spending habits remained moderate despite their new income and/or that the money was insufficient to substantially increase their spending. Others (13/80 16 percent) were caught before they could spend the money and the remaining two-thirds (54/80 67.5 percent) of the sample report extravagant spending sprees.

DRUG USAGE AND GAMBLING

It is difficult to classify and measure illicit drug usage and drug dependency, particularly when it is based on an offender's self-evaluation of drug and spending habits. Despite the crudeness and subjective nature of these estimates, distinct patterns and causal sequences appear to exist. Ten men in this sample (10/80 12.5 percent) describe themselves as drug addicts (heroin, speed, cocaine) and three offenders admit to using marijuana excessively prior to robbing banks. All thirteen admit that part of their motivation to rob a bank was to maintain their drug habit. This oversimplifies matters, however, since two were illegally at large and needed money to support themselves; three men were under pressure to pay drug debts; and all wished to begin or maintain a partying lifestyle.

In addition to the men who described themselves as drug addicts or excessive users, an additional two-thirds of the sample (54/80 67.5 percent) admit to using drugs occasionally or moderately prior to becoming involved in bank robbery. None of these men, however, specifically mention drug usage as part of their initial motivation to bank robbery. Most explain their reasons for continuing in this criminal activity, however, as including a desire to continue partying—an activity that for them involves the use of illicit drugs. Almost half report that their drug usage increased significantly after they began robbing banks while the remaining half maintained previous levels of consumption. For most drug users, drug usage is described in the context of drinking and partying and their crime spree is intended to support this lifestyle.

The remaining offenders did not use drugs before or after bank robbery and many stated that they preferred alcohol.

Gambling appears to follow the same pattern as drug usage. Gambling is the main expenditure in six men (6/80 7.5 percent) in this study yet only one subject attributes his initial motivation to gambling. All six report that they gambled before they robbed their first bank, yet excessive gambling occurred after bank robbery in five of six cases. Each of these men admit that the motivation to continue robbing is strongly related to the desire to continue gambling. All six frequented the racetrack, bet heavily on longshots with correspondingly poor odds, and lost thousands of dollars. A police search of one offender's home uncovered a dozen $100 losing stubs on a 60-to-1 longshot. A 30-year-old compulsive gambler recently paroled from prison committed 14 bank holdups in eight weeks before being arrested. He netted close to $40,000 and gambled it away at the racetrack. Suspecting that the person responsible for these crimes might have a "monkey on his back" [an addiction], the Hold-Up Squad posted plain-clothed officers at the entrance to the racetrack. Using a photograph of the offender taken by a bank camera, the police spotted the culprit but lost him in the crowd. The offender claims in his interview that he saw the police before they saw him and was lucky enough to get away. Two weeks later, he was chased by a bank manager and held until the police arrived to make the arrest. When interviewed, this subject was living in the protective-custody unit of a medium-security penitentiary because his life had been threatened due to unpaid institutional gambling debts. His addiction is evident when he compares the thrill of gambling with the "high" obtained from robbing banks.

> Have you ever played poker? Then think back to a hand that stands out. I'll bet you even money that you bluffed and won a pile of cash. That's what I do when I rob a bank. The threat is a bluff and I walk out with a lot of money. It's a great feeling.

These data reveal that gambling/drug addictions do not generate the initial motivation for robbery for the large majority of bank robbers in this study. Illicit drug consumption and gambling tend to precede bank robbery but excessive drug usage and gambling will most likely occur after they've robbed a bank and have money to blow. In the case of drugs, most men who rob banks admit to using drugs, in some cases to excess, but few attribute the need to support a drug habit as a reason for robbing that first bank. After taking care of debts, buying some items, paying their rent, and settling a few bills, most bank robbers begin to spend money on alcohol, drugs, restaurants, gambling, taxis, hotel rooms, women, friends, and sex. Drug usage and gambling may be an expensive part of this lifestyle but are only one part. The decision to rob again is more a wish to continue the lifestyle than a result of drug dependency or an addiction to gambling. However, the fact that drugs and gambling are expensive means that the money dissipates quickly and the offender commits more robberies in quick succession. These data show that a drug or gambling addiction better explains the motivation to initially commit a holdup. Given the lengthy criminal background of the majority of subjects in this sample, these data are also consistent with the "criminalization" hypothesis discussed in Chapter Two, which suggests that criminal associations precede and give rise to drug usage.

A PARTYING LIFESTYLE

Most offenders describe spending money on "partying." Partying involves the pursuit of fun and friendship typically by frequenting bars, purchasing drinks and drugs for themselves and others, staying up late, getting up late, and repeating the pattern each day. Offenders also spend money on clothing, gifts, taxis, sexual favours, and hotel rooms. Relatively few robbers purchase expensive material goods or make investments but instead prefer to party away the money. A 22-year-old man describes his spending spree as: "Out of control. Total abandonment of all moral and monetary principles."

The bar scene entails partying with others and many bank robbers realize (often retrospectively) that some people are attracted to the money and take advantage of their generosity. One young man observes:

> When you have a lot of money, you have a lot of friends. People notice, sure. And you spend it quicker because they're around and you don't care because you know there's more. I was always buying people beers.

An offender who robbed 61 banks describes himself as an alcoholic and admits to spending most of his time and money in bars. He acknowledges that people used him but appears unconcerned:

> I was buying rounds at this hotel and a friend who was working there took me aside and said, "Rob, I've known you a long time and I like you. What are you doing with all these goofs?" There were 22 people at that table and I hardly knew any-

body... I'm a soft touch for a woman who's sitting down telling me she hasn't got anything for the kids to eat... I give her a couple of hundred, "Here, go shopping." I gave it away and I loaned out thousands. I'll never get that back.

A man convicted of three armoured-vehicle heists in which he obtained and spent hundreds of thousands of dollars reports spending it in a few months. He also says he gave it away:

How did I spend the money? Stupid, stupid, stupid. A businessman cannot do a holdup and a holdup man cannot do business. I spent $400,000 in eight months and I was giving it away like I was Robin Hood... to everybody and anybody. You've got a lot of friends when you've got a lot of money. Maybe I was trying to buy my friends, I don't know. Maybe it has something to do with my coming from an orphanage. It's a problem I have to work out for myself... I spent a lot my last time out, probably $800,000... $400-a-night hotel rooms. I'd buy cocaine and give it away. I don't sell it.

His partner describes this man's spending prior to their arrest:

I would say he spent a million, easy... gives it away! "Go buy this for me." He gives you $500 for something that costs $300 and he don't want no change. If you order drinks for people and it costs $60 and you tip $10–$15 then you don't have much left out of a $100 bill and you have to break another 15 minutes later because your glass is empty. He liked the big life... and kids. Sex with kids. What I call a kid is a guy who is 16–18, looking young. He's a kid... street kids. Go downtown... those kind of kids. It's going to cost you a thousand bucks to pass the night with a kid—three or four hundred on coke. He don't mind prison because he has that inside and dope too.

The value of money appears to diminish the more one has and the easier it is to obtain. Bank robbers increase their spending largely because they no longer worry about money, "Why should I worry? There's more where that came from." Many become addicted to the money and the corresponding lifestyle that easy wealth brings and are reluctant to give it up. A young gambler describes his spending and accompanying attitudes:

I paid the rent and filled the fridge and the rest was for partying and going to the racetrack. I had some pretty bad days. I was hoping for one night where I could go in there with maybe $1,000 and bet $100 a race and maybe hit a couple of long shots but it never happened. I got to the point after my second bank that I didn't really care about the money I lost because I could always go back to the bank and make a withdrawal. I have an unlimited supply, "Why should I start saving it?" I think I had about 30–40 losing nights in a row. I didn't care.

A man accustomed to robbing armoured vehicles and spending large sums of money similarly describes and explains his extravagance:

That's probably the main reason I love to steal—I love to spend money. One of my partners, he wouldn't spend a dime to see an earthquake. I do stupid things... I remember once, I'm in Miami with this babe and I know I'm going to be hung over in the morning and I'm going to the West coast to meet these two guys. I'm having a drink and I'm on the phone reserving two first-class plane tickets so I wouldn't have anybody there bothering me at 6:00 a.m. on the champagne and orange juice flight to Los Angeles. You do stuff like that which you wouldn't do if you work for your money. I'm sure.

Women are part of a partying lifestyle and another expense for many bank robbers. Some men purchase the services of prostitutes, others buy drinks for women in bars, while others spend their money on a girlfriend. In some instances, the offender's girlfriend or wife will await his release from prison but most relationships end with the offender's arrest. A few women will write and/or visit but most eventually terminate the relationship. In one instance, an offender I was scheduled to interview cancelled the meeting because a former girlfriend arrived at the prison to visit him. I recognized her as an ex-girlfriend of another bank robber, a man I had known for several years. In a further coincidence, the subject who substituted for the interview was a friend of both men. When I made my observation, he laughed and told me that the woman was also presently involved with a friend of his who was also a bank robber. "She must like bank robbers," I remarked. "She likes money," he corrected.

Although women may have taken advantage of them, few robbers express bitterness. Men who have established long-term intimate relationships are disappointed when the affair ends but others claim that they either did not care about the person or they did not expect the relationship to last. For many, the women are only one part of a lifestyle that is not sustainable.

Except for the men who rob armoured vehicles, few offenders report spending time and money on travel. Those who do travel report visiting nearby cities, the Caribbean, Mexico, and other sites throughout Canada and the United States and limit their holidays to a few days or weeks. Most bank robbers prefer to party and spend their ill-gotten gains in familiar surroundings.

Overall, the career of most bank robbers is short-lived and characterized by a series of holdups done in quick succession to support a hedonistic lifestyle. The fact that most squander the money and have no alternative income indicates that they are unlikely to retire from bank robbery. Only five men report saving or investing stolen money. Most adopt a "live for today" philosophy or fall into this pattern without realizing it. The fact that few men purchase material goods perhaps indicates an awareness that they will not be around long enough to enjoy them. Most bank robbers prefer transitory pleasures—drugs, alcohol, sex, companionship, and attention or status. Few invest with the intent of retiring and reverting to a law-abiding life and many admit that they would probably have continued robbing banks until the police stopped them. Their attitude towards money is "easy come, easy go," and they spend freely and foolishly because "there's always more where that came from." This careless and carefree attitude eventually leads to their demise, since most of them would not have been caught or convicted had they stopped their criminal activity at an earlier time.

RECIDIVISTS—MEN WHO COME BACK

Once a person has been arrested, imprisoned, and then released, why does he or she repeat the crime? Why are persons who have been convicted of several robberies, received a lengthy prison sentence, and face even greater time if reconvicted, not deterred by the possibility of more time? Their reasons for re-offending are often identical to their initial motivation and the motivation to continue. They need or want money for specific purposes—often being broke after their release from prison—and they aspire to the lifestyle that they once enjoyed. In addition, they continue to view the crime as easy and relatively safe despite their arrest and conviction. A subject who believed that his arrest for robbery the first time was due to bad luck, robbed again and was re-arrested. He explains: "I just figured that lightning doesn't strike twice in the same place."

THE DECISION TO LEAVE CRIME

Most research on criminal careers has focused on the process by which persons become initially involved in crime. Much less is known about the pathways out of deviance and processes of disinvolvement. Criminologists do know, however, that there is a direct connection between age and crime and that the crime rate decreases with age, beginning in late adolescence and continuing throughout adulthood. Even among career criminals, desistance from crime is a frequent occurrence. Cusson and Pinsonneault (1986:73) argue that since most offenders give up crime eventually, to die a criminal, one would almost have to die a violent death.

Researching the motivation to leave crime, Irwin (1970) interviewed 15 ex-convicts and found that they had terminated their criminal involvement because of (1) the fear of further imprisonment; (2) exhaustion from years of a desperate criminal life and a deprived prison life; (3) a reduction in sexual and financial expectations; (4) an adequate and satisfying relationship with a woman; and (5) involvement in extravocational and extra-domestic activities. Meisenhelder (1977) interviewed 20 incarcerated property offenders about earlier periods of their lives when they had temporarily terminated their criminal behaviour. Their motivation to discontinue crime included a fear of doing more time in prison and a subjective wish to lead a more normal life. In addition, successful exit from crime was assisted by the establishment of meaningful bonds to conventional persons.

Shover (1989) interviewed 36 previously convicted and incarcerated property offenders, focusing on their reasons for ending a lengthy criminal career. He concluded that during their late thirties to early forties, most began to take stock of their lives and accomplishments and realized for the first time that their criminality had been an unproductive enterprise, and that this situation was unlikely to change. The aging process results in a redefinition of their youthful criminal identity as self-defeating, foolish, or even dangerous. Most of the men became acutely aware of time as a diminishing, exhaustible resource and began to plan for the remainder of their lives. As this new perspective developed, the future became increasingly valuable, and the possibility of spending additional time in prison especially threatening. They dreaded a long sentence, but believed that because of their previous convictions, any prison terms they received would be lengthy. The men began to view the entire criminal justice system as an apparatus that clumsily but relentlessly swallows offenders and wears them down. Furthermore, they grew tired of the problems and consequences of criminal involvement. Shover also found that respondents reduced their aspirations and goals and no longer strove for the same level of material fulfilment and recognition that they had sought when younger. These changes produced a disenchantment with the activities and lifestyles of their youth, and an interest in and a readiness for fundamental change in their lives. Successful participation in relationships and/or jobs provided personal rewards and reinforced a noncriminal identity. For many, the development of a commitment to someone and/or employment gradually generated a pattern of routine activities that conflicted with, and left little time for, the daily activities associated with crime (Shover, 1989).

In interviews with 17 thirty- to forty-year-old Canadian ex-robbers who had not been arrested in the five preceding years, Cusson and Pinsonneault (1986) similarly note that an interesting job and satisfying family ties give meaning to life and provide an incentive to respect the law. Their study also found a succession of arrests and incarcerations eventually have an effect. Men who for years could not be intimidated despite many severe punishments decide to go straight mainly because they do not want to go back to prison. This "delayed deterrence" gradually wears down criminal motivation and engenders a pervasive fear. Delayed deterrence has four components: (a) a higher estimate of the cumulative probability of punishment; (b) the increasing difficulty of doing time; (c) an awareness of the weight of previous convictions on the severity of the sentences; and (d) a spreading fear. Cusson and Pinsonneault note that with age, criminals raise their estimates of the certainty of punishment and acknowledge that the more crimes they commit, the greater the cumulative probability of arrest. Ex-offenders unanimously acknowledge that, with age, it is increasingly difficult to do time and that they are wasting time and ruining their lives. Criminals also realize that the more extensive their criminal record, the greater the risk of a long sentence. The fear of incurring a long prison term the next time influenced their decision to stop. Cusson and Pinsonneault report that the decision to give up crime is not so much a positive decision, the desire to go straight, but a negative one, a desire to never to go back to prison. The prospect of dying in prison is seen as the ultimate failure (1986:78).

SUMMARY

Research on the motivation to cease criminal involvement indicates that with increasing age and years spent in prison, offenders develop a self-critical, objective view of their lives. In their youth, they equate the chances of being caught to the probability of being arrested for a single crime. With time, the career criminal eventually recognizes that the probability of being caught is much higher since it is calculated on the total number of crimes committed. The realization that the law of averages works against them leads aging offenders to conclude that crime has a high risk. Their reasoning is clearly more rational and objective than when they were younger and many admit that the rationale and assumptions that motivated them to commit crimes in their youth were fundamentally flawed. Aging offenders re-examine their lives and conclude that crime does not pay. The increasing pain and fear of imprisonment, combined with a satisfying job and/or relationship motivates them to go straight. It appears that rational choice, deterrence, social control, and differential association theories help to explain criminal disinvolvement.

Cusson and Pinsonneault describe offenders who had given up their criminal careers as more realistic, more prudent, and more mature than younger criminals. Their temporal perspectives were broadened and they had evolved to where their lives had ceased to be a series of disconnected episodes and had become future-oriented. "Like rolling a film backward, we see the aging offender take the threat of punishment seriously, reestablish his links with society, and sever his association with the underworld" (1986:80).

From the perspective of rational choice theory, it is clear that robbers exercise a degree of rationality in their decision to commit crime. Research indicates, however, that offenders seldom approach robbery in a purely calculating manner. Rather, their rationality is limited to what seems reasonable at the time, given their financial needs and the limited alternatives and opportunities open to them. In addition, there is frequently an element of desperation, fatalism, impulsiveness, and opportunism in the life situation of people who commit robbery.

C   H   A   P   T   E   R   **4**

Modus Operandi

INTRODUCTION

The term "modus operandi" (M.O.) refers to the methods of operation used by robbers in the commission of their crimes. Robbery is an offence that pays small dividends and consequently is repeated by offenders typically in the same manner. Emboldened by early success, robbers commit a string of similar style robberies, become overconfident and careless, and are arrested shortly afterwards. Most robbers choose to rob either individuals, commercial establishments, or financial institutions—but usually not all three. Typically, offenders will develop a distinct modus operandi that includes selecting the same type of target for each score. Bandits who rob taxi drivers will seldom rob a bank and vice versa. This degree of specialization is reflected in the manner in which Hold-Up Squads assign cases to investigators. Officers are assigned to work either (a) muggings and robberies of small commercial establishments, or (b) financial institution and armoured-vehicle holdups. Although many of the offenders who commit muggings also commit commercial robberies, few will rob banks. Robbers usually choose an M.O. and consistently repeat the crime in the same manner. Since offenders seldom significantly vary their M.O., the police can build up case files on individuals or crews through their brief robbery escapades. Occasionally it even helps in their capture. More frequently though, the routinized repetition of M.O. is useful in clearing cases by linking the offender to most, if not all, of his or her crimes. This chapter examines the different modus operandi used by robbers in muggings, convenience-store robberies, and bank and armoured-vehicle holdups. Also discussed are issues related to target selection, control of victims, the use of weapons and violence, solo versus group robbery, and the spending habits of robbers. A detailed typology of three types of bank robbery M.O.s based on interviews with 80 Canadian bank robbers is presented at the end of the chapter.

MODUS OPERANDI AND THE ROBBERY OF PERSONS, STORES, AND FINANCIAL INSTITUTIONS

(1) MUGGINGS

The term "mugging" is derived from criminal and police parlance in the 1940s and refers to a certain manner of robbing and/or beating a victim for his or her money and/or property (Lejeune and Alex, 1973:260). A mugging originally meant a strangle or choke-hold applied to the victim from behind while his or her wallet was being stolen (Maurer, 1964). Today, the term "mugging" is commonly used to refer to acts of robbery committed in public places against individuals. Mugging is a personal crime that frequently involves direct violence, emotional trauma, and bodily injury to the victim. The offence lacks the finesse, skill, or cunning characteristic of other types of criminal activity such as fraud or embezzlement. Influenced by media reports of crime and images of villains lurking in hallways, elevators, parking garages, and parks, many citizens fear being mugged and adjust their lifestyle to ensure personal safety. The mugging symbolizes the breakdown of social order and the way that crime or the fear of crime can limit one's freedom. As the incidence and visibility of mugging and other street crimes have increased, urban residents believe that they are no longer safe in public places. At the same time, the limited protection offered by law-enforcement agencies has made it clear to citizens that they must protect themselves from predators.

For victims, the mugging represents an unexpected terrifying encounter with one or more strangers. In contrast to a commando-style assault, some offenders initially approach victims in a nonthreatening or less threatening way by panhandling or requesting directions. During the mugging, the victim is likely to experience shock and disbelief, which can cause rapid deterioration of scenes from benign to malevolent. Such an experience, uniformly reported by victims of muggings (Lejeune and Alex, 1973:265–76; Lejeune, 1977:137–38) is also perceived as a management problem by the mugger. Although some muggers realize that the victim may not initially comprehend what is happening, many interpret the victim's momentary disorientation as resistance and treat it accordingly. The elements that initially normalize an encounter (e.g., polite conversation, respectable dress) accentuate both the victim's disbelief and consequently the mugger's management problem during the confrontation phase. A trouble-free execution of the act requires that the mugger quickly and unambiguously define the situation to the victim.

The use of some physical force by young and frequently inept robbers, particularly among those who execute robberies without weapons, occurs more frequently than not (Conklin, 1972:102–22; Mulvihill et al., 1969:234–38). The mugging is essentially a violent encounter where there is always a possibility that the victim(s) will be seriously hurt. Violence represents either a means of gaining control or a loss of control over the victim. In the first instance, force is used as an initial tactic in anticipation of any resistance by the victim. In the second instance, force is used in response to perceived resistance by the victim. Lejeune (1977:141–43) classifies the perceived rational use of force among respondents as either pre-emptive or reactive. The mugger, he suggests, will tend to use pre-emptive force to quickly define the situation as a robbery to the victim when he or she is, or feels, unable to control the situation by other means. The younger, inexperienced mugger is more likely to rely on pre-emptive force. Reactive force, however, is used when the robber fails to obtain or loses control over the victim. It is typically precipitated by victim resistance such as when the victim screams, fights back, or refuses to give up the money.

The mugger defines the situation as one in which he or she attempts to instil fear and communicate to the victim that in return for his or her cooperation, the use of force will be limited. After establishing a "coercive exchange" (Goffman, 1971:329), albeit one that the victim may not understand or may not be able to fulfil, the mugger is likely to define any failure to comply to expectations as a justified cause for a violent response.

> At other times, people I went to rob, they gave me a hard time. To get the money that I wanted to get I had to stab them (Lejeune, 1977:143).

A victim may also be blamed for not having any money to give the robber.

> Sometimes we would get somebody and they would have nothing [no money]. And a lot of times we would get—well a lot of times we would get mad, so mad that we wanna hurt the person that has nothing. You're saying: "I'm going

through all this for nothing." That's how a lot of times, you know, things happen (Lejeune, 1977:145).

Since both the mugger and the victim are often inept in the performance of their roles, each unable to predict the behaviour of the other, the likelihood of tragic consequences is always present.

Lejeune (1977:133) reports that the mugger relies on knowledge and skills learned in play, sport, and everyday street interactions with peers. The interactional skills that are critical to the management of the mugging are acquired on the street in an environment where being cool and tough are requisites for survival. The chosen victim is one whom the mugger perceives as unlikely to resist and likely to yield an acceptable payoff. The success of the first few muggings enables the mugger to lower the estimate of likely risks entailed in future confrontations and the crime becomes redefined as "easy" or "routine." Repeated success breeds self-assurance. From the mugger's perspective, the police, the victim, and witnesses are possible sources of danger during a mugging. Of the three, the victim is perceived as potentially the least predictable and least controllable threat. Bank robbers, in contrast, have little fear of victim resistance since they assume that tellers will comply with their demands.

Lejeune (1977:145) concludes that mugging is a primitive form of criminal activity practised by those who are too young, unskilled and inexperienced to execute other crimes. Furthermore, mugging is often a group activity in which the threat or use of force is substituted for cunning, deception, and expertise. Muggings occur with encouragement of associates who discourage the outward manifestation of fear and encourage acts of bravado. Fear is managed through peer support, by carefully selecting victims, by defining the crime as low risk, and by attempting to control the elements in the mugging situation to reduce risks.

In recent years, two new types of muggings have received considerable publicity due to their violent nature. In Florida, robbers have been targeting tourists in rental cars who stray off the main highway. The bandits cause a minor car accident and rob tourists who stop to investigate. Several highly publicized killings of foreign tourists have led to a major police crack-down and legislation that prevents companies from displaying symbols that indicate the vehicles are rental cars. In Toronto, a frightening new form of robbery has emerged in which offenders break into the victim's home while residents are there and steal their property under threats of violence. Several of these "home invasions," as they have become known, have resulted in serious assaults and injuries to victims.

(2) CONVENIENCE-STORE ROBBERIES

The same factors that make convenience stores attractive to customers also make them easy prey to holdups. Local groceries, gas bars, beer and liquor stores, and other small merchants are located in areas of the city and operate during hours that are most convenient to their customers. To the would-be robber, these stores are attractive and vulnerable targets because they have easy access and escape routes, are open late at night, are relatively isolated, and have readily available cash. The stores are especially vulnerable since the clerk is not shielded by bulletproof glass and there are few customers/bystanders to be controlled. Frequently a robber will appear as a prospective customer, enter, loiter for a few moments, and then make his or her move. This allows the robber to observe the clerk's movements, wait for customers to leave, and evaluate any security devices.

Offenders typically assess target vulnerability in terms of (a) location for easy access and escape; and (b) the probable degree of control that can be exercised over staff and customers to prevent resistance. Control relates to the number of staff and customers present, physical characteristics of the store, the number of offenders, and the weapons used. The presence or absence of security measures influences the degree of control the robber perceives that he or she has. The more vulnerable characteristics that a target has, the more it will attract the armed robber.

Ciale and Leroux's (1983) study of armed robbery in Ottawa indicates that the preferred or most vulnerable targets are small businesses connected with food distribution, e.g., restaurants, groceterias, chain convenience stores, and corner stores. Fully 35.5 percent of these stores were victims of armed robberies in the year of their study. Next in order of preference are individuals (17.5 percent of all robberies) who are robbed in public places, financial institutions (15.5 percent), and other commercial establishments (15.5 percent). The researchers calculate that some chain convenience stores have a risk coefficient of .95 (total number of robberies divided by the total number of stores). Financial institutions were next with a risk coefficient of .403 and drug stores at .229 (1983:24).

(3) ROBBERIES OF FINANCIAL INSTITUTIONS

An analysis of bank robberies in Canada indicates that the majority were committed by lone bandits (81 percent in 1991; 78 percent in 1992; and 81 percent in 1993) and that most of these offenders are men. Women were involved in less than three percent of all bank holdups in this period. Bank robbery is usually committed without much sophistication or planning. Most bank robbers were not disguised (76 percent wore no disguises in 1991; 67 percent in 1992; and 67 percent in 1993) and many use a holdup note (45 percent in 1991; 40 percent in 1992; and 26 percent in 1993). No weapon was seen by the victim 50 percent of the time in 1991, 45 percent in 1992, and 48 percent in 1993. A weapon was simulated in 27 percent of 1993 holdups. When a weapon was displayed, 67 percent of the time it was a handgun. Only one employee was directly victimized in 74 percent of the 1991 holdups, 61 percent in 1992, and 63 percent in 1993. About 80 percent of the dollar losses incurred were taken from the teller's cash drawer. Some physical injury was reported in only six of the 1,609 robberies in 1991; in 10 of 1,530 robberies in 1992; and in only 7 of the 1,641 bank holdups in 1993. Bank robberies are fairly evenly spread over the 12 months but the most popular days for holdups are Thursdays and Fridays (Ballard, 1992; 1993; 1994).

U.S. Bureau of Justice statistics (1988) indicate that in more than three-quarters of bank robberies, offenders used no disguise, despite the widespread use of surveillance equipment. Similarly, 86 percent of bank robbers did not inspect the bank prior to the offence. In his study of bank robbery in the United States, Camp (1968:112) found that offenders expect four things in a bank robbery: (1) no resistance from employees; (2) to be observed by the employees; (3) the police will be notified during the robbery or immediately thereafter; and (4) the robbery will be easy. In only half of the robberies did they disguise themselves. Bank robbers perceive the crime as easy and actually experience it as easier than they had anticipated. Camp (1968:126) also notes that one major effect of success is that the offender returns repeatedly. In addition, the robber believes that one more robbery will make little difference in terms of the severity of the punishment.

In a study of 500 convicted bank robbers in the United States, Haran and Martin (1984:50) note that bank robbery is primarily a small-group activity. Solo bandits consisted of 22.3 percent of cases, two robbers included 15.9 percent, three robbers 23.3 percent, four 13.9 percent, five 11.3 percent, six 6.2 percent, seven 3.0 percent, and eight or more only four percent of the time. Certain patterned roles are evident in bank robbery. The money grabber leaps over the bank counter and scoops up the money from the teller's cages. Many of the robbers wore sneakers to make vaulting easier. The floorman remains positioned at a strategic point commanding the entrance to the bank and bank personnel, displays a weapon, and shouts commands to the tellers, customers, and other partners. Haran and Martin note that these roles are often blurred or interchanged depending on the circumstances involved. Lookouts were also used to watch for police or to prevent customers from exiting while the robbery was in progress. There were also "wheelmen" who drove getaway cars for quick escapes.

The end of this chapter outlines typologies that characterize the modus operandi of three types of bank robbery: (1) the note-pusher or beggar bandit; (2) the solo gunman; and, (3) bank robbery crews. Also discussed are crews who commit armoured-vehicle robberies.

Planning The Crime

"We were just praying that it would work."

—*A 21-year-old bandit shot by the police*

The media image of robbery is one in which professionals meticulously plan their robberies and escape with large sums of cash. Research suggests that the typical robber is anything but professional. Unlike other crimes such as fraud or safecracking, robbery does not require much planning, skill, or knowledge. The basic requirements are nerve and the use of threats or a weapon to frighten victims into compliance. The targets are usually convenience stores and other small businesses. The offender's lack of sophistication is shown by the fact that most are young; the crime is completed within a matter of seconds; offenders often wear minimal or no disguise; most robberies bring no more than a few hundred dollars and frequently less; and robbers do little planning prior to their robbery.

Based on interviews with 113 Californian robbers, Feeney (1986) reports that most robbers appear to take a highly casual approach to their crimes. Over one-half said that they did no planning and another one-third reported only minimal preparations such as finding a partner, thinking about where to leave a getaway car, or whether to use a weapon. This minimal, low-level planning generally occurred the same day as the robbery and frequently in the few hours preceding it. Some robberies had an impulsive, opportunistic nature to them. Feeney (1986:59) also found that only 15 percent had any kind of planned approach and the largest number of these (9 percent) simply followed an existing M.O. Fewer than five percent of the robbers planned in any detail. These robbers, all adults who committed commercial robberies, stole getaway cars, planned escape routes, detailed each partner's actions, evaluated contingencies, and observed the layout of prospective targets. Commercial robberies were planned more often than individual muggings (60 percent versus 30 percent). Robbers' comments as to how they chose victims also indicate minimal preparations. Over 20 percent said that they chose their victim because of convenience, 15 percent said that the victim appeared to have money, and another 15 percent chose their victims because a fast getaway was possible or the risk otherwise appeared to be low. Others gave mixed reasons or did not know why they had chosen particular targets. The casual attitude is also illustrated by their lack of concern over the possibility of apprehension. Over 60 percent said they had not even considered getting caught before the robbery; another 17 percent said that they had considered the possibility but did not believe it to be a problem; and only 21 percent were concerned about getting caught and many of these were first-time robbers (Feeney, 1986:60–62). The majority express little concern about the risks involved, assume that they will execute the crime quickly, and have escaped before the police arrive.

Haran and Martin similarly observe that robbers are not Willie Sutton-like professionals and that robberies are basically hit-and-run affairs with little planning. A full 21 percent were caught in the act at the scene or later the same day (1984:51). Camp (1968:112) similarly reports that the planning of bank robberies is rather casual. Slightly more than half the time, the culprit has never been inside the bank before robbing it. In addition, robbers express little concern with internal aspects of the bank, such as alarms, cameras, or marked money (1968:113–14). The present study also found that less than half of the bank robbers interviewed enter the premises before committing the robbery partly because banks have predictable architectural designs that can be assessed by looking through the window or walking through the door.

> I never went in the bank to check it out. It doesn't matter
> how the bank is set up. I'll find the money and the door out.
> Those are the important things.

When I began this bank robbery research, I was surprised to discover how little planning offenders put into their crimes. Given the risks involved and the severe sentences, I had assumed that bank robbers would be highly cautious. Much later in the research, I was surprised whenever I found a subject (usually a solo gunman) who had taken precautions and put effort into planning and executing their scores. I had become so accustomed to interviewing robbers who had done little planning that when I later listened to the recorded interviews, I heard myself asking questions like: "You went to all that trouble just to rob that one bank?" In earlier interviews, I was more apt to ask: "You mean to say that you didn't even wear sunglasses or a hat to disguise yourself?"

SELECTING A TARGET

"It was such a beautiful bank."

—*A bandit who robbed the same bank six times*

One of the most important tactical choices that a robber must make is whom to rob. Consequently planning often begins with the selection of a target. Preparations consist of obtaining firearms and disguises, observing the site, determining the roles of each participant, and planning the getaway. Choices are circumscribed and limited by the weapons, disguises, partners, and vehicles at hand. Robbery is a crime that is often made up as it goes along and robbers have few contingency plans. Target selection is based on the individual's familiarity with potential targets, the amount of money believed to be there, perceptions of victim vulnerability, chance encounters, and on variables related to escape. Some offenders prefer to rob in areas of the city in which they are familiar. Feeney (1986:62) reports that despite the risk, over one-third of the robbers attacked victims close to their own residence. Although a nearby site is obviously convenient and familiar, it also carries the highest risk of recognition. More cautious bandits will travel outside their home area and commit crimes in other districts and/or in nearby cities. In most cases, the target and getaway route are selected only a few moments or hours before the robbery.

Although the amount of money is an important factor, robbers normally state that the minimization of risk is their principal goal. Commercial robbers are on the lookout for surveillance cameras, patrol cars, and customers who might interfere or alert the police. Convenience-store robbers typically wait until times such as late at night when retail outlets have no customers. Crow and Bull's (1975) study found that in 82 percent of the robberies, no customers were in the store at the time of the robbery. This means that there are fewer witnesses and less chance of interference. Ciale and Leroux (1983:26) found that 58.8 percent of commercial robberies occur at night between 7 p.m. and midnight, when business is slow.

Lejeune (1977:135) observes that the mugger is influenced by the particular range of victims likely encountered "on the stroll." Among opportunity factors, the mugger's geographical location is likely to limit his or her choice of victims. The mugger is usually too young or poor to own a car. He or she may use public transportation to seek out victims, both in transit and in distant neighbourhoods. But typically the mugging takes place within walking distance of hangouts where escape routes are known. Lejeune (1977:128) further notes that the takeoff of a crime is greatly affected by the immediate contingencies of the mugger's situation at the time he or she experiences a need for money. The mugger will consider such particulars as the neighbourhood in which he or she hangs out; the time of day; the immediate availability of associates judged to be capable of assisting in the takeoff; the characteristics of vulnerable strangers; and the ecological and architectural features of the area that provide cover and getaway opportunities. Usually these and other elements are "pieced together" in the form of a loose plan that can be modified as the action develops. The mugging is usually planned immediately prior to its occurrence. Typically, a mugging occurs from conception to completion within the span of a few minutes. Often the decision is made on the basis of impulse, circumstance, and opportunity (Lejeune, 1977:128).

A major risk in committing a mugging is the possibility that patrol officers may pass by while the robbery is in progress. Robbers will select victims in locations and at times so as to shield their actions from the view of police or bystanders under the cover of darkness, or by attacking in remote areas and enclosed spaces (Newman, 1972). Thus, muggers usually look for a single victim in an isolated place to minimize the possibility of resistance and interference. If their attack is visible to witnesses, they may rely on citizen apathy and fear to deter them from intervention (Freeman, 1966).

Lejeune (1977:135) reports that the mugger is influenced by values that make a particular type of victim more or less emotionally acceptable as a target. The set of predispositions that guides the selection of victims includes values for or against mugging women (generally against); old people (generally against); or whites rather than blacks (generally for); or the rich (generally for). The ideal victim is the relatively young, affluent, white male. In practice, such predispositions appear to play only a secondary role in the selection process when compared with more vital concerns of reducing personal risks and locating a victim within the usually limited temporal and spatial scope of the stroll. Thus while the predisposition to mug men rather than women is verbalized by most respondents, this preference is easily eroded in the attempt to select the most accessible or vulnerable target. On the other hand, contempt or hostility towards certain types of persons facilitates the neutralization process. Lejeune (1977: 136) reports that homosexuals and drunks are both favourite and frequent targets and are most likely to be seen as deserving victims.

Robbers who rob banks also express values that justify their selection of targets. As previously discussed, these values include the argument that they are stealing from institutions and not ordinary persons who work hard for their money; banks are deserving victims that exploit the common person; and banks can easily afford the loss. The extent to which these techniques of neutralization contribute to the motivation to robbery and the selection of particular targets is difficult to assess. In some cases they may be significant while in others, they may be no more than post-factum rationalizations that are used to justify a course of action already decided upon and influenced by other variables.

ROBBING IN THE CITY VERSUS THE COUNTRY

Robbers prefer targets in large metropolitan areas rather than small towns because they often commit robberies in areas of the city in which they live and/or are familiar; congested areas allow them to blend into the crowd; and there are more escape routes. Whereas one can get lost in a crowd within minutes in the city, country roads and highways can be easily and quickly blocked by the police. Roger Caron, a former bank robber and author of *Go Boy* and *Bingo* explains his disdain for country banks.

> I never liked country banks. One thing about a city, when you're one block away you are part of 2,000 people. When you're two blocks away you're part of 6,000 people. When you're three blocks away you're part of 10,000 people. When you're six blocks away, you're part of 100,000 people. You're safer every hundred feet you travel in a city. You become part of a bigger and bigger crowd until you become anonymous. But in the country, you drive one mile and you're nowhere. You drive two miles and you're still nowhere. You drive three, four, five, six miles and it feels like you're driving forever. That's the chilling part of doing a country bank and that's why I look for a city bank.

PLANNING THE GETAWAY

> When those subway doors clear and that train starts moving, it is such a wonderful feeling, it's better than an orgasm.
>
> — *The Subway Bandit*

Robbers generally agree that the getaway is their primary consideration. Some bandits will spend several days looking for targets with the perfect getaway. Most, however, typically spend only a few minutes searching for an escape route and ensuring that there are no police in the area and only a few passersby (Gabor and Normandeau, 1989:200). A bank robber describes how quickly the task can be done.

> The whole planning process would take five minutes. Find the bank, look around, up and down the street. Time of day, where you wanna go when it's done. This is really quick planning. There's nothing really to plan.

Bank robbers in this study often selected targets in areas where public transportation is readily available—near taxi stands or in downtown areas where they can hail a cab, catch a bus, or board the subway. Several men, for instance, only robbed banks located along subway routes. If escape will be on foot, robbers prefer targets in areas that have heavy pedestrian traffic so they can easily get lost in the crowd. Alleys and underground passageways are also popular escape routes. When getaway cars are used, robbers look for a parking spot with an exit on to the street, few stop lights, light traffic, and a quick route out of the area. Using a motor vehicle also allows offenders to move throughout the city or change cities. When one bandit with a distinct M.O. stopped hitting banks close to subway stops and began robbing them in a nearby suburb, police correctly assumed that he had purchased a car with his earnings. Although the selection of a target and the choice of one's getaway affect one another, most bank robbers decide first on the type of getaway, then select the target accordingly. The choice of transportation out of the area determines whether the target provides a decent getaway.

Most robbers are unconcerned about alarms because they typically take no more than a moment or two to commit their crime and have ample opportunity to escape before the police arrive. Crow and Bull's (1975:23) study of convenience-store robberies, for example, found that robberies occur so quickly that in only 10 percent of cases did a customer enter the store while the crime was in progress. Their research also indicates that in most cases, the robber does nothing to prevent pursuit. A few robbers will warn the clerk not to follow or have him or her lie down or move to the back of the store. In some instances, the robber may even tie up the victim to facilitate escape and delay the time the police are notified (Crow and Bull, 1975:39). In the present study, some bank robbers warned staff and customers not to follow them but in no case did the offender tie anyone up. Although some bank robbers consider the proximity of police stations in selecting a target and their getaway route, most do not. This oversight occasionally contributes to their arrest near the scene of the robbery.

APPROACHING THE TARGET: SURREPTITIOUS VERSUS COMMANDO-STYLE ATTACK

Solo gunmen and crews who use a commando-style attack modus operandi typically wear masks or balaclavas to prevent identification. They don their masks as they enter the premises and remove them before they hit the street. Robbers who use an overt commando-style M.O. report that the decision to proceed with the robbery occurs after a preliminary assessment of the scene. After some initial hesitation, there is the moment of commitment. For some, the physical and psychological threshold to be crossed is one and the same—the moment they open the door of the bank, all tentativeness is abandoned and they proceed with the robbery.

Almost all bank robbers in this study report that their first robbery was frightening and difficult to commit. Summoning up the courage to enter the bank sometimes takes hours. One man describes the effort it took to commit his first robbery.

> It took me 3 1/2 hours to go in and do my first bank. I kept circling the block and went in five minutes before closing time—almost got locked in. I think that my first three bank robberies were very close to closing time as I tried to get up the nerve.

After the first few holdups, bank robbers become confident in their abilities and no longer find the experience terrifying. Gone is the mad, rushing fear they experienced in their first few scores.

A more discrete type of robbery often begins with a "walk-in entry" in which the offender acts as a customer. The decision to rob is still tentative and depends on various contingencies. Bank employees report that it is not uncommon to find crumpled demand notes in the wastebasket, presumably from offenders who have changed their minds. Crow and Bull's (1975:29) study of convenience-store robberies found that in 57 percent of the cases, the robbers posed as customers and loitered inside the store. Sometimes they even pretended to make a purchase and then announced the robbery when the till was open. The modus operandi of the note-pusher in bank robberies is structured so that only the bandit and the teller know that a crime is being committed. The offender's appearance and demeanour are such that he or she attracts little attention. The robber waits in line, approaches the first available teller, passes a note, makes a verbal command if necessary, takes the money, and calmly walks out of the bank. His or her normal dress and appearance contribute to the impression that nothing unusual is happening. Being calm and controlled not only presents an image that nothing is amiss, according to bank robbers, but it also helps the teller to remain calm.

CASE EXAMPLE

Nobody Does It in Gucci Shoes Anymore

This 20-year-old man from an upper-middle class background robbed several downtown banks wearing a suit, tie, and Gucci shoes. He was proud of his exploits and boasted that he committed his holdups with style—unlike other bandits who didn't even know how to dress. He describes his M.O. and the rationale behind it.

I'm very comfortable in a suit. You mingle very easily in a suit in the downtown. You blend in. Appearances can be deceiving. My appearance would subdue anybody. A man in a suit looks more professional and he looks like he knows what he's doing. I robbed all my banks in the downtown where they're very busy and have a lot of cash flow. Preferably in an area where there are a lot of underground passages, lots of stores, lots of shoppers, lots of businessmen in suits. If you have a fairly good appearance, the police aren't even going to notice you. You don't have to be Galileo to figure that out. I always walked out of banks, I never ran. A man running out of a bank is likely to be tripped by some decent, law-abiding citizen. You have to casually do the entire robbery with grace and ease because if you are at ease, they will be at ease. And if you're dressed like a business-man—well can you imagine the police sending out an alert: "Man in three-piece navy suit wanted for bank robbery"—you're going to have every lawyer in the city locked up. I wasn't concerned about the possibility of anyone playing hero. How many men in three-piece suits would jump other men in three-piece suits? Very few.

Offenders who initially pose as regular customers cannot wear a mask or balaclava to avoid identification. Camp, for instance, found that only half of the bank robberies in his sample disguised themselves (1968:114–15). Canadian Bankers' Association data for 1991 indicate that 76 percent of bank robbers were not disguised (Ballard, 1992). Many robbers use no disguise or employ simple, unsophisticated disguises such as a hat, glasses, beard, moustache, and a change of clothing. Some will avoid targets with surveillance cameras; others will look away from the camera to prevent a clear shot of their face; and some are not concerned about being photographed. As one subject says, "A picture doesn't have your address on it. It doesn't tell the police who you are if you're not in their files." Even minimal disguises such as a hat, glasses, or facial hair are believed to be sufficient to prevent a positive identification from a photograph. These disguises only partially conceal their features, however, and robbers are often identified with the aid of camera photos. Banks have found that the best photographs of robbers are taken as they make their exit—occasionally smiling to themselves as they walk out with the money. Robbers will often change and/or discard clothing immediately afterwards on the assumption that the police converging on the scene will have a description of the suspects.

BANK ROBBERY M.O. AND THE INFLUENCE OF THE MASS MEDIA

Data from interviews with 80 bank robbers indicate that once the decision to rob a bank is made, offenders often use information gleaned from the media to draft a plan of action. More than one-half (44/80 55 percent) of the sample, including all men who originate the idea to rob a bank from the media, used specific information obtained from news reports and media portrayals of bank robbery to develop and implement their M.O. Three significant patterns are apparent in this study: (a) the majority of men who originate the idea to commit a bank robbery from the media operate unarmed; (b) of the 46/80 men who were armed, only two attribute their decision to media influence; (c) several bandits indicate that their decision not to arm themselves was influenced by information obtained in media reports. Of the 25/80 who originate their idea to rob a bank from the media, 7/25 (28 percent) used a gun on their first robbery. Most of the 18/25 chose not to arm themselves because media reports led them to believe that tellers and customers do not resist nor do they challenge bank robbers who claim to be armed. Given the violent nature of today's movies and television programs, it is surprising that media reports of bank robbery appear to influence bank robbers against using a gun.

In addition to this potentially fatal decision, offenders report other ways in which the media influence their behaviour. Some bank robbers avoid cameras for fear of having their photograph displayed in newspapers or on television. Some men leave town if their crimes receive excessive publicity: in one case, a highly sophisticated crew of five fled to the United States because of media "heat" over their prison escapes and bank robberies. Several robbers reported travelling to other Canadian cities to commit holdups because of concern that press reports describing their M.O. would make them recognizable to potential informers. Other decisions made on the basis of media reports or portrayals of bank robbery, the police, or bank policy include the following: the wording of the note, the choice of getaway, the area of the city, the choice or avoidance of certain banks, and the use of bulletproof vests and police scanners. Some bank robbers review media accounts of their crimes searching for mention of evidence they may have left behind, and a few report making slight changes in their M.O. afterwards. This is uncommon, however, since most follow the same rigid pattern until they are caught. The reason most often given: "I didn't want to tamper with a winning formula."

Despite the fact that the majority of bank robbers report learning a variety of tricks from the media, few of them simply copy another offender's M.O. because there is seldom sufficient detailed information to do so. A number of men who rely on media reports as the basis for action further complain about inaccuracies and sensationalism. The irony appears to be missed by some but is recognized by others:

> When you read stories you have to be very careful of what
> you accept. I can usually pick out what I think is accurate.

This man accepts some facts reported in the media as true, dismisses others as false, and expresses confidence in his ability to differentiate. Most bank robbers discriminate in the ideas they borrow, modify the M.O. of others, and develop their own particular style by evaluating it on their own, or, if they have accomplices, discussing it with them.

Although it is difficult to measure the media's effect on behaviour, some additional observations can be made. Based on offenders' reports, it appears that the more specific the information disclosed, the easier it is to use and the more enticing bank robbery appears. In particular, disclosing the amounts of money taken makes the crime appealing. What appears to be a small sum of money for most persons (e.g., $1,500), may be exactly what a potential bank robber needs to solve his or her financial problems. It is also seductive to know that bank policy requires tellers to obey a bandit's instructions and dispense money without resistance. Perhaps most significant is the image created through media reports that bank robbery is relatively safe because few robbers appear to be caught. On the basis of this study, it may be suggested that the banking community, in collaboration with the police should (a) avoid releasing specific information related to bank robbery; (b) avoid publicizing the bank's policy of nonresistance in robbery situations; and (c) attempt to correct the erroneous impression that most bank robbers escape justice.

This study indicates that the media have a significant influence on bank robbery behaviour both in originating the idea and in influencing robbery M.O. It can also be argued that the figures presented above underestimate the role of the media because some respondents could not recall how or when ideas or assumptions originated, suggesting that they were swayed by media presentations at one time or another.

THE DECISION TO USE A WEAPON

Einstadter (1969:77) argues that robbery requires little skill or ability partly because all a robber needs to be master of the situation is a gun. In their study of convenience-store robberies, Crow and Bull (1975:35) found that weapons were used in 87 percent of the cases, with a handgun being the weapon of choice in two out of three robberies (64 percent of cases). In 13 percent of offences, a weapon was not visible although robbers stated that they had a weapon. Feeney (1986:63–64) reports that 80 percent of his sample used some kind of weapon: 53 percent used guns, 19 percent knives, and 8 percent other weapons. Most said they were trying to intimidate their victims and control the situation rather than harm or dominate the victims. Most felt that merely showing the weapon was enough to accomplish their purpose but were prepared to use force if the victim resisted or the police intervened. Nearly 30 percent of those who used a gun used an unloaded or simulated firearm. Most wanted to ensure that no one was hurt and explained that if they had no bullets in the guns, they could not accidently shoot anyone. A few offenders deliberately chose not to use a weapon for moral or legal reasons. In the present study, 46/80 (57 percent) bank robbers were armed and 11/80 used replica firearms.

Studies based on official statistics tell us whether weapons were used but cannot tell us how often guns that are displayed are real or replicas or what proportion of robbers carry weapons without producing them. Canadian Bankers' Association data on bank holdups indicate that a weapon was displayed in 50 percent of the 1991 robberies; 55 percent in 1992; and 52 percent in 1993. It must be noted that approximately 80 percent of bank robberies in Canada today are committed by lone individuals and the vast majority of these are men who pass notes and/or make verbal commands to a single teller (Ballard, 1992; 1993; 1994). These offenders may claim to be armed but only 3/31 (9.6 percent) of beggar bandits in the present study actually carried a weapon and an additional 5/31 (16 percent) brandished an unloaded or replica firearm.

The use of a weapon, particularly a gun, creates a buffer zone between the offender and the victim; intimidates victims and helps to gain their cooperation; can be used to harm the victim and eliminate the threat that he or she presents; and facilitates escape by deterring anyone from following and/or intervening. Conklin (1972:109–11) reports that the decision to use a weapon depends less on the psychological state of the robber than on the instrumental gains to be had. Offenders seldom give expressive or psychological reasons—feelings of power, omnipotence, masculinity—for using a weapon and refer instead to instrumental advantages. Guns, however, may be used for both expressive and instrumental purposes. From self-reports of criminal histories, Wright and Rossi's (1986) questionnaire survey of 1,874 inmates isolated a group of intensive offenders whom they dubbed "handgun predators." These men indicated that the single most important reason to carry a gun was that "when you have a gun, you are prepared for anything that might happen." Gabor et al. (1987:63) indicate that for a few subjects, the feeling of power evoked by possessing of a firearm is an additional motive for committing a robbery.

Factors such as the availability of guns, one's modus operandi, and the number of victims that must be controlled in the holdup will influence the decision whether to use a weapon. The commando-style attack on targets such as banks requires a firearm to control the large number of customers and staff. Standing in line and passing a note, on the other hand, may not require a weapon since a threat is often sufficient to gain compliance. Robbers who would prefer not to use a weapon will choose or develop a modus operandi that allows the robbery to succeed without being armed. This entails selecting victims who are weak and vulnerable, unlikely to resist, and without nearby assistance or possible interference. Robbers who prefer convenience stores, for example, will wait until customers have left and target a woman or an adolescent if possible.

Most note-pushers are attracted to bank robbery in part because the offence does not require a weapon. A few, however, will carry a firearm or a replica to prod the teller into action. Sometimes tellers will ask to see the gun before he or she will give up the money. An offender explains the psychological impact of the gun:

Bank robbery is part mind-game. The gun drives home the point. What am I going to do if the teller refuses to give me the money—jump across the counter? No. If she refuses and I'm standing there, it's a stalemate. You're losing precious time and you're also losing face. So the gun breaks the stalemate. Show it to her and it's simple. "Oh, all right," and out comes the money. The gun is a symbol of dominance in the game of psychology. They realize that maybe this person means business.

Since robbery is seldom planned in detail, offenders are likely to use whatever weapons are at their disposal. Conklin (1972:105) found that juveniles are more likely to rob without a weapon than adults, perhaps due in part to the difficulty they may have in obtaining firearms. Conklin also found that robbing with accomplices reduces the need for a weapon for self-protection, since the group itself acts as a functional equivalent of a weapon. Lone offenders are more apt to use firearms or other weapons than are groups of offenders, since solo robbers feel more vulnerable to victim resistance (1972:107).

The perception of the victim as armed and/or likely to resist influences the decision to use a weapon. Feeney (1986:64) found that 90 percent of the commercial robbers and 70 percent of those who robbed individuals used a weapon of some kind. He also found that 80 percent of commercial robbers used a gun and 80 percent of these men used a loaded gun. Only a third of the muggers carried firearms and only half of these used a loaded gun. Since convenience stores are frequently owner-managed, the probability of resistance is high. If the owner is believed to be armed, determined robbers may decide that they too need guns to prevent them from being shot. Crow and Bull found that one-quarter of convenience-store clerks had weapons in the store but they were hardly ever used (1975:x).

CONFRONTING AND CONTROLLING VICTIMS

Luckenbill (1980) explains that robbers must establish co-presence (approach the victim) and communicate intent. The offender can either use speed and stealth to rush the unwitting victim or, alternatively, manage a normal appearance to get close enough to surprise and overcome the target. The offender and victim in a robbery must have a shared definition of the situation for it to proceed smoothly. To avoid death or injury, the victim suppresses opposition and permits the offender to take his or her goods. Despite an inherent conflict in interests, the two cooperate to bring about a successful conclusion. Robbery breaks down when the robber fails to communicate intent and/or the victim experiences momentary shock and disbelief and delays action. Lejeune and Alex (1973:261–65) report that in the initial stage of a robbery, mugging victims are often taken by surprise and do not recognize the true purpose of the encounter.

Most robbers immediately inform their victims in simple terms that they are being robbed. Typically, they will state "This is a robbery!" or "This is a stickup!" followed by a command "Don't anyone move!" or "Hand over the money!" Katz explains that this moment of declaration is necessary to ensure their cognitive control of the event (1988:177). Luckenbill (1980:364) indicates that in opening the interaction, offenders will use one of three modes of intimidation: (1) a command for compliance backed by a threat of force, (2) the use of prodding force, and (3) the use of incapacitating force. The threat of force includes gestures that inform the victim that failure to comply with a directive will bring death or injury. Prodding force is pain that falls short of debilitating or immobilizing the target. Pushing, shoving to the floor, and slapping with or without a weapon are the most common types of prodding force. Both threat of force and prodding force constitute a level of limited force and are meant to intimidate the target against resistance and into compliance. Incapacitating force is pain that debilitates or immobilizes and physically eliminates the target from the event. Luckenbill (1980:365) also reports that most offenders consider the use of lethal force morally unacceptable and would rather forfeit the robbery than seriously hurt anyone. In addition, they reason that the use of deadly force increases the risk of apprehension and harsher sentences. In those instances in which offenders shoot or stab the victim, the use of lethal force often follows target resistance that jeopardizes the offender's wellbeing.

Robbery is a crime in which offenders concern themselves with the actions of victims. Their aim is to use enough force to control the victim so that he or she will not resist but will instead cooperate for the successful completion of the crime. Based on their interviews with robbery victims, Gabor and Normandeau (1989:202) found that direct threats were made at the outset of the robbery in 40 percent of the cases. Overwhelmingly, the most common first reaction by victims was immediate compliance with the perpetrator's demands. The next most likely reaction was shock and numbness. A victim's refusal to cooperate also increased the likelihood of threats during the event, but such refusal at the outset was rare.

A common technique for gaining compliance is the use of verbal commands and/or threats on victims who resist, hesitate, stall, or refuse to hand over the money. Bandits often bark out their commands: "Hurry up!" "Move it!" "Back up!" "Hand over the money or I'll shoot!" Many report that they act mean and tough by using a gruff and intimidating tone of voice. Intimidation is also achieved with obscene language and nonverbal gestures such as menacing looks. These verbal commands and body gestures frequently shock and frighten the victim into compliance and may even prevent the incident from escalating into a physically violent confrontation by deterring resistance. Lejeune (1977:141) notes that when a threatening posture is effectively enacted in the mugging, it tends to reduce the likelihood of physical injury to the victim; but when it fails as a primary method of control, the mugger is likely to turn to violent means.

Feeney (1986:64–65) reports that around 15 percent of the robbers in his study used physical force at the outset to establish initial control over the situation by striking the victim without warning. One-third of the robbers assaulted victims during the course of the robbery. Robbers of individuals hurt their victims more than twice as often as commercial robbers. Juvenile offenders harmed their victims more often than adult offenders. Most of the offenders who struck victims said they did so because the victims resisted and they chose to hit them with their fists or a weapon rather than to shoot or stab them. A sixth of those encountering resistance did, however, take drastic action: shooting, cutting, or spraying liquid into the eyes of their victims. Around 10 percent of the offenders hurt their victims unintentionally. A quarter of those who hurt someone did so in an attempt to recover money they had some claim to (1986:64).

Lejeune (1977:146) reports that the central theme that emerged from interviews with muggers is their sense of vulnerability. Victims who are under direct attack are anticipated to react in ways that may jeopardize the mugger's safety: by screaming or in other ways resisting, the victim can make the attack more visible to the police, or perhaps strike back and physically injure the attacker. Because of their concern with controlling victims, muggers are likely to use force to intimidate and/or incapacitate.

Incapacitating force is common in muggings, less common in commercial robberies, and uncommon in bank robberies. The present study found that bank robbers rarely use incapacitating force to disable bank personnel. There are three main reasons for this: (1) bandits expect and receive cooperation from tellers and do not need to use force; (2) robbers require the active assistance of staff in the transfer of money from the tills; and (3) most robbers do not go behind the counter and are therefore separated from tellers by a physical barrier that would make the use of incapacitating force difficult to apply. In the 1,609 bank robberies committed in Canada in 1991, only six bank employees suffered physical injuries (Ballard, 1992).

Luckenbill (1980:366–67) found that when the offender possesses a lethal weapon such as a firearm or knife, a threat or warning or prodding force is sufficient to manage the target. Limited force will bring immediate compliance if the robber appears to have the capacity and determination to use massive force. If the offender holds a club or is unarmed—no lethal force—then he or she envisions that opposition is likely. Therefore, the offender may open the interaction with incapacitating force, attempting to fell the target immediately.

Gabor and Normandeau (1989:200) similarly found that robberies committed with inferior weapons, such as knives, paradoxically have the highest incidence of violence. It would appear that crude weapons make resistance by the victim more likely as they do not afford the perpetrator the same credibility as do firearms. The simple display of a firearm will likely gain compliance. The analysis of 1,266 instances of armed robbery in Montreal reveals that firearms were discharged or victims assaulted in only eight percent of cases. Three percent of the cases caused injuries requiring medical care and about 1.5 percent of the incidents resulted in hospitalization or death. Those in this last category were more likely to be suspects than victims (Gabor and Normandeau, 1989:199).

Other studies also indicate that the use of force decreases when offenders are armed and targets appear weak (such as a woman) and increases when offenders are unarmed and targets appear strong (such as, a group of young men) (Conklin, 1972; Letkemann, 1973; Weir, 1973; MacDonald, 1975; Lejeune, 1977). Feeney (1986:65) concludes from his research that robbers usually do not use gratuitous force. In some instances, the force applied was greater than necessary but generally robbers do not appear to take any abstract pleasure in hurting people. The existing research on robbery strongly indicates that the use of force by offenders is instrumental rather than expressive and aimed at disarming, intimidating, and controlling victims. Studies that ask culprits about their actions similarly indicate that most robbers are motivated by the money and attempt to avoid harming victims as much as possible.

Give Me My Money

This 30-year-old solo gunman is serving sixteen years for sixteen bank robberies.

In the last one, I fired a shot in the bank. There was a car chase around town and I got stopped in a road block with nowhere to run. I fired the shot because the teller wouldn't give me the money. She backed up and hid behind this partition and I got mad. Indignant. I figured it was my money. I had a lot of close calls and things that didn't go right but that was the worst. It was the first time I was ...[pause]... denied [Laughs]. After I stake out a place and that's the place I'm gonna do, it's like I've already done it. If something comes up in the process, well it's screwing up your plan.

I used to figure that by the time they rung the alarm or knew there was a robbery, I'd give myself about 45 seconds and whether or not I had the money, I was going to leave. But I got so sure of myself near the end that I must have been in there three or four minutes altogether. One of the things I did wrong was letting off that shot. When you're trying to apply force, there's an optimal amount you can apply before everyone starts getting freaky and they can't even hear what you're saying. Half the customers ran out of the bank and everybody started ducking down. I had to wait for everyone to get their common senses about them before I could get the money. I waited around and told the tellers to get up and get me the money instead of just leaving myself. I got the money but I didn't get away.

If the victim resists, some robbers will retreat and forfeit the venture. Others may repeat or increase the threat by using prodding or incapacitating force. Violence, therefore, is not merely a function of the offender's inclinations; the level of violence also depends on the reactions of victims and bystanders. This does not mean that victims are responsible for their own injuries. It simply means that robbers will often increase their use of force to overcome the resistance or interference of victims and bystanders. As Gabor and Normandeau (1989:199–200) point out, robberies are fluid, dynamic events in which understanding the interaction of the parties is vital in making sense of the outcome.

Offenders who wish to accomplish the transfer by themselves have no use for the victim and will force him or her into a passive role. Luckenbill (1981:32–33) points out that when the victim is considered unnecessary, the offender is more likely to open with incapacitating force to ensure that the victim cannot intervene. The choice of openings also depends on the offender's perception of how victims are likely to respond. It is not surprising that force is used more often in muggings than in commercial or bank robberies. Individual targets are more unpredictable and more likely to react defensively if accosted. Gabor and Normandeau (1989:200) point out that bank robberies and muggings are polar opposites in the degree of violence used to gain victim compliance.

DOING IT ALONE VERSUS DOING IT WITH OTHERS

The reasons for going solo are simple: there is (a) no need for assistance, (b) no split with a partner, (c) no potential informant, and (d) no qualified candidate. Offenders who operate alone explain that they do so because their M.O. does not require a partner; they will not have to share the rewards; partners create an additional risk since they may eventually inform on you; and there are no suitable trustworthy and experienced persons available.

The decision to commit a robbery with partners may be strategic or mundane. A few robbers in the present study explained that they robbed banks with partners mainly because they were friends and partied together. Others use partners to minimize resistance and maximize gains. In cases in which there are two or more robbers, planning necessarily involves discussing the roles that each will play. Each individual must perform particular tasks to successfully execute the job. For example, when two offenders are committing a commercial armed robbery, one usually collects the cash and the other controls people at the scene. Using a partner as a getaway driver allows the crew to park close to the target, helps to ensure that they don't get boxed in by other vehicles, and provides a lookout. Gabor and Normandeau (1989:200–201) report from their study that the driver of the getaway vehicle does not generally have the same status as those executing the crime. Similarly, bank robbers in the present study also define the robber's role as more important and difficult than the driver's job. Nonetheless, they usually divide the crime proceeds equally.

Einstadter (1969:67–70) interviewed 25 serious criminals who considered themselves robbers, operated in gangs, and had committed several armed robberies. He found that certain norms and patterns of activity exist among robbery crews:

(1) Gains are equally shared.

(2) Robbers give little thought to arrest and make little preparation for this eventuality.

(3) If arrested, members are expected to not inform on their

partners although the arrest of one frequently leads to the arrest of them all.

(4) The group is a fluid and loose confederation.

(5) Relationships are transient.

(6) There is no confirmed leadership.

(7) Members are not held responsible for events they cannot control.

(8) The concept of fate is evident in their view of the world.

Einstadter (1969:67–70) describes robbery as a "get-rich-quick enterprise" and consequently offenders need to strike swiftly when the opportunity arises. The armed robbery crew is not a cohesive, tightly knit group with fixed personnel and standards of behaviour. Instead, the social relationships are tenuous and transient and robbery crews consist of partners who share equally in the risks and profits of the operation.

In his analysis of the leadership and social organization of robbery crews, Einstadter (1969:69) notes that any member may leave the group at any time and may also "sit one out" if he or she judges a particular robbery to be too dangerous, although this is not a frequent practice. Einstadter also found that robbers generally do not consider the possibility of arrest while actively engaging in robbery. Should a partner be arrested, however, he or she can expect no assistance from his or her partners. Conversely, the group expects the arrested member to remain silent but also realizes that members may reveal their crime partners' identities in exchange for a more favourable disposition. This knowledge creates considerable anxiety in the group when a member is arrested. Most robbers realize that the arrest of one member usually spells the end for all (1969:70).

THE DIVISION OF LABOUR IN ROBBERY CREWS

From its conception, the strategy or engineering of a job is a group product and must be viewed in an interaction context (Einstadter, 1969:72). Although there is little discernable evidence of distinctive leadership roles, previous experiences of members are recognized. Experienced members may be more persuasive than others but dictates from partners are frowned upon and do not constitute the basis of action. When disagreements occur, there is majority rule of sorts, but the partners also try to appease dissident members. To force an unwilling member to join in a robbery would only endanger the whole group, since its ultimate success depends on cooperative effort. The group, then, is a partnership of equals, each with a voice; and leadership comes from mutual recognition of an individual's expertise, which serves the group's goals (Einstadter, 1969:72–73).

The present study also indicates that bank robbery crews operate as partners; there are typically no defined leaders; and members exhibit mutual respect and deference. Each member of the crew has an equal voice in planning robberies. No one is forced to go along with a plan he or she doesn't approve nor is there criticism of members who back out of particular robberies. On the contrary, gang members are easily spooked by the "bad vibes" that partners occasionally experience since they too report such feelings. Given that they have typically committed several robberies together, instances in which one member gets "cold feet," are not interpreted as evidence of the person losing his nerve.

CASE EXAMPLE
Go Boy

Roger Caron, author of Go Boy *and* Bingo *describes the dynamics involved when serious old–style 1960's Montreal bank robbers would plan a heist.*

We'd sit around and discuss it. We'd know each person's capabilities. Everybody would be pretty straight and they would know what was expected of them. If they weren't qualified to do this or that, they wouldn't argue about it. It's not like in the movies where someone says, "I'm the boss and I'm running this outfit" because these guys are all hotheads and they'll say, "You run this you asshole." Nobody talks tough. That's only in the movies. I've never heard of a gang where one guy says that he's running the show and the other guys have to follow him. There's no one leader. One guy will contribute 15 percent of wisdom or experience, that guy puts in 45 percent because he's more respected, and this guy puts in 20 percent. Somebody might put in nothing and he knows it. He knows this is serious stuff and this is no time to be a prima donna. It's not the time to be stupid. Everybody is pretty reasonable. Pretty damn reasonable. The attitude is serious and its mutual respect.

I did a couple of banks with a guy who was recommended. I was the senior partner, the guy with the experience. I planned the job and established the rules. The junior partner goes along with the rules. He wouldn't be robbing a bank without someone to do it with. He needed me more than I needed him and he was there to learn. With my normal partner, it was equal and we decided things together.

Deliberations over a particular robbery are usually informal and are likely to occur in places such as a car, a bar, or a motel room. It is a rational and deliberate, albeit haphazard, process of decision-making. The planning varies in the degree of care and time that goes into it. Prior to any robbery, each partner is assigned a role to play based on his or her skill and experience. This decision is reached through group interaction; no single individual assigns positions without group and individual consensus (Einstadter, 1969:73). A loose type of specialization results that can adapt to various circumstances. Individuality is never completely relinquished by the careerist. Partners cooperate but are never subjugated. They fit into the allocated roles to accomplish certain purposes but attempt whenever possible to carry them out on their own terms (Einstadter, 1969:74).

AN UNCHANGING M.O.

> I was going out that day and I was trying not to rob a bank—
> if you know what I mean.
>
> —*First-time offender attempting to explain that he never
> intended to rob six banks and kept trying to stop*

The fact that most robbers do not vary their modus operandi greatly assists the police, who follow the pattern of individual bandits through their brief escapades. Occasionally it even helps in their capture such as when the police stake out banks in an area in which the offender is operating. But the routinized repetition of the M.O. is most useful in clearing cases by linking an apprehended offender to most, if not all, of his or her past offences and obtaining evidence and admissions of guilt.

Why do robbers repeatedly use the same M.O.? Why don't they vary their modus operandi to confuse the police and to disassociate themselves from previous scores in the event that they are caught? Bank robbers have a number of reasons for continuing to use the same modus operandi: (a) since the M.O. works so well, they have no wish to tamper with a "winning formula"; (b) they do not believe they can improve on it; (c) some robbers are superstitious and believe that any change could end their good-luck streak; (d) since they intend to quit soon anyway, there is no need to develop and improve their modus operandi; (e) offenders do not believe they will be caught and are not concerned about being linked with other crimes in court; and (f) many are unaware of the distinctive nature of their M.O. and are shocked to realize that the police can link them to each of their crimes.

Bank robbers feel confident and secure in their M.O. because they believe that the variables are known and controllable. Most contend that the only thing that can upset their plans are unforeseeable incidents that "could happen to anyone." Consistent with this view is the belief that arrest will come only if one is unlucky (or very careless). Bank robbers believe that their modus operandi allows them to control the situation and they will not get caught if they do things right. Although there may be unforeseen events that trip them up, these are regarded as small risks that are worth taking. Bank robbers express confidence in their abilities to control the situation and handle incidents as they occur. Even after experiencing several close calls and/or being caught, they still view their demise as resulting from bad luck.

Einstadter (1969:69) observes that robbers tend to have a fatalistic attitude toward life. Walsh (1986:47) similarly notes that robbers fatalistically accept that hazards may overcome them, which are beyond the offender's control. Errors and accidents are accepted as part of the fortune of life: the "breaks" are what count and you either have them or you don't. Einstadter notes that many robbers perceive fate as controlling their destiny: "When the cards are right, when the dice are right, when the setup is perfect, nothing can go wrong but if luck is against you, you haven't got a chance (1969:69)." He also observes this fate motif does not lessen as the robber becomes more proficient, learns to reduce the hazards, and better controls the situation. No matter how well a robbery may be planned, it always presents the possibility of uncontrollable hazards and hence uncertainty.

TYPOLOGIES OF THREE TYPES OF BANK ROBBERS

The following typologies are based on interviews with 80 convicted and imprisoned bank robbers across Canada. Three distinct types of modus operandi are evident in bank robberies. Beggar bandits (note-pushers) discreetly pass a note to a single teller demanding money; bank robbery crews, consisting of two or more robbers, burst into the bank and terrorize staff and customers with threats and a gun; solo gunmen similarly use a commando-attack strategy to obtain money and deter resistance. Of the 80 men interviewed, 31 operated as note-pushers, 35 worked with partners, and 14 committed armed robberies of banks on their own. Eight men who operated in crews and two men who operated as solo gunmen also robbed armoured vehicles and their experiences are also discussed separately. The reader should remember that a criminal typology combines and blends the most significant characteristics shared by a number of offenders. This is an "ideal-type" construct based on real cases but it is, by necessity, a simplification of actual experiences. Besides indicating the similarities that characterize each of these three types of M.O., the following typologies also describe the differences between them.

(1) PATTERNS AND VARIATIONS AMONG BEGGAR BANDITS

CASE EXAMPLE

Travelling Salesman

Age 47, described by police as a jovial person, this French Canadian businessman was convicted of robbing 49 banks. Always polite to tellers, he dressed in a suit, passed a note indicating he was armed, and made his getaway by car. By moving from city to city and province to province, he evaded police efforts to capture him for two-and-a-half years.

A lady followed me out of the bank and took my licence-plate number. The police pulled me over on the highway and let me go. Later they arrested me in my hotel room. I always used a note and it was always the same. It was like: "Give me your money and there won't be any problems. No shooting." I might say in the note, "Don't panic", or "Hurry up." Sometimes, I would come in the bank and give the note and the girl would say "No!", and I'd have to walk out. [Laughs.] I didn't have a gun or anything but sometimes I use a toy gun and I stick it in a newspaper. I take the newspaper and wrap the gun so part of it shows. What they see is not a real gun but they can't take a chance.

I always had my own business and when you have a business, you have to work sometimes 20 hours a day. After a few years, my wife says I don't give her enough time. She met one guy, he was a millionaire, so she left me for him. And so I say, "Okay, I can make money too." That's how I got started. I got the idea from a film, a movie. The guy in the film gave the teller a note and he didn't have a gun either. [Laughs.] It was something I remembered and I tried it two or three years later. I never thought about it but it just came to me. I was mad one day and I was going to get some money. I got mad about my wife and the time I spent working. I...[long pause]...I wanted to prove something. At first I never think I can do it. So if something happens, she's going to have to take the blame. The blame was hers. It worked. I was surprised. [Laughs.] Before I tried that, I figured it's all bad guys who rob banks. Guys who kill. A kid can do it. [Laughs.]

I used to have a business selling office supplies and I travelled through four provinces. If I don't make a sale, I do this to pay the bank. I have to have money to pay the bank so I rob the bank to pay the bank. [Laughs.] I was a seller and my English is not very good so it was tough to make sales. I used to go against some big companies and it's hard. If the business don't work, I go for something else. [Laughs.] My second career. After, I feel relieved. Not nervous, not good, I feel relieved. I can pay what I have to. Before, I'm nervous because you never know what could happen. [Laughs.] I didn't like it. I did banks because I was obliged to get money to pay things. Sometimes I was in the motel the night before and I was saying to myself, "Why are you doing this?" [Laughs.] I'd talk to myself. I'd try to talk myself out of it but the next day, I'd get up and go do it. I had to. I had bills.

If the girl would say no, I would leave. In one, the note was in English and she was French. She took the note to see the manager and I walked out. [Laughs.] Another, the girl yelled. I was surprised. I walked out. Don't run, always easy. [Laughs.] I'm scared but I don't get discouraged. You can't discourage me in anything. [Laughs.] I'm an optimist. [Laughs.] You can't put me down, it's impossible. I'm confident in everything I do. I didn't think I'm going to get caught. Every time I do one, I tell me, "This is the last one." I want to stop. Every time I stop, it's the last time. I stopped at each one and I always said it's going to be the last one. I don't think I do so many. I never counted. I did them one by one and said to myself, "I need some money. This is going to be the last one." The first one was supposed to be the last one. [Laughs.] If the business had done good, I would have stopped. I wanted to stop. I always take a bank with an exit close by so I can park and nobody

can see the car. I take my car and go. I just kept it easy, not too much trouble. One time, I get the money and when I go to leave, the door is locked! This lady came and opened it and said to me, "Bonjours Messieux. Merci." [Laughs]. I was stopped six times in roadblocks. The money was in the spare tire under the carpet or in my coat under the seat. They never searched the car. They looked and that's all. They ask me what I do and I say I'm a salesman. I show them my wallet and so they say, "Well, he can't be the guy." [Laughs.] I was nervous but they didn't know I was nervous.

Most of the time after I do a bank, I go to the racetrack to change money. I would take only two or three races, the best races of the night, and bet money on them. Sometimes $600 or $700 on a horse, sometimes $2,000 to place or show so then I have two or three chances to win. I usually win some money. That night, I win $300. The police who arrested me sent that money to my girlfriend. It wasn't the bank's money.[Laughs.] I made a mistake when I confessed because I got ten years. The police told me that I should get it off my chest but if I had pled guilty for the one, I would get maybe four years on that. The judge told me they should have caught me the first time. [Laughs.]

This offender had previously been convicted of robbing banks and sentenced to three years in prison. He waited until his parole had expired before beginning his latest round of bank robberies. He never changed his M.O., averaged $2,000–$3,000 per robbery, and made his getaway in his own car which he parked at a discrete location close to the bank.

"My note was simple: "I have a gun. Give me the Money." That says it all: gun, money."

— *Beggar bandit*

I HAVE A GUN GIVE ME THE MONEY

Many beggar bandits like to keep their notes simple. *Courtesy Metro Toronto Police Hold-Up Squad.*

"Beggar bandit" is a term used by police to describe men who rob banks by using a note and/or making a verbal command. This type of bank robber is also referred to as a "note-pusher" and typically wears minimal or no disguise, stands in line with other customers, approaches the first available teller, passes a note demanding money, and then leaves. The M.O. exploits bank policy directives that advise tellers to cooperate with robbers, hand over the money, and push the silent alarm only when it is safe to do so. Using a calm and discreet manner, the robber assumes that the teller will cooperate and the transaction will occur without anyone noticing or interfering. Offenders believe that even if customers do "catch the play," people are unlikely to resist when they risk personal injury and have no money at stake. All bank robbers assume that they will have sufficient time to escape before the police arrive.

Of the 31 men in this study who operated as beggar bandits, 23/31 (74 percent) committed their robberies unarmed, 5/31 (16 percent) used replica or unloaded firearms, and only 3/31 (9.6 percent) used a loaded weapon. Twelve (12/31 38.7 percent) have previous convictions for robberies and eight of these men were convicted of robbing banks by passing notes. The following is a profile of the beggar bandit based on an analysis of the M.O. of 31 convicted offenders.

Similarities

Most beggar bandits have an initial and specific need for money, a poor employment history and job prospects, describe themselves as lazy, express a disdain for work, and see crime as a "shortcut" means of obtaining needed cash. Few describe themselves as financially desperate and most admit that they either could have done without the money or borrowed it from friends or family. They decide to rob a bank in part because they wish to be independent and obtain the money themselves. Most begin with the intention of robbing only one bank but quickly spend the proceeds from the first score and return for more.

Media portrayals of bank robbery as easy and nonviolent influence the majority (18/31 58 percent) of beggar bandits in this sample to commit this particular crime. They are extremely frightened during the first robbery but determined to go through with it. Some will take considerable time in this initial holdup to gather up the nerve to enter the bank, yet most are surprised at how smoothly and easily the crime proceeds. Subsequent robberies are not nearly as scary and most become increasingly confident and relaxed.

BORN LOSER reprinted by permission of NEA, Inc.

Witnesses report that beggar bandits sometimes engage in conversations and appear quite calm while waiting their turn in the customer line-up.

Note-pushers assume that tellers will cooperate and not raise the alarm until it is safe to do so. They patiently stand in line with customers, claim that they feel calm once they enter the bank, carefully observe customers and employees while they wait, prefer younger female tellers closest to the door, but approach and rob the first available teller. Most beggar bandits rob one teller only, hand him or her a note and/or ask for the money, and often indicate that they are armed. They describe the threat as an act, a bluff, or a performance; insist that they have no wish to harm anyone; explain that they only want the money; and emphasize that their goal is to get out of the bank without any hassle.

Beggar bandits dress and act as though nothing unusual is happening. They are discrete, quiet, and fast, often take no more than 30 to 60 seconds to complete the transaction, walk out with an average of $1,500–$2,500, assume the police need four or five minutes to arrive, change their appearance shortly after leaving the bank, and quickly leave the area. Most consider the getaway to be the most significant part of their plan. The majority walk away from the bank and disappear among the shoppers and pedestrians found on busy city streets. Men who have robbed several banks have usually experienced a "close call" in which they were almost arrested near the scene. Although initially frightened by the experience, the fact that they were able to remain calm in a tense situation reinforces their self-confidence. Some also see their escape as evidence that fate or luck is on their side. Bank robbers believe they are safe from arrest once they're away from the immediate area of the bank. They do not walk around paranoid after the event and most report that they don't even think about the crime until the money runs out and it's time to do another score.

Few bank robbers consume alcohol or take drugs before committing a holdup. Most emphasize that they would not risk robbing a bank while impaired. Typically, robbers prefer cities over small towns, put little time or planning into their robberies, choose their target the day of the crime, prefer to avoid banks with security guards and central tellers, wear minimal or no disguise, and seldom enter the bank before robbing it. They normally commit the robbery once they are inside the bank but will sometimes back out if there are too many people, bank cameras, suspicious-looking customers, or they feel that they are being watched.

Most beggar bandits are unconcerned about silent alarms and assume the alarm will be activated as they leave the bank. They are also not worried about fingerprints, bait money, or eyewitness identification since this evidence may help with a conviction but does not aid the police in their capture. Because their M.O. is discreet, they do not worry about others noticing and interfering in the robbery. They believe that even if someone does "catch the play," these persons will not risk their life to protect the bank's money. Bank robbers unanimously condemn "heroes," most express a willingness to use force against them, and the majority believe they could physically handle anyone who would be foolish enough to confront them. Imagining how they would act in similar circumstances, bank robbers assume that others will behave rationally.

> They know it's a holdup and you could be armed. They mind their own business. It's fear. They don't know what type of person you are.

Overall, bandits believe that the bank robbery is relatively safe and that most of the variables are known and are controllable. They see it as a low-risk crime and believe they can only be caught if an unforeseeable and uncontrollable event occurs, an informant notifies the police, or they are careless.

On average, beggar bandits rob one bank every two weeks but can range from four or five per week to one or two per month. Few bandits bother to check the location of police stations before targeting a bank. After several successful scores, they believe that they're on a good-luck streak; rob a number of banks in quick succession; spend their money quickly and foolishly; return again for more; and repeat their M.O. in the same distinctive way. Most will wait until they are broke or close to broke before they rob again and the majority plan to quit in the immediate future. Many robbers believe that each robbery will be their last. During their brief spending escapade, they lose their monetary values and "blow" the money on a hedonistic "partying" lifestyle that includes illicit drugs, alcohol, bars, nightclubs, and sex.

Beggar bandits think positively about their abilities and appreciate the simplicity of their M.O.; they never jump over the counter; they seldom change their M.O.; they use a similar getaway each time; they view their style of bank robbery as relatively nonserious; they rationalize their crimes as nonviolent; and portray their targets as large, impersonal institutions. Bank robbers typically do not like banks; they criticize their policies and interest rates as exploitive; and claim they would never (or prefer not to) steal a person's hard-earned money. Beggar bandits rationalize their crimes by cognitively breaking the offence into its component parts: they stand in line, pass the teller a note, and walk out with the money. They view the offence as nonserious because no one is physically hurt, the sums of money are not great, and banks are either insured or can afford the loss. Beggar bandits typically either do not consider or they dismiss the psychological trauma inflicted on tellers and justify any threats as a "bluff." Most describe themselves as bandits, outlaws, adventurers, and risk-takers.

Beggar bandits are shocked by the serious police response and heavy sentence and most are surprised that the police "know" about all or most of their holdups. They are typically linked to their previous robberies and make incriminating statements to the police. This type of robber will cooperate with the police in exchange for a guarantee that female accomplices will not be charged. Despite their arrest, conviction, and sentence, few bank robbers credit the police with competent and/or innovative police work. Most attribute their downfall to fate and/or bad luck, to informants, or to their own carelessness or stupidity. Most beggar bandits plead guilty to several bank robberies, receive lengthy penitentiary sentences, and believe that their punishment is harsh and unjust.

Variations

There are several ways in which beggar bandits differ: some have lengthy records and a criminal self-concept while others have little or no criminal background and do not perceive themselves as criminals. Most beggar bandits commit their crimes unarmed but a few use guns or replicas to gain compliance. A few bandits operate in pairs, taking turns robbing banks and sharing the proceeds, and some will use a partner or their wife/girlfriend to act as the getaway driver.

Although most bandits will avoid banks they have previously robbed for fear of being recognized, some will hit the same bank again because the location is convenient, they are too lazy to check out other targets, and/or they like the getaway. Some beggar bandits are concerned about their photograph being taken since they wear little or no disguise and will walk out of the bank if they notice surveillance cameras. Cameras do not deter all beggar bandits since some wear partial disguises such as a hat and sunglasses; look down and away from the camera to prevent a full facial shot; assume that the photos are of a poor quality; and/or realize that the photo will not lead to their capture since the police cannot identify them. Some robbers vary their dress each time while others repeatedly wear the same clothing or disguise.

Some beggar bandits prefer busy banks because there are more distractions, less chance of someone identifying them, and possibly more money in the tills. Others will target only less busy or empty banks because there is less chance that someone will observe what is happening and interfere. Whereas some note-pushers are polite and friendly with teller victims, others use vulgar language and intimidating gestures. Some bandits will walk away if the teller refuses to cooperate, while others make further threats to gain compliance. Some bandits maintain their precautions in every robbery, while others become overconfident and/or careless in subsequent robberies. Some men use a bag or briefcase to carry the money while others simply scoop the money into their pockets because a bag is too obvious and will impede their escape if they have to run. Some bandits claim to enjoy the experience itself while others find it terrifying and claim that the enjoyment comes from spending the money. A few note-pushers will commit their robberies in different cities or move within areas of the city to avoid detection but most prefer to rob only in familiar areas and neighbourhoods. Some offenders tell no one about their crimes while others inform selected friends that they're robbing banks. A few even admit to boasting about their exploits and in some cases, this has led to their downfall.

(2) BANK ROBBERY CREWS — THE COWBOY M.O.

Bank robbery crews consist of two or more partners whose modus operandi involves a division of labour, the use of a gun, disguises, threats, explicit verbal commands, and a getaway vehicle. In this type of robbery, the bandits rush into the bank and surprise staff and customers with a frightening, ("cowboy") commando-style raid that deters any resistance. The present study includes 35 interviews with offenders who robbed banks with other persons. In 31/35 cases, the robbers used loaded guns and in the other four crews, a replica firearm was employed. A total of 22/35 (63 percent) of these men have been previously convicted of robbery, including 10/35 (28.5 percent) for banks.

CASE EXAMPLE

Young Offenders

Age 19, this young man travelled from Montreal to Toronto with his partner, Jules, and robbed a bank in a nearby suburb. Two weeks later, they returned and robbed the same bank on the same day of the week using the same M.O. The investigating officer determined that the suspects had earlier escaped in an orange Volkswagen Rabbit driven by an Oriental male. On the chance that the bandits used the same vehicle, he alerted patrol officers to be on the

lookout and the suspects were arrested.

I knew from friends that Phil was doing banks and I heard that his partner got arrested in the subway. Then he talked to me about it one day and I thought about it and decided to give it a try. Things worked out well until we almost got caught. We did a bank and it was the best we ever did. A beautiful stack of bills! Then when we came out, the cops were sitting right there at a red light and they saw us take off the masks. We split up and we each got away but he had the money and said that he shot the money in the air so the cops would pick it up instead of chasing him. I don't believe that so that was the end of the partnership.

Jules heard that I had dropped my partner. He was into A.R.'s so he brought me out on an armed robbery and everything went cool. We got about $700 each for about 15–25 seconds work. That was pretty good so we did a bank—one that I had done three times before. Jules was right on. He was only 15 at the time but he knew what he was doing. We used these chicks we knew from detention to hold the cabs for us. The cab driver wouldn't know what was going on because it would be parked a block away around the counter.

I told Jules when I took him as a partner, "We're only in there for a certain amount of time and then we're out. I don't care! We're not there to empty every single till." Minimum time and we take the head till first. We start with the $100's and go downwards. Most people get caught because they stay in there too long. I threatened him a few times. I said, "If you're going to stay in there longer, I'm fucking leaving without you." That happened on two occasions. He's still over there collecting bills! Then I start yelling and screaming my head off. He'd be too greedy and be in there a little too long. There was no way I wanted to go down for bank robbery. He would practically get off because he was a juvenile and I'd be doing pen time.

We met Augie, our other partner, in training school. He was

doing banks before we were. I felt a little bit sorry for him because his partner got blown away by a security guard in a bank and he still wanted to do them. He had no partner so we took him in. All three of us were partners in the end but I never did a bank with him in the bank. He and Jules would do them and Jules and I would do them and he would set them up by going in the bank and checking for security guards, plan the getaway, and hold the cab. We were supposed to take turns setting them up but I never set any of them up. I don't like walking in the bank and have my picture taken. They're going to notice me because of my long hair. It's a heat score. Also, there's not as much excitement in doing that. It's exciting when you go in there. Everybody is in the palm of your hands and you're the master. You're the boss for a change.

Jules and Augie would hit banks at other times and I wouldn't be part of it because I had money to spend and I wanted to spend it. They'd waste their money. Jules would waste it on coke all the time. He'd spend $1,500–$1,700 at a time. In a three-day period it would be gone. Meanwhile I'd have half my cash left and I'd be partying and he'd want me to do a bank. That's one of the reasons why we had to get another partner, because I didn't want to do it so often.

Usually I feel calm in the bank. All the partners I ever had, they always wait outside until they psyched themselves up. I didn't like that because everybody looks at you. This one time, we get ready to go and Jules would say "No" then "Okay" then "No" back and forth like a yoyo.

By the time we went in, I didn't feel good and everything went wrong and I flipped out. I was yelling my head off. The teller didn't want to cooperate and everybody was pretending they were scared, all cowering in the corners and crying and everything. She didn't want to cooperate so I just pushed her with one hand and I didn't realize how hard I pushed her and she went flying face first into the till. They cooperated in the end. They could see how hyper I was getting and I guess they figured I'd go to extreme measures to get the money.

I'm afraid to go back to Montreal when I get out because the police will pick me up and shake me down. They raided my apartment already and they'll probably want to question me about other bank robberies. I think I'd like to avoid that.

INTERVIEW WITH JULES

Age 17 at the time of his arrest, Jules has five older brothers all of whom have served time for armed robbery. One of 16 children, he was placed in an orphanage when he was five years old and moved from foster homes to juvenile detention centres throughout his life. He began robbing banks at age 15 and estimates having committed over 50 robberies. He was re-arrested five years after this interview and sentenced to 15 years on four counts of bank robbery.

I don't want to hold the piece because I'm too hyper. My partner has the gun and I have the bag. As soon as he's in, I would go over the counter. Speed! I'm already over the counter rifling through the tills. I don't think about the money when I'm doing them, it's just time, time, time. I'm not nervous in the bank.

Lots of times we yelled at people. Not to hurt them, just to terrify them. Just to make them realize what's happening because they're all in a daze. They don't know what's going on. They're all stunned or daydreaming like robots. That's why you usually yell twice. I would come in and yell, "Okay, this is a robbery! Lie on the ground!" and they're all standing or sitting around looking at us like, "What are you guys doing?" [Laughs.] After they see someone jumping over the counter and holding a gun yelling and screaming, then they usually hit the ground. We start with a little swearing. The message we try to get across is to lie on the ground.

As soon as we go through the first set of doors everything is out. The masks are on just inside the door. We keep the nylon stocking in our shirt pockets folded in a special way. The stocking is rolled up and I use both hands to pull it over the chin first. What I learned to do is pull the stocking up starting at your chin, hold your head back and look up in the air with your eyes open. Then the stocking will push your eyelashes against your eyebrows and they won't get in your eyes. I perfected the technique by practising it in my room.

One time in a bank, I was yelling and screaming and this little old lady—I'm yelling but not at her, at someone else—and she's all freaked out. "It's okay old lady, it's okay. I'm not going to hurt you."

There were two of them on the floor hugging each other. I was embarrassed making an old lady do that.

Sometimes you have to grab a teller and bring her over to open her till because she's too freaked out to move. I've pushed people around in a bank. I've only done that once or twice because I was excited. The woman wouldn't open her drawers. She was yelling, screaming, and crying. You can tell if a bank has been hit a lot because they're calm and they know what to do.

Similarities

Bank robbery crews have a division of labour that typically includes two roles. The "doorman" or "gunman" stays near the door but out of sight of the entrance; displays a firearm; announces that a robbery is in progress; instructs staff and customers to stay where they are; ensures that no one leaves; orders anyone who enters the bank to remain inside; watches to ensure that no one interferes; yells when it is time to go; and enters the bank last and leaves immediately behind his partner(s). The "bagman" vaults the counter, removes the money from the tills, and places it in a bag; leaves the bank when he has all the money or when cued by the doorman—whichever comes first; orders customers and tellers to stand back but otherwise ignores them; does not usually carry a gun; and enters the bank first and leaves first. These bandits wear masks/balaclavas that they put on and remove as they enter and exit the bank. Although some members of bank robbery crews initially intend to rob only one bank, others are committed to crime as a way of life.

In most crews, there is no acknowledged leader who sets the rules and exercises authority over others. Partners are treated as equals but whenever experienced robbers and novices team up, the former will be given more respect and provide greater input into the planning and execution of the score. Because the doorman is armed, this role is often assumed by an experienced robber. Role allocation is also determined by personal preferences since one person may wish to act as the gunman while another may prefer to vault the counter. Athletic ability and age occasionally determine roles, with older and unfit partners requesting the physically less demanding doorman role. Partners typically inform the doorman/gunman of their expectations and make it clear that they do not want someone needlessly shot. It is not uncommon for members of a crew to deny this role to a partner they believe to be a "hothead" and unreliable with a gun. Most crew members state that their biggest fear is to have an innocent person killed because the doorman panicked. For this reason, a few gangs will use an unloaded or replica firearm to ensure that no one is injured.

Gang members believe that speed is the most important variable during the robbery, agree in advance how much time they will take, and generally spend only 30 to 60 seconds inside the bank. Robbers assume that the alarm has been activated; assume that it will take the police four or five minutes to arrive at the bank; and give themselves sufficient time to escape. They will agree in advance how much time they will take and rigidly conform to these self-imposed time constraints.

Bank robbery crews normally commit robberies in their home city; pick up an average $4,000–$10,000 in each holdup; escape in a car, particularly if there are more than two offenders; make their escape together; consider the getaway the most important part of their M.O.; choose target banks primarily because of the escape route; seldom enter the bank before robbing it; avoid small towns because of roadblocks; prefer banks with numerous access roads out of the area; drive away calmly; leave the vicinity of the crime immediately; and divide the money equally. These offenders are unconcerned about bank cameras, marked money, silent alarms, or staff/customer interference.

Robbery crews use a loaded or replica gun to control bank personnel and customers and to deter anyone from following. Many gangs explain that the gun is for the cops but few resist arrest when confronted by the police. Firearms are displayed and pointed but robbers seldom discharge weapons within the bank. It is extremely rare for crews to shoot anyone during a bank robbery. Most encounter no resistance during their holdups and many suggest that a gun lessens the likelihood of violence because people are deterred from resisting and therefore getting hurt.

Most bank robbery crews admit that their M.O. is frightening to staff and customers; define the crime as nonviolent since no one is physically hurt; dismiss the victim's fear as transient and harmless; insist that they have no intention of harming anyone; and claim that they only want the money with the least resistance possible. They operate with partners to collect the money themselves, rob several tills, and deter resistance. They also prefer banks that are busy enough to have a number of tills open at any given time. Most gangs will order tellers to open those tills that have been locked; steal money from only tills and not the customers; and do not enter the vault.

Bank robbery crews will "case" the area surrounding the bank for cruisers or suspicious vehicles but few gangs systematically locate police stations or make detailed escape plans before choosing a target. Crews occasionally postpone or back out of a robbery because traffic is heavy, the bank is too busy, there is a police cruiser or what appears to be an unmarked police vehicle nearby, or one or more of the crew experiences "bad vibes." If a member is reluctant to complete the score, partners will wait to see if the feelings pass. Partners are respectful of pre-robbery jitters since they too have experienced them and many are superstitious and easily spooked. Peer pressure is not used to persuade a reluctant member to proceed with the robbery. If the anxiety persists, then the robbery may be postponed. The bad feelings normally pass, however, and the robbery proceeds.

Most members of bank robbery crews admit to being terrified during their first robbery and, like the beggar bandit, they will wait several minutes and occasionally a few hours before getting up the nerve to enter the bank. Subsequent robberies are easier and most report feeling calm within the bank. This pattern is similar to the stomach "butterflies" experienced by athletes before a big game. Once the robbery begins, however, offenders become involved in the action and forget their nervousness. Some robbers also suggest that the feeling of calm relates to the sense of control they experience when the action begins.

Robbery crews believe that the chances of getting caught are slim and that arrest away from the scene is remote; they feel safe after their getaway and do not feel paranoid afterwards; and they believe that they are most likely to get caught through bad luck or informants. They dismiss good police work as an important variable in the apprehension of criminals. Bank robbery crews rob several banks over a short period and are caught within a few weeks or months. Since they typically maintain the same division of labour, choose banks in the same area, use the same disguises, bark out the same verbal commands, and use the same or similar getaway vehicles, the police can easily link them to their crimes.

Variations

While bank robbery crews commonly operate with two or three partners, some crews will include as many as six. Some partners are friends and party together after the score; others separate and only meet again for the next robbery. Some crews use their own car and park it in a discrete location while others drive a stolen vehicle and leave it outside the bank. A few will use a getaway driver who parks the car in a convenient spot, keeps the engine running, makes sure no one blocks them in, and acts as a lookout for the police. Some members will change clothing and/or hide in the car while driving away. Most crews share the money evenly with the getaway driver while others pay him or her a fee or percentage of the take.

Some gangs will use threats and vulgar language to frighten and intimidate, while others prefer to reassure staff and customers that no one will get hurt if they follow orders. In either case, victims are confronted by armed and masked bandits and do what they are told. Although some bank robbery crews attempt to prevent staff from activating the alarm, others concern themselves only with getting the money as quickly as possible. Some crews will check the vault for money or ask bank personnel to open the safe—something that usually cannot be done because of time-locks. Whereas most gangs will go behind the counter to collect the money, some will ask tellers to hand over the cash from their tills.

Although most bank robbery crews consider themselves non-violent and say that they would not shoot police or citizens who interfere, a few claim that they were prepared to use whatever force was necessary to escape. Some crews have discharged their weapons in the bank and a few bandits will push or strike customers or staff who fail to cooperate.

During the robbery, two common mistakes may occur: sometimes the gunman will panic and leave his partners behind; and occasionally, the bagman will disobey the command to leave and continue rifling through the tills. These mistakes will be discussed by the gang afterwards and the partner who has erred generally assures the others that the behaviour will not reoccur. Some crews maintain the precautions in every robbery while others become careless. Most admit to their crimes at arrest and implicate their partners but some offenders refuse to cooperate with the police.

(3) THE SOLO GUNMAN—A PROFILE

The modus operandi of the solo gunman is gutsy, aggressive, and overt as he attempts to accomplish independently what bank robbery crews do in groups. He enters the bank, displays a gun, controls staff and customers, and robs several tellers before departing. Of the 14 solo gunmen in this study, 12/14 (85.7 percent) used a loaded weapon and 2/14 (14.3 percent) used a replica weapon to control and deter bank staff and clients. A total of 13/14 (92.8 percent) have previous criminal records and 11/14 (78.5 percent) have previous robbery convictions, including 7/14 for banks.

Lone Wolf

Age 21, this solo gunman is serving 16 years on eight counts of bank robbery. Known as "The Wig Bandit," he was arrested by a police-surveillance squad on the steps of a bank he had just robbed. He has never worked and is suspected of having committed over 75 bank holdups in a five-year period.

I fired a gun in the one before. The teller was reaching her hand underneath the counter to press the alarm and I told her not to do it and I fired into the ceiling. This was the .22 and not the shotgun. I was always armed in case I walked out of that door and there is a police car waiting. That is why I had a shotgun. I don't mean to kill a cop or anything but if two police pull up, they are normal Joes. I mean they have a police badge and a gun but that is nothing. You just fire a shot into their car and destroy their windshield and they are not going to bother you. They have families, they have kids. I won't intentionally kill them. I'd make them know that I could do it. Take a blast at the car and then take off. They are not likely to chase me but if they do, that is not my fault. That is their own decision.

I'm not sure where I first got the idea of robbing a bank. I just thought this is the quickest way for cash. When I was a kid, I used to do crime and I used to get caught all the time. When I went to training school I started thinking, "Why do people get caught?" I looked at my area and 70–80 percent have losers put it on them

and tell the cops. One guy will get arrested and he'll tell on everybody else. I knew I never wanted to get caught again so I decided to do my crimes alone.

I'd usually take a stolen car and park it wherever I wanted it. The next morning I would take my vehicle and drive to the stolen car, get into the stolen car with my disguise on, and drive to the bank. Go in, take the money, and go out. Then I'd take the stolen car back to the good car and put everything in the trunk and drive off. Doing it is the easiest part. Getting away with it is what I consider the hardest. The first time I was nervous. After that it was just like I was going to my job. That sounds silly but that's what it felt like, getting up to go to work today. I used different kinds of disguises. I'd use scars, beards, moustaches, a wig, a balaclava a couple of times. I'd just go through the door, pull out the gun and make sure everyone knew it's a robbery. All I want is the money so I'd just make that point clear. I'd tell the tellers to step back and put the money on the counter. I'd give the bag to another teller and she'd walk by and collect the money. I'd hit however many tellers were in the bank. It doesn't really matter if it is busy because I stay away from the customers and I tell them to turn the other way. I'd take every kind of precaution before I'd go out and actually do a robbery. I'd buy a wig, beard, the weapon, get the car in place, and I'd have all my clothes ready the day before.

Then on the day, I'd just go and do it. I used to pay five hundred dollars for a stolen car and I had other costs. A brand-new gun would cost upwards of $600 depending. If I don't use the firearm, I give it back and pick up another one the next time. I just tell the person the gun has not been used. It would cost me an extra $200–$300 each time. And wigs are expensive—$340 for a good wig. I didn't believe they were that expensive. It would cost me $1,000 upfront before I did the score. It varies how much you get but I got about $10,000 on average. Sometimes I would do two a week and sometimes I would wait. I'd go up north, rent a cottage and do some fishing, and travel around. I don't know why I kept doing them because I never ran low of money. I started getting into drugs and that costs a lot of money. I'd buy an ounce of cocaine for $2,500 and that might last five to six days. I was injecting it and my money just went. It was costing $1,000 a day. It's a fucking waste. I was never stoned when I robbed a bank. You do dumb things with your money and it's gone. Once, me and a friend were up at a cottage and we bought two little motorcycles just to drive them off the cliff into water. I think they cost $1,700–$1,800 each, which is very foolish. We used to jump off this cliff all the time. There is a little trail and the cliff drops. We just went about 30 mph off the cliff. I didn't even jump off the thing. The bike fell faster and I went a lot further than the bike. You do things like that and I don't know why.

My girlfriend was a bank teller so they charged her with robbery. She never went down and robbed anything but they charged her with robbery. One time a friend of mine came over and gave her a package that had a gun. Now I was in the shower when this happened and he buzzed for her to come down and grab something because he has to go in a hurry. The police took a picture of her picking it up. They charged her with robbery but she beat it. There was some dumb charge that she pleaded to but she didn't get any time. She did lose her job.

Similarities

Because the solo bandit is more vulnerable to physical assault, he uses several techniques to minimize the possibility of interference: (a) like the crew, he brandishes a gun and warns people against resistance; (b) unlike note-pushers and bank robbery crews, he avoids turning his back on customers and staff to prevent a surprise attack; (c) he also maintains a safe distance by ordering them to move back; and (d) most refrain from jumping behind the counter to remain close to the door and prevent people from leaving the bank. Solo gunmen will order tellers to put the money on the counter and pick it up themselves or they will hand tellers a bag (or bags) and demand that it be filled. Men who leap over the counter and collect the money will order bank personnel to move away from the tills and keep a safe distance.

Solo gunmen claim that they do not wish to harm anyone but most are ready to use their gun to deter and halt any pursuit. One bandit says, "The gun is for the police," while another is more inclusive: "The gun is for anyone who wants to stop me."

Like other bank robbers, the solo gunman may have had close calls that bolster his confidence. After several robberies, he sees himself as being on a good-luck streak and does not believe that he will be caught. He considers himself more clever than the police, whom he views as inept at catching criminals. The solo gunman's modus operandi is more lucrative than most bank robbing techniques. Since he can obtain $1,000–$2,500 per till and will hit three or four tellers on each score, a purse of $3,000–$10,000 is common. This M.O. has brought in a reported low of $2,500 to as much as $50,000. The large score was obtained in a bank protected by an armed security guard that a solo gunman disarmed.

Most solo gunmen have an extensive criminal background and have committed other crimes. They have spent time in prison and view themselves as criminals. Unlike the note-pusher who assures himself that each bank robbery will be his last, the solo gunman views crime as a long-term career choice. Previous criminal experience makes these men knowledgeable of police practices. Most will locate police stations and will assess potential police surveillance and stakeouts before they enter the bank. They carefully prepare and frequently operate away from their home area so as not to be identified by their modus operandi. They will case several banks, disguise themselves, wear gloves, carry and display a gun, watch staff and customers attentively, execute the robbery swiftly, and plan their getaway carefully. They remove the mask as they leave the bank, discard an outer layer of clothing, and dispose of the gun and "bait" money.

It is uncommon for these robbers to confide in others. They are not paranoid after the robbery since they believe that having fled the scene, the police will have little chance of catching them. Solo gunmen are cautious to the end. This cautiousness makes them much more difficult to apprehend and consequently they tend to operate for longer periods than most note-pushers and bank robbery crews. Because they make more money from each score, solo gunmen re-offend less frequently and therefore face fewer risks than bank robbery crews and note-pushers.

A total of 13/14 (93 percent) solo gunmen have criminal records and 11/14 (78.5 percent) began their criminal careers working with others. The move to solo robbery from crews and partners was based on the following reasons: the loss of a partner and the lack of a suitable alternative; a view that partners are unnecessary and that the crime can be committed as efficiently and as safely alone; a belief that partners increase the risk because of the possibility of them informing, boasting to others, spending foolishly, or otherwise becoming a "heat score"; and because there is no split, the payoff is more lucrative. These men know that evidence based on the similarity of M.O. in itself is insufficient for conviction and consequently hang tough during interrogation, refuse to give a statement, and attempt to make the best deal possible with the courts.

Solo bandits are relatively calm during the holdup. After several robberies, they no longer experience intense fear before or after the score. In fact, this type of bandit is more self-assured and less apprehensive than other types of bank robbers. A few characterize the robbery as exciting but most simply regard it as work. They describe their mental state immediately prior to the robbery as aware, observant, confident, determined, single-minded, and psyched-up. Noticeably absent are terms such as nervous, scared, or paranoid. Solo gunmen are confident in their abilities to commit robberies on their own. Whereas crew members consider robbing a bank without a backup as risky, solo gunmen confidently plan and execute the crime by themselves. They believe that they can control staff and customers and deter potential resistance and heroes. All that is needed are the know-how, courage, and determination to do it alone.

Solo gunmen are serious criminals who exhibit a fierce resolve to complete the job. They enter the bank determined to obtain the money and to deter anyone from interfering. In almost all robberies, solo gunmen walk out with the money and escape unimpeded. The determination of one bandit is illustrated by the fact that he spent 52 minutes in the bank, cautioned the manager and head teller not to raise the alarm, demanded $50,000, counted the money, and left quietly. In the event that he should fail, his gun held one bullet meant only for himself. He describes his mood as suicidal—not in the clinical sense of despairing of life—but as a self-induced state that hardened his resolve. He was going to succeed or die trying.

Variations

Although most solo gunmen will order tellers to hand over the money, a few prefer to empty the tills themselves. Some are polite while others use threats and obscene language to gain compliance. Although most operate on their own, a few (4/14) report that they will occasionally use a getaway driver to assist them in their robberies. Two solo gunmen in this group are also included in the following analysis of armoured-vehicle robbers. Both men robbed their last bank alone but used an M.O. in which the bank manager was briefly taken hostage in his or her office and ordered to hand over large sums of cash.

ARMOURED-VEHICLE ROBBERS: SEEKING THE BIG SCORE

CASE EXAMPLE

Prolific

Billie is described by police as the most prolific bank and armoured-vehicle robber in Canadian history. Hold-Up Squad officers estimate that he committed over 300 bank robberies in his ten-year career. He worked with the Stopwatch Gang and teamed up with a variety of French and English crews to rob banks and armoured-vehicles across Canada and the United States. He was convicted of 95 bank robberies, six armoured vehicle heists, and has pleaded guilty to one count of murder. Billie received a reduced sentence in exchange for his testimony against 13 armed robbers and former partners.

In that bank, I used the scanner to stay from 8:15 a.m. to 9:20 a.m. We took the bank manager hostage in the morning and took the employees hostage as they arrived for work. The manager would open the door and bring them in and we put them in the vault. We had the police scanner on the counter so they could hear. I told them, "Listen, if anybody trips the alarm, we'll hear the police coming and we'll have plenty of time to kill twenty people and still get away." There were 27 employees and nobody gave us a problem. We put two girls on the telephone and they told people that everyone was tied up in a meeting having to do with counterfeit bills. When the time vault opened, we got the money and I left with $85,000. My partner stayed behind to give me a head start.

At one point I started using video equipment to help plan my scores. I had a van with tinted windows and I'd park it across the street from a bank with the camera focused where the doors were. I'd pick it up afterwards then watch the tape at home over dinner. I'd fast forward it and stop whenever I spotted something interesting like an armoured-vehicle delivery. So instead of having to sit on the bank and risk getting spotted, I'd just park the van and film the whole thing, go home at night, and play it back in 45 minutes. Next day, I'd move it to a new location. The van and video camera was a $30,000 investment.

Steve introduced me to big money. I was only 21 or 22 when I met him but I had been robbing banks for 6 or 7 years. I was just a normal...[pause]...bank robber but I never got caught. I'd jump over the counter but he taught me to go for the big score. I never robbed an armoured vehicle before that, just banks. I was in Canada and they were in the States. Steve would case a few banks and me and my partner would fly down, team up with the three of them and do the scores. He describes one in his book [*Jackrabbit Parole*]. We'd go in and Steve would have the stopwatch hung upside down on his neck. On the last road trip, we did five banks and one jewelery store. When Steve was arrested by the FBI in Arizona, he was on his way to pick me up in a hotel in Phoenix. We had a job planned in Phoenix but it never came off. The San Diego job was worth $300,000 and in the jewellery store we got over a million dollars in merchandise. In Florida, we followed some Brinks' guards and noticed that they would go to the Sears store for a pick-up, sign some forms, and walk out with the money. Steve and me got some Brinks uniforms, guns, the keys, big belt, the hat. We walked into the credit office and the lady threw us the bag of money. We walked out with $60,000.

Another trick I was taught was smashing through the windows. My partner and I wait outside the bank until they opened the night deposit safe. We're disguised, wigs, three-piece suits, and I've got a big flower box with a sledgehammer and a machine gun. When the time was right, I pass him the sledgehammer and take out my machine gun. We watch them load the bags on the cart and when they're done, smash the glass, step through, and take the cart. On our first one, all the women ran into the vault and left the money cart in the middle of the floor. My partner ran into the vault after the women thinking that they brought the money with them. I yelled, "It's here. It's here", and he ran back. We got $100,000

in that one and in another one, we got $165,000. Afterwards we'd drive to an underground parking lot, wipe off the make-up with a wet cloth, do a change of clothing, transfer the money into another car, he'd get into the trunk and I'd drive away. Drive back in front of the bank. They're looking for two guys, a different car, and we've got the police radios telling us what they're up to. Who's gonna drive past the bank? We're in a different car going in the opposite direction. If they're stopping cars, the guy in the trunk is ready. If it comes down to it, we've got machine guns. They wouldn't have to be dead, put it that way. You can take them easy and handcuff them just like you do a Brinks guard. I changed my M.O. all the time. You have to if you want to make a career out of bank robbery. You have to expand.

I broke up with my partner and got introduced to some big operators from Montreal. They wanted to do some trucks out west and they needed someone who was bilingual. I speak fluent French and English so I'd do the talking in English so nobody would know it was a Montreal gang. Helping to break Paddy out of jail was a big thing for my reputation and that's why I was asked to join these different crews.

These Montreal guys had a few scores in Edmonton and I went down for a month, talked to them, looked over the scores and then we did a few trucks. The armoured-vehicle guards have their guns in their holster so it's a simple thing to do because they don't have time to get to their guns. We choose an inconspicuous spot and in three-piece suits and disguises, you just stand anywhere. When they walk by, it's a simple matter to grab their guns and handcuff them to a railing. Only once did we get into a shoot-out. I grabbed one guard, and I took his gun and put him in front of me. My partners couldn't get to the other guard's gun in time. We told him to drop it. Instead of dropping his gun, the other guard starts shooting at us. He's shooting at me and I've got his buddy in front of me. Imagine! He was shooting while he was running away. One of my partners got shot in the ass. We picked him up, got the money, and got away. We knew a guy who was a cow butcher and we drugged him real good and this butcher had to dig deep into his ass to get the bullet out. He still walks with a limp but that's it. That was quite an experience. We kinda knew that guard was gonna be a cowboy. He had the look in his eyes like he was aching for somebody to rob him.

In my last year, I did six trucks besides the banks. We watched one truck make deliveries to a bank and noticed that the money would be locked into the vault. About ten minutes later, two women would go into the vault, take the bag, count the money, and put it into the safe. So we did the bank. After the truck left, we went in, got the girl with the key to open the door, and walked out with $200,000. I was always polite when I robbed banks and would tell people to have a nice day. If I went into a bank and I saw a teller push the alarm, I wouldn't get mad at her. I wouldn't even say anything. What's the point? I don't consider myself a bad bank robber.

SLEDGE USED BY DARING ROBBERS

LONDON, Ont. (CP)—Two bandits dressed in blue coveralls—one armed with a sledgehammer—pulled off a daring, early morning robbery of a London bank branch on Monday, wheeling an undetermined number of night deposit bags off to a stolen car in shopping carts.

No one was injured in the robbery, which began shortly before 9 a.m. in Westmount Mall when one of the men smashed the glass door of the bank to gain entrance.

Police Supt. Don Andrews said alert business people in the area phoned police immediately, but the "out-of-town pros" were gone before police arrived. Their getaway car, stolen Sunday in Mississsauga, just west of Toronto, was recovered later in an underground parking garage.

Sharon Hunniford, an employee at a dry cleaners beside the bank, said she heard two "smashes" and ran out to discover another robber wearing sunglasses and "something dark in his hand," apparently a gun.

"I've seen so much of this on television," she said, "I didn't stick around."

Source: Kitchener-Waterloo Record *(9 February 1982). Reprinted by permission of The Canadian Press.*

$1 MILLION ROBBERIES HAVE LONDON LINK

HULL, Que. (CP)—An Aylmer, Que., man has pleaded guilty in Hull provincial court to six armed robberies in Edmonton in 1982 which netted a gang more than $1 million in cash.

[The male offender], 27, will be sentenced April 30.

He had already pleaded guilty in connection with a bank robbery on July 9, 1984 in London when about $120,000 was taken.

London police raided his apartment in Aylmer near Ottawa on July 26 and found masks, surgical gloves, walkie-talkies, makeup, and semi-automatic rifles.

Police say he and his partners, who have not yet been charged, committed the Edmonton robberies between Feb.3 and Dec.29.

Police said a Loomis truck at the University of Alberta, four banks and a Brink's truck at an Eaton's store in Edmonton were robbed.

Security was heavy for [offender's name] court appearance. The courtroom was cleared of spectators before he was brought before Judge Bernard Dagenais.

Gene Assad, the Hull assistant crown attorney, said police used extra security because they are concerned for his safety.

Source: The London Free Press *(10 July 1984). Reprinted by permission of The Canadian Press.*

SLEDGEHAMMER ROBBER RECEIVES 12 YEARS IN JAIL

HULL—A Quebec man was sentenced Tuesday to 12 years in prison for his part in a string of robberies that included a bank holdup in London last July in which about $120,000 was taken.

[Offender's name], 27, of Aylmer, Que., earlier pleaded guilty to robbing the Westmount Mall branch of the Bank of Montreal last July 9. In the robbery, a sledgehammer was used to smash a glass door to gain entry shortly before the bank opened for the day.

He also pleaded guilty in March to six armed robberies in Edmonton during 1982 which netted a gang more than $1 million in cash. A Loomis truck at the University of Alberta, four banks and a Brink's truck at an Eaton's store in Edmonton were robbed.

London police raided his apartment in Aylmer, near Hull, on July 26 and found masks, surgical gloves, walkie talkies, makeup and semi-automatic rifles.

A co-accused in the London holdup is to appear in court in London on May 14 for preliminary hearing.

This photograph is taken from a Toronto Crime Stoppers video-taped reenactment of the robbery described in the following article.

DID YOU SEE THIS METRO BANK ROBBERY?

Sergeant Gary Grant
Metro Crime Stoppers
Two bandits used a sledgehammer to smash their way into a Scarborough bank and the Metro Crime Stoppers program want you to find them.

The robbery occurred Jan. 3, at the Bank of Montreal branch at Kennedy Rd., and investigators hope a re-enactment of the robbery, to be shown on CITY-TV newscasts tomorrow, will jog the memory of a witness.

It was 8.40 a.m. on the first working day after the New Year's holiday and the staff was preparing to open the branch.

Suddenly there was the sound of breaking glass and startled employees saw a man smashing a front window with a sledgehammer.

After breaking through the window, the man threw down the hammer and waved a handgun in the air as he rushed into the branch.

He was followed by a second man carrying a rifle, who stood guard just inside the shattered window.

The man with the handgun ran behind the service counter and yelled isntructions to staff members while demanding to see the manager.

The bank manager came forward and spoke with the gunman who demanded the night deposits.

The bandit was directed to a box that had just been filled with bags of money from the night deposit safe.

The gunman grabbed the box and ran with his partner from the bank.

They got into a green 1974 Chevrolet Impala which had been parked outside the bank, and sped off.

Bank employees last saw the vehicle travelling south on Kennedy Rd. and it was later found abandoned a short distance away on Eppleworth Ave.

A search of the area failed to turn up any suspects and investigations showed the getaway vehicle had been stolen.

So far, no witnesses have come forward, despite the fact the robbery occurred in broad daylight and the car dumped in the parking lot of a busy apartment complex.

The suspects are still being sought.

DESCRIPTIONS

Bank staff said the man carrying the rifle was white, between 26 and 27 years, 5 feet, 6 inches to 5 feet, 7 inches tall and weighed 135 to 140 pounds.

He had dirty-brown, collar-length hair and a skinny facd with a pointed nose.

They also said he was clean-shaven and wearing a green waist-length jacket and a green and brown woollen toque.

The other man was white, between 25 to 30 years, about XX feet, 7 inches tall and weighing 160 pounds.

He had dirty-blonde collar-length hair and was wearing a three-quarter length navy blue "parka-style" ski jacket with dark pants and a dark blue toque.

The preceding newspaper articles deal with the "sledgehammer" robberies and the apprehension of our case example "Prolific."

From the 1930s through the 1960s, most bank robberies in Canada were committed by career criminals who operated in armed crews and were considered the elite of the criminal world. Most of these bank robbery gangs worked out of Montreal and are described by the police and older bandits as professional bank robbers. They were serious, heavily armed gangsters who used commando-style tactics and frequently positioned a lookout with a machine gun outside the bank to deter police from approaching the scene. These bandits terrorized staff and customers, often obtained money from the vault, and would sometimes escape with more than $100,000. In the 1960s, banks responded by minimizing cash exposure in their tills and by installing time-locks for large amounts of money. This made bank robbery less profitable to professional criminals so many gangs changed their modus operandi and in the early to mid-1970s, bandits began to kidnap the manager's spouse and children, forcing him or her to obtain money from the bank. There were 120 such incidents in one year in Montreal alone. The banking community responded with new security procedures and employee training. The police initiated intensive investigations, formed surveillance squads to follow suspects, and made a number of arrests. Following some very stiff sentences, the underworld began to reassess the crime as a high-risk and heavily penalized crime that banks, police, and the courts would not tolerate. The brief flurry of robbery/kidnappings abruptly ended and this type of M.O. is now almost obsolete.

Prior to 1970, bank robbers commonly took the bank manager into the vault and had him or her open the safe. This can no longer be done since the safe is under a time-lock and bandits are in a hurry to leave. Nonetheless, some of the more skilled robbers operating today have developed techniques that allow them to control staff, deter them from pressing the alarm, wait for the time-locks to open, and seize large sums of money. The case example, "Prolific," describes such an incident. Overall, however, professional bank robbers have all but disappeared and been replaced by the more common beggar bandit. The decline of the professional and the rise of the amateur means that bank robbery is no longer a high-status crime in the criminal subculture.

PROFESSIONAL CRIMINALS

Criminologists have often used conceptual language from the sociology of work to portray crime from an occupational perspective. Letkeman (1973), for instance, describes crime as work and analyses it as a vocation. He also draws attention to the fact that property crimes are often carried out by individuals who lack legitimate opportunities to get ahead and differ little in their needs or psychological functioning from law-abiding citizens. Crime is seen as an illicit occupation and criminals are portrayed as engaging in criminal careers. In addition, the learning processes through which crime skills are acquired are depicted as similar to the socialization into work roles. Some researchers have also differentiated between "heavy" criminals who engage in robberies and burglaries, and occasional and amateurish petty criminals. Although it is possible to single out some predatory offenders as professional criminals, they are generally not crime specialists. The distinction between professional criminals and less sophisticated offenders is one of degree rather than kind. Some offenders may be clearly labelled professional while others are more difficult to categorize because technical skill, profits from crime, involvement in criminality, and criminal attitudes and values are matters of degree and may be difficult to measure.

The concept of a "professional criminal" was first outlined by Edwin Sutherland (1937) who later with Donald Cressey developed it into a typology of professional thieves (1955) containing five behaviour systems: (1) stealing is a regular business; (2) every act is carefully planned; (3) technical skills are used; (4) the thief is migratory but uses a specific city as a headquarters; (5) the thief has criminal associations involving acquaintances, congeniality, sympathy, understandings, rules, codes of behaviour, and a special language. Among men who rob banks in Canada, the term "professional" is mainly limited to those who commit armoured-vehicle robberies or target banks in which there are armed guards. These scores require higher skill and courage since the guards must be disarmed, but they also provide large rewards. The concept of professional is used among bank robbers themselves but not uncritically. A subject who operated in a heavily armed crew, robbed armoured vehicles in Canada and the United States, and published a book about his adventures called *Jackrabbit Parole*, uses the term professional but admits even the most accomplished bank robbers may be deficient.

> It's hard to become a true professional bank robber because how many times are you going to be in that situation? It is just that 30 seconds, that 60 seconds, or that 90 seconds where the guns are out and the drama is on. You can't do it enough to become a professional unless you've done it for 8 or 10 years by which time you've probably done 8 or 10 years in jail like I have. You can be a professional soldier because they spend millions of dollars in training. Bank robbers have no training except the real thing.

Police also have reservations about the term but nonetheless describe "pros" as career criminals who work in armed gangs; operate beyond their home city; use automatic weapons; bullet-proof vests; and police scanners; plan their robberies meticulously; take on armoured vehicles; obtain large sums of money; and are ready to engage in a shootout with the police if necessary. These are serious criminals who aim for the big score and spend accordingly. Defining someone as a professional is a compliment and most bandits confer this status exclusively on men who commit armoured-vehicle and armed-guard robberies. In addition, only men who rob armed guards define themselves as professionals. As one armoured-vehicle robber states, "You don't need balls to pass a note to a female teller. That's not a professional. But go after armed guards and you take your life in your hands. That's what separates the men from the boys." Another armoured-vehicle robber explains the status differential:

> You can't equate someone who's selling nickels and dimes [small quantities of drugs] on the street to someone importing a ton of hash. The higher you are, the more respect you have for each other. A guy who takes on a truck [an armoured vehicle] and a guy who takes on a grocery store are not in the same league. Not in here [prison]. Not on the street. Not in the eyes of the police.

Armoured-vehicle companies attract robbers because they deliver and transfer large sums of cash. They are difficult targets, however, since there are usually two or more guards who are armed and trained to be alert, cautious, and ready to respond with gunfire. The trucks themselves are steel-reinforced and the driver generally remains inside the vehicle, watching the operation. Drivers are also equipped with radio transmitters to communicate with other guards and headquarters if anyone is following them and/or they suspect trouble. Generally, only those men who rob armoured vehicles and risk their lives by confronting armed guards receive sums more than $100,000.

A DYING BREED—
THE LAST OF THE PROFESSIONALS

Many bank robbers in this study thought about, discussed, and even planned "the big score," but not many offenders are willing to take the risk. Because there are so few armoured-vehicle robbers, a special effort was made to interview them. Ten men in this sample (10/80) have been convicted of armoured-vehicle robberies and each of them meet most of the criteria listed in Sutherland and Cressey's typology of professional thieves. These men have a long-term commitment to robbery as a way of life; are heavily armed and highly skilled and prepared in executing their tasks; commit their crimes throughout the country and across national boundaries; and operate with other known gangsters. Although their technical skills are not great, they are knowledgeable about police practices, bank policy, and armoured-vehicle procedures. They also use automatic weapons, technological aids and police scanners and video cameras, disguise kits, and bullet-proof vests. The men in this group range in age from 27 to 64 at the time of interview. Their median age is 35 years and their average age is 39—almost 10 years older than the 29.8 year average age of the remaining 70 bank robbers in this study. All but one have lengthy criminal records for a variety of offences, have been in trouble with the law since their teenage years, and are presently serving prison terms that range from 14 years to life. One subject, age 64, has spent 50 years in prison and was the longest serving inmate in Canada when he was interviewed in 1983. He had recently escaped from prison, been recaptured, and was awaiting trial for several armed robberies of banks across Canada. All ten of these men have also robbed banks both with partners and alone, using the M.O. of the solo gunman previously described. Eight of these men are included in the analysis of bank robbery crews and two are included in the discussion of solo gunmen. This distribution reflects the last type of robbery that each man committed before being apprehended.

Only one of these ten men reports working at a legitimate job and attempting to go straight. This offender met a woman he fell in love with, decided to get married, found himself a job, and informed his partner that he was retiring from crime. His life was going well until he was enticed back into crime by what looked to be a lucrative and easy inside-job.

My wife was eight months' pregnant when I got caught up in a conspiracy. I didn't like the whole trip because a bank teller was involved and she knew me personally and the way it was going down was kind of shaky. I thought about it for days. My wife thought I was up to something and she told me she had a gut instinct that something was happening and it was bad. It was free money to me. But the teller watched TV the night before and some guy dumped his partner after stealing some money and she got to thinking that was going to happen to her. So she ended up telling. That was a turning point in my life. I was really bitter about that one. It was my own fault too. It was a costly, stupid, dumb error.

The ten men in this sample live in a criminal and violent world and each knows persons who have been killed in holdups, in prison, or because of "drug rip-offs." One subject is serving a life sentence for murder and his partner was acquitted on a separate murder charge. These two men also shot and wounded an ex-police officer who attempted to intervene in a bank holdup. All ten subjects have charges/convictions for other offences including narcotics, abduction and kidnapping, assault, attempted murder, break and enter, escape, resisting arrest, and extortion. Seven report having been beaten by the police and all but one have spent years in prison. Each of these nine men has also escaped or attempted to escape at one time or another; four have taken hostages in their escapes; two were charged with the shooting of prison guards; and all ten describe robberies in which shootings have taken place.

It is widely recognized that most serious bandits in Canada originate from Quebec and in particular from Montreal. Six (6/10) of the armoured-vehicle robbers in this sample reside and/or operated primarily in Montreal and the other four (4/10) originate from and/or operated out of Ottawa/Hull. There are major differences between these and the other bank robbers in this study. Professionals view armed robbery as a career or job; they seek large sums of cash; they are cautious, patient, and plan their robberies in detail; and they are not deterred by the possibility of violence although they attempt to minimize it. These bandits acquire partners through underworld connections, some of which are made in prison. Several also received "job offers" from established gangsters after pulling off a big score. Despite the variety of offences they have committed in their career, they primarily define themselves as robbers. They consider bank and armoured-vehicle robbery as a chosen profession or their area of expertise, specialize in this criminal activity, and engage in it on a sustained basis over various periods of their lives (usually interrupted by incarceration). They describe the move into armoured-vehicle heists as a transition from bank robbery to the big score. These bandits also report, however, that they will consider any target that is financially worthwhile and several have robbed jewellery stores, heisted transport trucks carrying meat, furs, cigarettes, and alcohol, and even committed a major gold-bullion heist. The rationale behind the big score is explained by one bandit, "You pay the same price in jail for doing a Brinks and getting $100,000 as you do for a bank and picking up $5,000. So you might as well do a Brinks. It's just as easy. It's the most dangerous scores that have the least money—the corner grocery store." Another states: "I go wherever the money is and wherever the danger isn't, if possible. I would do a tomato-soup factory if there was money in it."

Robbery skills are inevitably learned on the job and by trial and error: "You learn by doing." Referring to the time spent in prison, another comments, "The lessons are learned hard." All ten of these men work in crews and earn a reputation in the underworld as solid and competent robbers. The crews are exclusive but loosely organized groups in which everyone is treated with respect, no one gives orders, and everyone is equal. Bandits listen to one another and pool their ideas to develop the best plan possible. No one may drink or use drugs on the score and crews ranged from two to five persons. Fellow inmates respect these bandits because they have successfully completed robberies that involved planning, skill, and courage, and in which large sums of money were obtained. They are not deterred by danger but are respected as much for their intelligence as their courage. Their status is also based on a reputation for personal integrity, trustworthiness, and being solid, that is, an unwillingness to inform on others, despite the personal costs. They have status in prison and tend to associate with other gangsters. While free, they associate with other underworld figures. Only two of these men report ever having "straight" friends. Most of their associates are organized criminals, thieves, drug dealers, hookers, and other gangsters.

All ten of these men have committed robberies out of province and five have operated in the United States. When searching for scores in another city, the typical M.O. involves one or more bandits moving there, renting an apartment, searching the city for lucrative and vulnerable targets, planning the holdup, bringing in needed partners, explaining the score to them, and committing the robbery. Some offenders chose cities because they had contacts there who could provide accommodation and/or assist in planning the score. The case example ("Prolific") reports four armoured-vehicle robberies in Edmonton in a one-month period. A Montreal gangster who had escaped from prison had been living there for two years, set up the scores, and provided the apartment for the Montreal crew that flew into town. One of the heists was at the University of Alberta: "Every university has a little bank but at the end of the month the students have to pay their rent so the candy truck brings a bigger load of money for that week." Bandits commit out-of-town heists because they are known to the local police and would immediately be investigated if a major robbery occurred; they are already under investigation for previous scores and wish to avoid more heat; other cities have had few holdups and the armoured-vehicle companies take fewer precautions; robberies committed by out-of-town crews create many difficulties for the police to investigate and solve; and guards in provinces other than Quebec have their guns in a holster rather than in their hands.

PLANNING AND SETTING UP THE SCORE

Planning an armoured-vehicle robbery typically takes several months and may involve thousands of dollars of investment. Bandits will study maps of the city, locate all banks and police stations, familiarize themselves with streets and expressways, and search for a vulnerable and rich target. Armoured trucks are described as "cracker-jack boxes" because it is difficult to determine how much money they actually contain. Bandits locate large money transfers by identifying busy retail stores and banks that cash paycheques for nearby office or factory workers. Some robbers will use false identifications to open bank accounts, make deposits and withdrawals, visit their safety deposit boxes, and converse with the staff to gather intelligence on potential targets. "Is that real money?"—"That's nothing, you should see what they bring into the Elgin Street branch." "Why are you so busy today?"—"Today's payday for all the office workers."

Armoured-vehicle robbers will also visit banks or stores when guards make their pickups/deliveries and attempt to observe guards' routines, determine where the money is stored, who has the key, and whether it is left unprotected. Some robbers keep detailed records on armoured vehicles by noting routines and peculiarities, and timing their movements. Bandits are aware that people are creatures of habit and they look for and attack the weakest link. Planning an armoured-vehicle robbery involves searching for a security breakdown that can be exploited.

You have to do your homework. You have specific things in mind and you stick with it and just develop it. First you find the Brinks guy and you follow the truck, then you watch them make a delivery and you follow them somewhere else like down to the main branch. You might work backwards another day and then one time you'll find some way and say, "Beautiful. Here we go." The guy is alone and there's a hallway and he is blind and the truck is blind. Get dressed here, park the car here. Okay, we got him, let's go. Oh fuck, there is no money. The guy is taking only $35,000 a week, we'll pass. Then you find another one and something is not right and on it goes. You might look at the same truck in five different spots. I've had as many as eight in the book on the go at the same time. We keep track of the time, the place, estimated amount of money, the truck number. With an armoured vehicle, you have to be really confident in what you are doing.

Men who consider themselves professional gangsters argue that planning an armoured-vehicle heist requires self-discipline and work. Most report getting up at 6:00 or 7:00 a.m., Monday through Friday, and checking out scores all day long. Finding the right target can take months and requires money to live in the meantime. One bandit states, "You need financing, patience, discipline, and persistence—imagination comes later." Professional robbers will also change their M.O. from one score to the next. Since the majority of bank robbers in this study describe themselves as lazy, one reason that not many armoured-vehicle heists occur could be due to the discipline and planning that is required.

An ideal site for an armoured-vehicle robbery is one that allows bandits to blend into the surroundings and get close to the guards; provides little opportunity for the guards to manoeuvre; does not allow the driver to witness the robbery; is away from witnesses and possible interference; and provides a quick and safe exit. Because robbers need be close to the guards to disarm them, they cannot wear balaclavas or masks that would reveal their intentions. Disguises must allow them to look normal but not identifiable. Each of these men report purchasing and using makeup and costumes including fake tattoos, moles, eyelashes, beards, wigs, moustaches, coloured contact lenses, and hair colouring. One crew liked to wear business suits and the uniforms of janitors, construction workers, delivery men, postal workers, armoured-vehicle guards, and police officers. Although some bandits believe they can evaluate whether or not a guard is likely to resist, others caution that you should always be prepared for resistance and to never underestimate one's opponents. A bandit who specialized in robbing banks with armed guards describes how he passed on one score because he anticipated trouble:

> I've never had any trouble with guards. But some guards are very proud. They want to be a hero. There was one guard that I know was wild and special. This guard, I knew he would be a problem. I wanted him not for the money but for the challenge. I meant to do him many times but I always backed out. I backed out 10 times. I was sure he'd react. He was special this guard. I was right because I read in the papers that he was killed. That was two years ago. He was a big guard and I wanted to do him just to see if I could. But I said to myself, "Why try to prove something to myself? Why look for a problem?" That's why I didn't do it. After I read that he was killed, I said to myself, "I was right!" They had his picture in the paper.

Several of the robbers in this sample routinely secured police scanners, tuned into their frequencies, became familiar with police codes that indicate types of offences, and listened to police radios to glean information. On occasion, bandits will phone in a false robbery to observe and time the police response. They also routinely conduct dry runs, time themselves, and time the guards. On the day of the robbery, some gangs will use diversions to lead the police to another part of the city, or place roadblocks and detour signs to create traffic problems that will impede approaching patrol cars. The getaway is usually made in a stolen four-door car. This hot car is exchanged for a cool car a few blocks away in an inconspicuous place such as a parking garage and bandits usually remain together until the split is made. Before the robbery, offenders will obtain the licence-plate numbers of unmarked police vehicles and search for "ghost" cars before striking. Professionals look for stakeouts and are concerned about a police ambush. These subjects know bandits who were shot by the police and are aware of the danger. The possibility of a police ambush was brought home clearly to one crew whose highly publicized M.O. spawned a copycat gang whose members were shot as they emerged from a bank holdup. Gangsters are also on the lookout for plain-clothed police officers within the bank and one bandit claims to have twice spotted detectives during holdups:

> The first thing you have to look for when you go into a bank is an off-duty cop or he'll shoot you in the back when you leave the bank. I found them twice. I was pretty sure that I had spotted one and afterwards, I'm listening to the police scanners and sure enough, this guy was an off-duty cop. The other guy we actually disarmed.

During the course of this study, an armoured-vehicle company began using a regular van while one of their armoured trucks was being repaired. Two criminals noted the security lapse, waited for the guards to enter a department store, approached the driver with a gun, commandeered the van, drove it to an underground parking garage, emptied the contents, tied up the guard, and escaped with hundreds of thousands of dollars. Professionals in this study considered this to be a brilliantly planned and executed caper because the bandits spotted the opportunity and took advantage of a security breakdown. Furthermore, they scored big, injured no one, and got away cleanly. In their opinion, this was "a professional job" and "the perfect crime."

DISARMING THE ARMED GUARD

Like other bank robbers in this study, armoured-vehicle robbers claim that they only want the money and have no wish to harm anyone. These offenders realize, however, that both they and the guards are at risk in this type of robbery. Since guards carry guns, robbers may be killed. Alternatively, bandits may kill guards to avoid being shot themselves. A professional is defined in part by the skill exercised in the heist and this includes committing the crime without needlessly killing anyone. Most condemned the perpetrators of a recent armoured-vehicle holdup in which the robbers came up behind, shot, and killed two guards whose guns were holstered.

Part of the skill in committing armoured-vehicle robberies is to select a situation that minimizes the danger to both bandits and guards. The technique for disarming guards is simple: the robbers must be close enough so that they can simultaneously seize the guards' guns and incapacitate them with their own firearms. The act is accomplished in seconds and the guards are either left standing, made to lie down, handcuffed, or tied up. By grasping the guards' guns, the robbers prevent them from unwisely unholstering and firing. Armoured-vehicle robbers explain that if they were to attempt the robbery by simply pointing their weapons, the guards might draw and fire. An incident like this is described in the case example, "Prolific." It may be irrational or unwise for a guard to reach for his gun when robbers already have theirs drawn, but it can easily occur. No one can predict how people will respond when their lives are threatened. In such a situation, robbers may have to shoot the guards or be shot themselves. This appears to have happened in several of the armed-guard shootings that occurred during the course of this research.

The armoured-vehicle robbers in this sample report that they will avoid dangerous situations and pass on scores where injuries to guards are likely to occur. Two bandits state:

> We do everything we can so as not to have to take somebody out. Ambushing somebody is bad business. So we will pass on a lot of scores so as not to have to shoot anyone.

> I don't want to kill anyone. I don't want to be up for murder. I don't want to hurt people. If you're going to do one, why not do one with their guns in their holster?

Even though they attempt to avoid hurting anyone, all ten men admit that they would kill in "self-defence." Two bandits are even more aggressive and express little concern about killing. One states, "If you're going to rob a truck, you have to be ready to kill. You have to be more than ready to kill." A man who describes himself as a junkie on banks and a fanatic about guns asserts that being ready to kill is what separates the men from the boys. He also boasts that he was always ready to kill. This claim was no idle threat since he had served 15 years of a 25-year sentence for shooting an armoured-vehicle guard and had recently returned to prison for shooting another person in a gunstore robbery while on parole.

In Quebec, where so many armed robberies occur, security firms require guards to carry their weapons in their hands to deter robbery. Bandits unanimously condemn this policy as dangerous and blame it for the deaths of many guards. By actually holding their guns, the guards give robbers little opportunity to disarm them. This may deter some, but will lead others to simply shoot guards to obtain the cash. One man in this study described how a former partner shot two armed guards, killing one. He offers this advice: "They're best not to carry guns in their hands 'cause they'll be fuckin' wasted. That's why guards get killed. If somebody is going to rob them, he's going to shoot." Another robber similarly warns:

> You carry your gun in your hand, you carry your life in your hand. Who is going to take a chance? You're not going to say, "Stick 'em up!" when just a slight reflex on his part will kill you. Guys who go after Brinks are not fooling around. They figure that whoever is holding a gun in his hand is getting a bullet in the head. The best advice for a guard is to holster his gun.

These bandits also argue that real professionals will recognize and pass on dangerous scores. Amateurs, they suggest, are more likely to kill because they are less able to evaluate risk and select appropriate targets; they are more likely to panic if things go wrong; and they are less skilled at disarming guards and controlling resistance. A professional will take extra precautions, plan the score so he doesn't have to shoot anyone, and catch the guards with their guns in their holsters or in a position where they cannot be drawn.

All bandits in this group agree that bank robbery is no longer a smart or profitable crime. Nonetheless, they still view armoured vehicles as targets that are both lucrative and relatively easy to rob. One gangster suggests that whereas banks have become better at protecting their cash, armoured-vehicle companies haven't changed much in decades: "Banks are getting more sophisticated but trucks are not. They're albatrosses. They're dinosaurs. They don't change. They're not that hard to knock off." Despite this optimistic view of armoured-vehicle robbery, all ten men agree that drug dealing provides greater amounts of money with less risk and that most serious criminals today have moved into this area.

AUTHOR'S NOTE: Stephen Reid's *Jackrabbit Parole* and Greg Weston's *The Stopwatch Gang* depict a professional bank robbery crew in operation. Everett Debaun, a former bank robber, describes a 1940s style bank holdup in "The Heist: The Theory and Practice of Armed Robbery" *Harper's Magazine,* February 1950, 69–71. One older gangster recommends the book (and movie) *The Friends of Eddie Coyle,* by George V. Higgins as an accurate depiction of an old style bank robbery crew.

SUMMARY

Despite their differences, beggar bandits, bank robbery crews, and solo gunmen share several characteristics: they are initially motivated by need but continue robbing banks because of greed; most have criminal records, few job prospects, and poor employment histories; and they commit several robberies in quick succession after "blowing" the money on a hedonistic "partying" lifestyle. Few bank robbers consume alcohol or take drugs prior to committing a holdup. Most view bank robbery as a relatively non-violent crime and argue that financial institutions can easily afford the loss. Bank robbers are frightened during their first robbery but become progressively more confident; are unconcerned about silent alarms, fingerprints, bait money, or eyewitness identification; and consider the getaway to be the most significant part of their plan. Robbers prefer cities over small towns, assume that it will take the police four or five minutes to arrive, and give themselves sufficient time to escape. Overall, bandits believe that bank robbery is a low-risk crime; that most of the variables are known and can be controlled; and that arrest away from the scene is unlikely. Most dismiss competent police work as an important variable in the apprehension of criminals.

There are also significant differences between beggar bandits and the aggressive modus operandi of bank robbery crews and solo gunmen. Beggar bandits appear to be less serious criminals in a number of ways. The note-pusher uses a modus operandi that relies on subtlety and discretion whereas crews and solo gunmen use speed, surprise, and weapons in a terrifying commando-style attack on bank personnel. Most note-pushers use no weapon (23/31 74 percent) or replica gun (5/31 16 percent) whereas the majority of crews (31/35 88.5 percent) and solo gunmen (12/14 85.7 percent) use loaded firearms to commit their robberies. Fewer beggar bandits have previous robbery convictions (12/31 38.7 percent) in comparison to bank robbery crews (22/35 63 percent) and solo gunmen (11/14 78.5 percent). Whereas beggar bandits are more likely to originate the idea to rob a bank from the media (17/31 54.8 percent) than through association with others (8/31 25.8 percent), crews and solo gunmen are more likely to be enticed into bank robbery through association with criminals (31/49 63 percent) rather than through the media's influence (8/49 16 percent). Members of bank robbery crews and solo gunmen are more likely to be involved in crime as a way of life.

Considering the large number of holdups committed by the men in this study, the modus operandi of all three types of bank robbers effectively prevent staff and customers from interfering. Of the 101 instances in which bank robbers were caught, only five were physically accosted by bank staff or customers. Since four of these five incidents involved beggar bandits, the aggressive modus operandi of bank robbery crews and solo gunmen appears to deter resistance more effectively.

Robberies are typically unskilled, low-paying crimes that are committed by young offenders who spend the money foolishly and repeat the offence until they are caught. Research indicates that most robbers do little planning, take few precautions, choose convenient targets and leave the scene as quickly as possible. This chapter has looked at the different modus operandi used by offenders in the commission of muggings, convenience-store robberies, and bank holdups. Also examined are a number of issues that potential robbers confront in deciding how to commit their crimes: selecting a target; making a getaway; using a surreptitious approach or a more aggressive commando-style attack; using threats and/or force to control victims; using a weapon; deciding what weapon to use; confronting and controlling the victim; committing the robbery alone or with partners; and allocating roles within a crew.

This chapter has also examined the reasons why robbers use the same M.O. in each holdup and the consequences. Also reviewed are research results from the present study on bank robbery detailing the influence of the mass media on the modus operandi of bank robbers; the spending habits and partying lifestyle of most bandits; and typologies of three types of bank robbers: (1) beggar bandits; (2) bank robbery crews, and (3) solo gunmen. The chapter ends with a discussion of professionals who target armoured vehicles.

The Victims of Robbery

VICTIM-CENTRED THEORIES OF CRIME

Robbery is attractive to novice offenders for a variety of reasons: there are many targets/victims available; it requires few skills; it is quickly accomplished; and it provides instant cash. The theories discussed so far have focused primarily on the offender and variables related to his or her criminality. In recent years, however, theories and research have examined the situational nature of victim-offender interactions and attempted to understand crime as a product of the exchange that occurs between the victim and the victimizer, rather than a product of offender motivation only. Marvin Wolfgang (1958), one of the first researchers to examine victim-offender interactions, coined the term "victim-precipitated" to refer to criminal homicides in which the victim is the first to show and use a deadly weapon or to strike a blow in an altercation. Although the idea of victim-precipitation focuses attention on the situational determinants of criminal incidents, it is criticized by some as victim-blaming. Fattah (1991:290–93) argues, however, that most of the criticism results from a failure to grasp the distinction between exculpatory and explanatory concepts. When correctly understood, victim-precipitation is a legitimate effort to understand the criminal's motives, the dynamics of victim-offender interaction, and the events that lead to the act of victimization. Whereas the term "provocation" is exculpatory, concepts such as precipitation, facilitation, and participation are explanatory and do not necessarily imply a value judgment.

Recent victimology research has given rise to theories of crime that focus attention on the structure of opportunity for crime. Whereas previous theories assume a steady supply of victims and attempt to explain the behaviour of offenders, victim-centred theories are more likely to assume a steady supply of offenders and attempt to understand the behavioural characteristics of victims.

LIFESTYLE-EXPOSURE THEORY

Hindelang et al. (1978) have developed a theory of personal victimization that examines vocational and leisure activities and the mechanisms that link lifestyle with victimization. The theory consists of eight propositions:

1. The probability of suffering a personal victimization is directly related to the amount of time that a person spends in public places (e.g., on the street, in parks, etc.), and particularly in public places at night.

2. The probability of being in public places, particularly at night, varies as a function of lifestyle.

3. Social contacts and interactions occur disproportionately among individuals who share similar lifestyles.

4. An individual's chances of personal victimization depend on the extent to which the individual shares demographic characteristics with offenders.

5. The proportion of time that an individual spends among non-family members varies as a function of lifestyle.

6. The probability of personal victimization, particularly personal theft, increases as a function of the proportion of time that an individual spends among nonfamily members.

7. Variations in lifestyle are associated with variations in the ability of individuals to isolate themselves from persons with offender characteristics.

8. Variations in lifestyle are associated with variations in the convenience, the desirability, and the vincibility of the person as a target for personal victimization (Hindelang et al., 1978:251–64).

Lifestyle-exposure theory argues that certain types of lifestyles and daily work and leisure activities bring people into contact with potential offenders, increasing their chances of victimization. Lifestyles may be defined as the patterned ways in which people distribute their time and energies across a range of activities. People differ with respect to how they spend their days, how they spend their leisure time, how often they go out in the evening, where they go, and with whom they routinely associate. Hindelang and his colleagues argued that some types of lifestyles are more likely to put people at risk of criminal victimization. For example, if a person is on the street or in bars late at night, or is regularly with people who have the social and demographic characteristics of typical offenders, the risk of criminal victimization increases. Young members of minority groups, therefore, have a higher level of victimization than middle-class retirees because the lifestyle of the former entails much more exposure to victimization risk. In addition, variations in lifestyle and occupations disproportionately expose occupational groups such as cab drivers and convenience-store clerks to relatively high risk of becoming the victims of crimes such as robbery, assault, and murder.

ROUTINE ACTIVITIES THEORY

Whereas the lifestyle-exposure theory focuses on victim lifestyle, "routine activities theory" (Cohen and Felson, 1979) emphasizes the importance of the physical environment. Borrowing from the ecological perspective, the theory proposes that the minimal requirements for predatory crimes are (a) motivated offenders, (b) suitable targets, and (c) the absence of capable guardians against crime converging nonrandomly in time and space. Thus, a motivated offender makes contact with a suitable target in the absence of a capable guardian who might otherwise prevent the crime. Routine activities theory argues that crime occurrence is affected not only by the absolute size of the supply of offenders, targets, or guardianship, but also by the factors affecting the frequency of their convergence in space and time. Predatory-stranger offences such as robbery depend on the opportunity created in places where offenders converge with vulnerable victims and low surveillance (Sherman et al., 1989:47).

Routine activities theory assumes that some people are inclined to break laws and does not attempt to explain motivation. Although people have desires and inclinations, they cannot always carry them out. The opportunity structure of society limits human ability to act, including acting on inclinations to commit crimes, or to avoid victimization. Moreover, changes in community life can produce more crime without the motivations of the likely offenders changing (Felson, 1986:120).

Routine activities theory uses regularities in behaviour to explain criminal victimization. According to Cohen and Felson (1979), much behaviour is repetitive and predictable. Routine daily activities affect the likelihood that property and personal targets will be visible and accessible to illegitimate activities.

Routine activities theory has been characterized as "place-specific" or as a "theory of place" because it attempts to explain the tremendous imbalances in crime risk that exist in different areas of the city. These "hot spots" of crime appear to draw or assemble offenders and targets, producing an excessive number of offences and victims.

Routine activities theory is compatible with several bodies of literature. Felson (1986), for example, attempts to provide a synthesis among routine activities, social control, and rational choice perspectives. Rational choice theory deals mainly with the content of decisions whereas routine activity approaches deal with the ecological contexts that supply the range of options from which choices are made. Felson argues that we cannot understand the rational structure of criminal behaviour by considering the reasoning of only one actor in the system. People make choices, but they cannot choose the choices available to them nor can they predict the chain of events that follow their choices, or others' choices. Routine activities theory provides the context within which choices are made. The structure of opportunities sets the stage for criminogenic choices and influences whether these choices result in successes or failures. Even though an offender may prefer to violate the law, his or her preference can be thwarted by decisions made by others, regardless of whether they realize that they are preventing a crime.

Felson (1986) also links routine activity theory to Hirschi's control theory. He summarizes Hirschi's four elements of control theory—commitments, attachments, involvements, and beliefs—with the concept "handled." By forming social bonds, society gains a handle on individuals to prevent rulebreaking. People have something to lose if others dislike their behaviour, if their future is impaired, if their friends and families are upset with them, if they are occupied with conventional activities, or if their beliefs can be situationally invoked to make them feel bad every time they break a rule (Felson, 1986). The "handled offender" is an individual who is susceptible to informal social control by his or her bonds to society, and the "intimate handler" is someone with sufficient knowledge of the potential offender to grasp the "handle" and exert control.

The handle is a necessary condition for informal social control. If an individual lacks commitment to the future, attachments to others, or conventional beliefs, he or she has no handle to be grasped, and informal social control is impossible. Although some offenders may have no social bonds (hence are not subject to informal social control), other offenders are handled, having a social bond to a parent or some other intimate handler who is able to seize the handle and impose informal social control.

Unfortunately for crime victims, handled offenders can evade their intimate handlers, thus avoiding informal social control for many hours each day. This evasion links routine activities to informal social control. As Hirschi (1969) notes, social bonds prevent delinquency; yet as Felson notes, such prevention is difficult to accomplish by remote control. In general, a potential offender must first shake loose from a parent or handler, then find a target for crime that is unmonitored by a guardian (Felson, 1987:913).

Social control, opportunity, routine activities, and lifestyle-exposure theories of crime and victimization examine the characteristics of target vulnerability and, for robbery, these characteristics apply most appropriately to muggings. They each assume that if illegitimate opportunity arises (i.e., a lack of social control on offenders or victim vulnerability), crime occurs. None of these theories attempts to explain the robber's motivation, which is taken as a given. The theories instead focus our attention away from motivation toward a greater effort to understand the structure of opportunity for crime, or more specifically, the availability of suitable targets for crime in the absence of (informal) guardians capable of preventing the violation.

Because these theories have many similarities, sociologists often use the term lifestyle-exposure and routine activity interchangeably or refer to them as theories of victimization opportunity. Victim-centred theories have generated much empirical literature in recent years, particularly for direct-contact, predatory offences such as robbery. In so doing, they have overcome some of the obstacles facing traditional offender-based explanations of such behaviour. Moreover, such accounts are well supported by the existing body of empirical evidence (Garofalo, 1986; Maxfield, 1987). The following chapter applies lifestyle exposure and routine activities theories to a range of issues including a discussion of target selection, modus operandi, victim injury, victim resistance, and robbery prevention programs.

MUGGINGS

From interviews with mugging victims, Lejeune and Alex (1973:261–64) found that citizens—or at least middle-class citizens—expect that in their own territory, they will be relatively free from the threat of attack by others. For most people, the mugging is an unexpected event that challenges the victim's prior assumptions about his or her vulnerability. Mugging calls into question assumptions about themselves, about others, and about their surroundings. It also calls into question basic assumptions about social order. Lejeune and Alex report that despite the high degree of public awareness of street crime, most victims are surprised at being mugged. Individuals who are aware of crime do not experience a sense of personal vulnerability. Prior to the mugging, most victims trusted others and did not see themselves or their neighbourhood at high risk to street crime. In fact, potential victims felt essentially positive sentiments toward the settings in which the mugging occurred.

FILLIPS reprinted by permission of Jim Phillips.

This cartoon depicts the robbery of an individual, which is known as a "mugging."

The mugging encounter begins with a verbal and/or physical invasion of the victim. Yet because of the newness of the situation, its unexpectedness, and its ambiguity, many victims initially have difficulty interpreting both the nonverbal gestures that precede the threat and the verbal demand for their possessions. People are evidently reluctant or unwilling to define an invasion of their space and person as a physical threat; they would rather define it in more understandable and less dangerous terms. These initial misdefinitions are not simply denial by the victim, however, since the situation is unexpected and often ambiguous.

The initial stage of robbery (the "takeoff") is dangerous because the victim is surprised and may act unpredictably. Quite often the robber fails to communicate intent and/or the victim experiences momentary shock and disbelief and delays action. Sometimes the victim will ask: "Is this a joke?" or "Are you serious?" Verbal commands, threats, force, obscenity, intimidating gestures, and weapons quickly define the situation as a robbery. Despite an inherent conflict of interest, the victim usually cooperates to bring the encounter to a fast and successful conclusion (Luckenbill, 1981:31).

From the offender's perspective, robbery breaks down when the victim resists, is perceived as resisting, or when others intervene. Criminals either respond to resistance by retreating and forfeiting the venture or by attempting to salvage the robbery by repeating or increasing the threat and/or using prodding or incapacitating force. Research clearly indicates that the victims' resistance, and/or attempts by victims or other bystanders to obstruct robbers, increase the likelihood of violence (Gabor and Normandeau, 1989:199–200).

Luckenbill's (1981) study of mugging indicates that offenders may cast the target into one of two roles: an acquiescent role, which requires the victim to remain passive, not interfere, and allow the offender to take his or her money; or a participatory role, which requires that the victim assist in the transfer of cash. An acquiescent role eliminates the victim from the undertaking while the participatory role enlists his or her help. The target's assistance may also be used to maintain the protective membrane that surrounds the robbery scene (Luckenbill, 1980:371).

Crow and Bull's (1975:39) study of convenience-store robberies found that the robber typically requires that the clerk open the cash register and hand over the money. Robbers may also require victim cooperation to maintain an image that "nothing unusual is happening" (Emerson, 1970). For example, if the robber moved behind the cashier's counter or teller's cage to obtain the money, bystanders would be alerted that something is wrong. Robbers who wish to be discrete, like those who pass notes in bank holdups, require victim participation to obtain the money but also to create the appearance of an ordinary transaction.

In open settings such as banks and convenience stores, staff and customers can monitor the interaction between robber and victim. Consequently, the offender may attempt to create an impression that a normal transaction is occurring. Striking the victim or moving behind the cashier's counter or teller's cage to obtain the money oneself would signal to others that something is wrong. The target's assistance may also be needed to accomplish the transfer from the safe or the till. In deciding between incapacitating force and a command backed by a threat of force, the offender considers the benefits of managing normal appearances as well as the target's value to the transaction. When the victim is considered unnecessary, the offender is more likely to open with incapacitating force (Luckenbill, 1981:32–33).

MUGGINGS AND VICTIM PRONENESS: LIFESTYLE-EXPOSURE THEORY

In interviews with 90 mugging victims, Conklin (1972:96) found that 42.2 percent had previously been victims of another crime. He also found that two-thirds frequented the area daily (Conklin, 1972:94). Although this finding is based on a small sample, it suggests, quite dramatically, a victim-proneness of certain individuals. Sacco and Johnson's (1990) analysis of patterns of criminal victimization in Canada shows that there is a direct relationship between the risk of robbery and the number of evening activities engaged in outside the home. As the lifestyle-exposure theory would predict, those involved in 30 or more evening activities outside the home in an average month were more than twice as likely to be robbed. Forty-two percent of the robberies occurred in a public place where victims are less protected by familiar surroundings and acquaintances. People who were most likely to be robbed were men, younger people, those who engaged in the largest number of evening activities outside the home, those who were students during the preceding year, and those who had not completed secondary school. Single people were more than twice as likely to be robbed. The risk of robbery was marginally higher among urban than rural residents (Sacco and Johnson, 1990:26). Hartnagel and Lee (1990:178) similarly found that some routine activity patterns directly affect the level of crimes in cities. In fact, the predictor with the largest effect on crime was criminal opportunity: as the opportunity for crime increases, so does the rate of urban violence. Cohen, Kluegel, and Land's study (1981) indicates that income—not income dispersion—is inversely related to risk of assault, directly related to risk of personal larceny, and parabolically related to risk of burglary victimization. With controls for several risk factors, the affluent had the highest risk of victimization for each of these crimes. These results suggest that income level rather than income inequality may be the more critical variable since, given similar exposure to risk and lifestyle patterns, the affluent are the more attractive crime targets (i.e., the number of rich persons in the city increases the number of attractive opportunities). The researchers interpret the results as suggesting that such social power resources as age, income, and race relate to criminal victimization only insofar as they indicate differences in exposure to risk, guardianship patterns, proximity to potential offenders, and identification of lucrative targets.

As the incidence and visibility of mugging and other street crimes have increased, many urban residents now believe that they are no longer safe in public places. At the same time, their perception of the ineffectiveness of law enforcement has made them aware of their personal responsibility to protect themselves from street crime. There is also a community-based movement that sees crime prevention as a cooperative effort. Many neighbourhoods have adopted programs such as "neighbourhood watch" to look out for one another. In addition, groups have formed to lobby government for street lighting, better police services, and other social and physical changes to prevent or deter crime in their neighbourhoods.

Conklin (1972:185) suggests that providing improved street lighting will help to deter robbers who steal from people who walk alone on dark streets—although he acknowledges that robbers may simply shift their locale. Even though many preventive measures may shift rather than stop robbery, individuals can take measures that will reduce their chances of becoming robbery victims, help minimize financial losses, and avoid personal injury. Just as homeowners may lock their doors, individuals can make themselves less vulnerable to robbery through common-sense measures. Parking the car in a well-lit area and avoiding walking down dark, deserted streets alone at night will reduce an individual's vulnerability and exposure to crime. Other safety recommendations include carrying less money; carrying money in unexpected places; keeping a small sum separate that you can give the offender if you are robbed; using credit cards instead of cash to minimize losses; and purchasing insurance so that your losses are compensated and you are less likely to defend your property and consequently endanger your life. Insurance is a small cost that guards against a larger loss. Walking with others, carefully choosing public places, or staying at home can help reduce risk but many people are unwilling to make these changes.

CONVENIENCE-STORE ROBBERIES

Local variety stores, groceterias, gas bars, beer and liquor outlets, and other small merchants are located in areas and operate during hours that are convenient to their customers. These retail outlets present tempting and vulnerable targets because they are open for long hours, particularly late at night, are relatively isolated, and have cash and/or valuable merchandise. These stores are even more vulnerable when there are few employees and customers in the store. In addition, staff are more likely to be assaulted since they are not shielded behind the metal cages or bullet-proof glass that are found in jewellery stores and some banks. The robber has easy access since the doors are open and there are no barriers to entry. The robber can walk in, pretend to be a customer, loiter, observe the clerk, wait for customers to leave, evaluate security, and then strike.

The more vulnerable characteristics a target has, the more it will attract the armed robber. By locating along busy streets, convenience stores facilitate the robber's escape. The probable degree of control that can be exercised over staff and customers also influences a target's vulnerability. This control relates to the number of staff and customers present and the physical characteristics of the store. The presence or absence of security measures also influences the robber's perception of control. Ciale and Leroux's (1983:24) study of armed robbery in Ottawa indicates that the preferred or most vulnerable targets are small businesses connected with food distribution including restaurants, groceterias, chain convenience stores, and corner stores. By dividing the total number of robberies by the total number of stores, they calculate that chain convenience stores have a risk coefficient of .95, meaning that each store is likely to be robbed on average once a year.

SUPERMARKETS AND DEPARTMENT STORES

Although supermarkets and department stores are known to handle large amounts of cash on a daily basis, they are not the favourite targets of bandits. The potential gains may be high but they do not outweigh the risks involved. The vulnerability of large stores is low because of a number of factors. Supermarkets are more likely to have security guards, surveillance cameras, two-way mirrors, and offices that overlook the cash registers. Supermarkets typically have many employees and customers in the store at any given time; high aisles of groceries that block the view of would-be robbers; and two or more entrances. Customers or staff may surprise the robber or escape from the store to notify the police. The task of controlling the movement of staff and customers in a supermarket is difficult and time-consuming, if not impossible. In addition, cash registers are visible from the street, increasing the likelihood that the police may be alerted. The large number of persons present in a supermarket also creates the possibility that an off-duty or plain-clothed police officer may be in the store. Many supermarkets are located in shopping centres, which may impede escape routes, due to pedestrian or vehicular traffic. Within the supermarket, cash registers are separated from one another by counters, making it time-consuming and difficult to hit more than one till. The practice of locking cash registers when they are not in use requires that the robber must enlist the cooperation of staff, which also takes up precious time. If the offender chooses to rob only one cashier, then he or she will probably obtain the same amount of cash as from a convenience-store holdup. So why take on a much more formidable target if there is little chance of any appreciable gain? It is not surprising that offenders generally avoid large supermarkets and department stores since these targets offer too little money with too many risks. The possibility of identification, resistance, and pursuit discourages many would-be robbers.

PROTECTIVE MEASURES FOR BANKS

Banks are concerned with ensuring that systems and procedures to prevent robbery do not interfere with normal banking operations. Bank officials resist the use of armed guards since they are expensive, create an intimidating atmosphere, increase the likelihood of a shootout with bandits, and endanger the safety of bank employees and customers. Most banks and financial institutions in Canada reject the idea of creating impregnable fortresses. Bandit barriers such as bullet-proof glass partitions between tellers and customers are expensive to install, foster a false sense of security since the glass is not actually bullet-proof, and detract from a bank's friendly and convenient service atmosphere.

Banks are reluctant to implement these expensive protective measures since robbers gain little money, while the preventive measures can involve thousands of dollars. Because losses from robberies are insignificant, banks can afford to cooperate with bank robbers. Some banks discourage employees from activating the silent alarm until after the robber has left so as not to provoke violence and place people in danger through a shootout or hostage-taking incident. Obviously this delay makes it more difficult for the police to apprehend the offender.

The prime locations of banks make them attractive targets since robbers give priority to the getaway. Although banks cannot control these external factors, some bank branches have been closed due to the number of robberies. Banks look to the police to investigate, solve, and prevent bank robberies, and they perceive themselves as playing only a minor role as agents of control. Within banks, prevention measures include the use of visible surveillance cameras. But while cameras may aid in eventual capture, they do not appear to have a significant deterrent effect. Robbers report little concern for such surveillance devices. The major weakness in the physical structure of the bank is the ease with which the bank robber can get to the teller. Low counters afford the teller little protection from an assault. However, robbers are concerned about witnesses noticing unusual activity and the low windows and visibility into the bank interior allow pedestrians from the sidewalk and street to witness any unusual activity.

Banks instruct their tellers to comply with robbery demands to reduce potential risks. Aside from the occasional use of permanent and obvious "bandit-barriers," banks have not provided tellers with screens or protective devices that they might retreat behind during a robbery. This follows the banks' avowed policy to get the robber outside the bank without incident as soon as possible. This is also why "interlock zones" on double sets of doors are not used to detain robbers when they leave. Police are instructed not to try to interrupt a robbery in progress even if it is detected. Instead, the robber is apprehended upon exiting the building. At the same time, the doors are locked immediately behind the robber, to prevent the robber from returning, to keep witnesses from leaving, and to deter pursuit by unarmed bank customers and personnel.

CASE EXAMPLE

Death Of A Teller

Only one bank teller has ever been killed in Canada during a bank robbery. Her killer describes the events that led to her death.

I didn't go in there with the thought of killing anybody. The whole thing with the gun was if the cops came 'cause I'm not going to stand there and just let them shoot at me. I didn't even know she was dead until 2:00 that afternoon. I just thought I grazed her head 'cause all I saw was like a little bit of blood come down to about her eyebrow. And then she just like... she disappeared. She

disappeared! I didn't see her collapse. I just saw her there and then she's not. I actually thought I grazed her. I didn't think it went in her head. Then I went out to the van and told Toby, "Come on, let's go. I think I shot her."

Then I was walking. I went to see an old teacher of mine and asked him if I could do a refresher course in drafting and he said no problem. I continued my day. I just thought, "The gun went off. She'll be okay. They'll take her to the hospital and fix her up." And then I heard! I stopped at the water fountain to get a drink and the janitor's office is right there and I heard on the radio something about a bank. I didn't hear it all so I stuck my head in the door and I asked a girl sitting there what they said. She said, "A bank teller got shot and killed in a bank!" I didn't even change expression. I just turned around and I walked out of the room. I almost missed the bus and all the way to my parole officer's I was paranoid, I was freaking out. I was on parole for some B & E's and had to report once a month. Today was that day. My parole officer asked me why my hands were all sweaty and I was shaking. I told her I was exhausted. "I haven't slept." Around 8:00 that night, the police came. They kicked the door and it hit me in the forehead. I ended up face down with a 12 gauge in the back of my neck. This cop says, "Move and you're dead!" In the car, this cop turned around and says, "Hey you cocksucker, we're going to take care of you at the police station. I'm the one who had to talk to the woman's husband." I didn't say a fucking word. I didn't know what to say to that. Got to the station, they didn't do a thing. I got through better than I expected and better than I read about in the papers about killers getting beat up. They didn't lay a hand on me.

I was nervous from the moment I woke up. I had the shakes, shaking involuntarily. Then it would stop, start again, stop. It just kept going like that until we got to the bank and then it was constant. It's funny, walking in the bank I was pretty calm. Then I had the mask on and I started shaking all over again. Gil and Paul talked me into this and sent me in there. I've been a follower all my life. Someday I'll

put my foot down. Gil and Paul talked Toby into it too. I never even met him before we did the bank. He had a stolen van. I met him that day, that very day. That morning. Me, Gil, and Paul went over to Toby's and I jumped into the van. I gave him $10 to fill it with gas. He was sitting in the van, warming it up. Toby had stolen the van the night before. Gil and Paul went in their car and led the way. They had told us there's one bank on this side and one on that side so I just said, "Go to this one. There's no intersection and no stop light." He parks right in front of the bank.

They could have prevented that from happening, the bank tellers, the bank, the bank manager. A guy comes in there with a gun, he shouldn't even have to ask for the money. I told them, "This is a holdup. Everybody freeze. Put the money on the counter." I'd never seen anybody freeze from shock. The way the bank teller was looking at me was like to say, "Well fuck you. I'm not giving you nothing." That's the way I was seeing it so that's why I put the gun closer and I cocked the hammer. I figured she's gonna say, "Well, he's not fucking around. This is a gun and it's loaded." She just didn't move! I never used a handgun in my life so I don't realize that once you pull the hammer back, the trigger is more sensitive than with the hammer down. You just got to touch the trigger and then the hammer will drop, "Bang!" I was holding the gun and I was shaking and then it just went off! In a way it's not my fault! Call it criminal negligence or whatever. Like they should tell them it's not their money. They're insured. Fuck. Give up the money. I'm no fucking killer! I'm not! I was scared. They said in court I was nervous, I was shaking, that I wasn't an experienced bank robber. And after I shot her, the next bank teller was throwing the money in the air. There was a guy who chased me but he would have been sorry if he had caught me 'cause I probably would've went for the gun again. These people think they're fucking heroes.

When I came into the Pen, I wrote a few letters but I didn't get no answers. I wrote this close friend but she didn't respond. Like what do you say to a guy who murdered a bank teller? Even the guards here figured that this bank-teller thing would play on my mind. But it doesn't bother me 'cause it was an accident. Last week, we were coming from court and there were six or seven of us in a van. The guys enjoy it because you're away from the Pen. So we started rocking back and forth in the van to make it fishtail. The driver had to slow down and when we get back, we start ribbing him and he says to me,

"Well I'm not going to lose no sleep tonight, I get paid overtime. With your charge I figure you'll lose the sleep." I said to him, "Why the fuck should I lose sleep?" I know he was referring to the bank teller thing and the fact that it was a woman that I shot and killed.

This offender, age 21 at the time of the robbery, received a life sentence for second-degree murder, making him eligible for parole after 15 years. The getaway driver, age 23, received a 10-year sentence as an accomplice and the two men who planned the crime, age 22 and 24, received 10 and 12 years respectively. Their victim, a 28-year-old part-time teller, probably froze out of fear rather than defiance as this novice bank robber assumed. Experienced bandits explain that they have learned to repeat their commands because a teller's initial reaction is often shock. The second verbal command brings them out of shock and they begin to respond as instructed.

INJURY TO VICTIMS

It is difficult to assess injuries that result from robbery for a number of reasons: standard definitions of injury are not applied; there is typically no follow-up of victims; it is hard to distinguish between degrees of injury; and emotional harm is not recorded nor is it easily measured. Not surprisingly, there are conflicting results reported by researchers who attempt to measure the incidence of injury to victims of robbery.

Gabor and Normandeau (1989:199) report that about 30 percent of robberies involve physical force including jostling, punching, and tying up victims. Sacco and Johnson's (1990) results from the 1987 General Social Survey show that while a weapon was present in only 28 percent of the robberies, victims were attacked in almost three out of four attempted and actual robberies. In almost two of three of these attacks, the victim was hit, kicked, slapped, or knocked down, and in over half the victim was grabbed, held, tripped, jumped, or pushed.

Ciale and Leroux's (1983) study in Ottawa notes that the most likely to be injured are lone individuals attacked in the open as they are depositing money or walking home late at night. Conklin (1972:121) similarly found that victims engaged in noncommercial roles are more apt to be injured than victims occupied in commercial pursuits. A person who is mugged is more frequently hurt than a clerk in a store or a bank teller, partly because the offender applies preemptive force and/or the victim offers resistance.

In a U.S. study of 500 convicted bank robbers (Haran and Martin, 1984: 49–50), 381 (76.2 percent) used weapons and 7 percent fired their guns in the bank. Two bank guards were killed and 19 other victims were injured, twelve of them through gunfire. There was no instance of direct firing at bank personnel or the occupants of the bank but robbers did not hesitate to use their weapons against interfering bank guards or pursuing police personnel. In one instance, a bank guard and robber shot and killed each other. In another case, a robber killed a bank guard and wounded a police officer who interrupted the robbery.

Some studies report that most robberies occur without any physical injury to victims. Crow and Bull (1975:14) found that in 95 percent of the robberies studied, no victims were injured and only slight injuries occurred in the rest. They also note that data from a major U.S. convenience-store chain over the period 1970–75 indicate that 69 deaths occurred in 17,649 robberies, a rate of one death in every 256 holdups.

PSYCHOLOGICAL/EMOTIONAL HARM

Studies frequently suggest that the effects of crime for the majority of victims are shortlived and that fear, anger, or distress subsides within a few weeks (Pointing and Maguire, 1988:8). But long-term research on the effects of serious physical, and in particular sexual, assault indicates that many victims show lasting fear, depression, and behavioural changes for months and sometimes years (Shapland et al. 1985; Burt and Katz 1985: Kilpatrick 1985 as found in Pointing and Maguire, 1988:8). Maguire (1984:221) notes that several researchers have already demonstrated that residential burglary produces a damaging impact upon the health and peace of mind of many victims. Common effects include immediate shock or panic, fear that the offender will return, difficulty in sleeping, inability to stop thinking about the offence, and a lasting sense of insecurity and suspicion of

I AM ARMED & DANGEROUS

& WILL SHOOT YOU IF YOU

NO DON'T GIVE ME ALL YOU'RE

MONEY. THAT INCLUDES 50 $100

BE QUICK

Dear Mam Do Not Panic!
Tommorrow I go to jail
for 10 years. I don't
want to SHOOT someone
Please empty drawer
I don't want to SHOOT YOU

In both of the above notes, the offenders attempt to portray themselves as desperate and each threatens to shoot the teller. Police report that explicit and violent threats help to ensure teller compliance but also traumatize victims. Judges often sentence offenders more harshly, however, for using explicit threats. *Courtesy Metro Toronto Police Hold-Up Squad.*

strangers. Women in particular report symptoms of shock or distress from being burglarized and nearly two-thirds report that the event was still affecting their lives four to ten weeks later. The study indicates that most victims consider the emotional impact on their lives as more serious than their financial loss.

Oblivious

All three of us had guns. A guy would have to be a complete imbecile to try to jump anybody. You're only there 30 to 40 seconds and you're gone. It's that simple. I did 28 banks and each has it's own individual trip. I remember once, the guys were doing the tills and I had my back to the wall checking everything out. I had a .38 automatic and if somebody comes in, they stay in. They don't go out. So I went, "Bam. Bam. Everybody hit the floor!" In French and in English. Fire the gun in the ceiling and you make people aware it's not a toy. It makes such a racket, people just freeze. You're telling them it's for real. I told them to hit the ground and they did. Everybody but this one lady who was behind the till just walking around. She had papers in her hand and she was in shock. I thought at first she must be deaf mute or something. I yelled at her to hit the ground but she continued to walk around as though nothing was happening. So I just let her go and we did the bank and left. She didn't even look up. She didn't see us. She wouldn't even recognize us. Everyone else is on the floor and she's walking around with her papers, oblivious to what's happening. I remember that trip. Weird.

While physical injury or harm are relatively infrequent occurrences in robberies, the emotional consequences of being a victim of a holdup may be significant. One only has to imagine the helpless victim confronted by a gun-wielding bandit to realize that even if he or she escapes physical harm, the victim may recall the trauma long after the event. The traumatic effect of facing assaultive, threatening, masked, armed robbers is difficult to measure, but doubtless, it is a harrowing experience. Even the polite, unarmed bandit is threatening to the victim, who experiences the interaction in robbery as a psychological assault.

Unfortunately, there are few studies on robbery victims, particularly longitudinal studies, that measure emotional harm. Lejeune and Alex (1973:286) interviewed 17 victims of muggings and found that one effect of the mugging is to significantly increase the victim's sense of vulnerability and feelings of powerlessness. Victims are shocked and angered and many report feeling shame for not resisting or blame themselves for not having been careful enough. Victims also believe that the environment that they previously perceived as benign has become a jungle, that appearances are deceiving, and that trust is an inappropriate attitude for survival. Lejeune and Alex (1973:272–73) suggest that the police may even contribute to this image of the neighbourhood or city as a dangerous place by communicating to the victim the ordinariness of his or her plight, the unlikelihood that he or she will recover any losses, and the probability that the offender will not be caught. The police are perceived as unable to solve the crime problem and the streets become feared as dangerous places.

Armed robbery may leave its victim with residual physical and emotional disorders, and personal difficulties. Gabor and Normandeau (1989:202–3) report that two-thirds of the subjects in their study experience one or more of the following complaints after a robbery: chronic nervousness, insomnia, nightmares, headaches, loss or gain of appetite. Over 90 percent of the respondents stated that the event disturbed them emotionally. The most frequent complaints were a growing fear of holdups, a general distrust of others, greater aggressiveness on their part, moodiness, and depression. These emotional disorders tended to last longer than the physical complaints. Almost a quarter of the respondents also mentioned that the experience resulted in a change in their lifestyle, led them to consider changing jobs, or produced other personal problems.

Sacco and Johnson's (1990) analysis of Canadian victimization data shows that three-quarters of the robbery victims had some difficulty carrying out their main activities after the incident. Victims of robbery typically report that the robbery has led to some changes in their attitudes or behaviour. Conklin (1972:95) found that a common response to being victimized is for victims to curtail their social life. Over half of his subjects report that their social life was no longer the same and that they were more likely to stay home at night, avoid meeting people, move their residence, quit their job, and/or cease frequenting certain locales and business establishments. The social cost of individuals avoiding certain areas is that it produces an atomization of city life (Conklin, 1972:96).

Crow and Bull (1975:x) found that one-third of convenience-store robbery victim-employees quit after being robbed, with one-half attributing it to the robbery. Similarly, Ciale and Leroux (1983:4) note that the stress of victimization in robbery may only be relieved by seeking other employment.

Although some communities have responded to rising crime rates with vigilante action, citizen patrols, and the banding together of neighbours for collective protection, these efforts have had little appreciable effect on the crime rate or citizens' fear of crime. The major modes of adaptation to victimization that result from the robbery remain primarily individualistic. Even police warnings to the public emphasize that people must take responsibility for their personal safety.

FEAR OF CRIME

Many persons are influenced by media reports of crime and violence in evaluating the risk of being victimized by crime. Frightening media images cause many to fear crime. News reports expose us to people who, in telling us about an event, show us greater risks than we thought we knew, and a world less safe than we assumed. Although most people may ignore the risks in everyday life, dramatic and violent crimes in one's community often become matters for public discussion and remedial or preventive action. The problem of the fear of crime is usually formulated as the relationship between the high crime rate, which is an objective fact, and fear of crime, which is a subjective attitude. Researchers frequently note that even though men experience crime in higher numbers, women report greater fear of crime. Women appear to have an objectively low rate of victimization along with a subjectively high fear of crime. Some critics dismiss their concerns about personal victimization as irrational and unwarranted. Researchers note, however, that women have different experiences in public places than do men, particularly when they appear alone (Balkin, 1979; Clemente and Kleiman, 1977; Gardner, 1990; Riger and Gordon, 1981). Whereas men may fear becoming the victim of a robbery, women must take precautions to avoid situations that make them vulnerable to both robbery and sexual attacks. It is not surprising that women are more fearful of crime of strangers than men since they are more likely to be victims of sexual assault. The fact that women are less physically capable of defending themselves than men also contributes to their greater concern with personal safety.

Carol Brooks Gardner's (1990) review of the popular literature on crime prevention along with in-depth interviews with 25 women concerning their fear of crime leads her to conclude that women are frequently advised to be distrustful of strangers and men and to act prudently in public places. This advice includes being escorted by men, dressing in nonprovocative ways, and maintaining mental and physical vigilance in public (e.g., avoiding or not living in certain areas, carrying keys in your hand as a weapon). Gardner (1990:311–12) notes that women occasionally report a low-grade guilt over their paranoia toward other citizens, who, in retrospect, may be viewed as meaning no harm to them. She also notes that crime prevention strategies require women to act in ways that involve negative contingencies such as relying on others or time-consuming preparations (1990:311). Because they are fearful of crime and it is difficult to reliably judge the many strangers that one encounters, except by appearance, women rely on social cues to assess a situation. Women must be crime-conscious and intensely aware of the many possible dangers of public life.

Fear of crime and concern with personal safety often keep women at home, where they feel more physically safe. Gardner argues that fear of crime is a form of social control that keeps women in the home, where they have traditionally belonged. Radford (1987:43) similarly suggests that a woman who is not perceived to be controlled by one specific man in public can and will be controlled by any man. Fear of victimization extends to major life decisions such as choosing a home or apartment. Gardner (1990:325) suggests that a further effect of crime prevention beliefs is the portrait they paint of men. The obligation to behave in a crime-conscious manner can undermine women's trust in the majority of quite innocent men whom women observe or with whom they come into contact in public places. These "sadly necessary measures," Gardner states, spoil public places not only for women, but also for men.

Critics argue that the public should have a balanced picture of crime because excessive anxiety detracts from people's lives. However, Jock Young (1988:167–69) is critical of the use of victimization studies that argue that the public's fear of crime is irrational, exaggerated, and disproportionate to the "objective" probability of victimization. He points to the fact that in victimology surveys, victims view about half of all unreported crime as serious. Young also notes that police statistics and victimology data are skewed both quantitatively and qualitatively because certain crimes are disproportionately represented while others are unrepresented. He concludes that for some groups, women and the elderly in particular, the fear of crime cannot be dismissed by objective evaluations of the probability of victimization based on official statistics and victim surveys since there is a hidden dark figure that is not measured and these persons are affected differently by victimization.

VICTIM RESISTANCE TO ROBBERY

Based on interviews with robbery victims, Conklin (1972:113) found that their most common reaction was fear. Others experience disbelief when confronted by the robber and some report that their mind went blank. One in ten responded by resisting, either by refusing to cooperate or by using force against the offender. He found no relationship between victim resistance and the use of a weapon or the type of weapon used by offenders. Conklin (1972:115) also found that if the victim does resist, the offender is somewhat more likely to use physical violence. Offenders define the robbery situation as one in which they take certain risks to obtain money; if they are blocked from reaching that goal by the victim, they may elect to use force to overcome the obstacle.

Many victims who did not resist had force used against them nevertheless. Robbers with weapons are much less likely to use force than unarmed bandits. In three-quarters of the unarmed holdups, offenders used force against their victims. Often this involved restraining the victim to prevent him or her from escaping or calling for help. Offenders who use a knife use force in 40 percent of cases while those with a firearm use force about 20 percent of the time. Offenders tend to use less force as the weapon becomes more threatening to the victim. Conklin (1972:116) suggests that without a weapon to intimidate and threaten the victim, physical force is used to show that they "mean business."

Gabor and Normandeau (1989:202) found that victims resisted robbers through verbal and/or physical means in a quarter of their cases. Resistance was rarely based on sound logic; that is, a rational calculation of the odds by the victims. Employees were more likely to resist than owners; victims did not tend to consider either the number of offenders or the number of witnesses in the decision to resist; and even the type of weapon used hardly affected their behaviour. The most influential factors were the victim's feelings of anger, the presence of threats, and even their prior experiences with robbery (Gabor and Normandeau, 1989:202). Conklin (1972) found that even when threats of force are employed to assert control of crime outcomes, victim resistance still occurs. He also found that victim resistance is unrelated to the robber's possession of a weapon and that a weak relationship exists between victim resistance and offender use of force. Cook's (1976) finding that victim resistance is related to the value of the victim's property implies that robbers may be faced with a situation in which they must inflict severe injury when the property is of substantial value.

Gabor and Normandeau (1989:202) conclude that resistance can be beneficial in that robbers were almost four times as likely to leave the scene with no money. But resistance increased the likelihood of injuries sustained by the victim by a factor of ten. Luckenbill's (1981) study of robbery similarly indicates that victims are more likely to be hurt in attempted, rather than completed, crimes. The victim, of course, is more likely to foil the completion of a holdup if he or she resists, but is also more likely to be hurt than if he or she acquiesces to the robber's demands.

Some researchers argue that resistance by victims, especially forceful resistance, is generally useless and even dangerous to the victim (Block, 1977; Yeager et al., 1976). Police typically advise prospective victims to cooperate rather than resist in robbery. Some criminologists, such as Lipman (1975:84), even suggest that potential robbery victims should carry a sufficient amount of money to satisfy the robber's immediate needs. Not everyone agrees that the best advice to potential victims is to cooperate and hand over their money. The victim's main goal is to avoid injury as well as property loss. Ziegenhagen (1985:675) argues that policy prescriptions that limit the range of responses open to victims may be harmful to both the victims and the interests of society in controlling crime. Conventional definitions of deterrence, he suggests, are often limited to the crime-prevention effects of legal punishments, arrest, and prosecution. The literature on deterrence of criminal behaviour focuses on the effect of public criminal justice agencies but largely ignores the extent to which victim resistance, including private ownership and use of firearms, acts as a crime deterrent. Victim usage of guns may be one of the most serious risks that a criminal will face and this may be an effective deterrent (Kleck, 1988:1–2).

An analysis of 3,679 robbery incidents in 13 U.S. cities indicates that victim resistance to robbery is not often associated with serious injury but is linked to preventing the successful execution of the crime (Ziegenhagen, 1985:675). The data also show that only 50 percent of attempted robberies are completed successfully, and almost all unsuccessful robberies result from victim-offender interaction rather than police or third-party intervention. Such interaction can be seen as both thwarting and deterring the crime of robbery. From this perspective, victims of crime can be viewed as agents of social control. The more effectively victims control crime outcomes, Ziegenhagen argues (1985:676), the less likely criminals and prospective criminals will engage in unprofitable, frustrating, and, in some cases, dangerous criminal behaviour.

Frank and Ernest

FRANK & ERNEST *reprinted by permission of NEA, Inc.*

Police advise against resistance in robberies. In addition, research indicates that resistance to robbery increases the likelihood of victim injuries.

ARMED RESISTANCE

Since the police admit that they are unable to protect all persons and businesses from criminal predators, some argue (Green, 1987:77) that citizens should have the means for self-defence and that legal defensive violence by private citizens with firearms is a significant form of social control. In the United States, a hotly debated topic within and without the criminal justice community is the extent to which citizens should have access to firearms. Does allowing citizens to own guns increase crime by providing a ready source of firearms for persons to use criminally or does gun ownership reduce crime through specific and general deterrence? Guns are potentially lethal weapons whether wielded by criminals or crime victims. They are frightening and intimidating to those they are pointed at. Guns thereby empower both those who would use them to victimize and those who would use them to prevent their victimization. Consequently, they are a source of both social order and disorder, depending on the user, similar to the use of force in general. There is clearly a tradeoff between the number of firearm accidents and any deterrence or usage for self-defence.

Kleck (1988) argues that the assumption that victim resistance is generally useless and even dangerous does not apply when victims have access to a gun. He argues that private gun use against violent criminals and burglars is common and about as frequent as legal actions like arrests. He also argues that it is a more prompt, negative consequence than legal punishment, and is often more severe. Victim resistance with guns is associated with lower rates of both victim injury and crime completion for robberies and assaults than any other victim action, including nonresistance. Kleck (1988:1) suggests that criminologists have ignored the extent to which being armed with a deadly weapon is an important element in capable guardianship. He further argues that victims with guns who resist robbers are less likely to lose their property than victims who use any other means of resistance or who do nothing. Kleck's analysis of robbery and assault data indicates that victims who used guns for protection were less likely either to be attacked or injured than victims who responded any other way, including those who did not resist at all. Only 12 percent of gun resisters in assault and 17 percent in robberies suffered any injury. After gun resistance, the course of action least likely to be associated with injury is not resisting. However, passivity is not a completely safe course either since 25 percent of robbery victims and 27 percent of assault victims who did not resist were injured anyway.

Using National Crime Panel data on 3,679 cases in which victims of robbery had face-to-face confrontations with robbers, Ziegenhagen (1985:683) found that robberies in which there is only one victim and that result in property loss without injury most often involve the offender's possession of a gun, no victim resistance, and no attack by the offender. As one may expect, forceful resistance is less likely when the offender is armed. Apparently, these linkages support advice to victims to cooperate. However, incidents in which there is only one victim, no injury, and no property loss involve forceful resistance by the victim and no attack by the offender. He criticizes policies that advise victims to cooperate and not resist robbery as well-intentioned but ill-conceived. Individuals, it is suggested, may be better able to size up the situation and choose among a range of responses. Encouraging victims to resist robbery is as misleading as encouraging them not to resist, and probably as ineffective. Victims and the robbery situations with which they are confronted vary far too widely to be controlled by prescriptions of public policy. Promoting cooperation is contrary to the interests of victims and society (Ziegenhagen, 1985:693).

Only slight and indirect empirical evidence for deterrence exists in the area of citizen gun ownership. Deterrence is related to an offender's perceived likelihood of randomly meeting a target who is armed, willing, and able to use that weapon in self-defence. The offender's perception is the relevant independent variable. Although research (Green, 1987:67) indicates that criminals will avoid crimes against victims perceived to be armed, unless a victim is a security guard who is obviously carrying a weapon, it is difficult for offenders to determine whether a victim is armed. One could even argue a counterproductive escalation effect associated with citizen-owned guns because as Wright and

Rossi (1985:23) found, among those who had used a firearm in criminal activity, half saw the "chance that the victim would be armed" as a very important reason to carry a gun (Green, 1987:71). In addition, firearm accidents increase with gun ownership (McDowall and Loftin, 1985) and many criminals steal the guns used in crime from citizens (Wright and Rossi, 1985). The crime-reducing effects associated with public policies that support civilian gun ownership must be balanced in light of other, negative public-health factors associated with citizen-owned guns (Green, 1987: 63).

It is difficult to assess the risk or effectiveness involved in victim resistance through the use of firearms. It is even more difficult to estimate the deterrent effect of defensive gun ownership. How can we determine the number of crimes that are never attempted because of the criminal's fear that the victim may be armed? If there is a deterrent effect of defensive gun use, it would depend on a criminal realistically anticipating a potential victim using a gun to disrupt the crime. Retail stores and banks with guards represent the most likely places of gun resistance for would-be robbers. But in many of these incidents, the offender takes the initiative, often surprising the victim. Furthermore, the situation develops too quickly for victims to get their guns. An armed-victim population, however, creates risks itself since some victims are also offenders and their possession of guns may embolden them to commit assaults and other crimes they would otherwise not have attempted (Kleck, 1988:18). Canada has clearly chosen to regulate gun ownership and usage, preferring instead other measures of social control and deterrence against crime.

ROBBERY PREVENTION

> Once a robbery has begun, the robber's and the victim's purposes are identical—to complete the robbery as quickly, successfully, and smoothly as possible. This recommendation of cooperation with one's assailant flows from the dominance the robber holds over the victim and the priority of victim safety over money loss. Robbers should be dissuaded before the fact and caught after the fact, but afforded full cooperation during the event itself (Crow and Bull, 1975:71).

Crime prevention efforts are typically aimed at: (1) reducing opportunities for offending; (2) improving the social conditions that are believed to influence criminal motivation; and (3) deterring crime through police action, sentencing, and legal prohibitions. Situational crime prevention refers to methods that seek to prevent crime by altering the environment, the community, or the potential victim, as opposed to focusing on the offender's motivation. In this sense, crime prevention efforts attempt to reduce opportunity by increasing the risk, decreasing the reward, or increasing the difficulty of committing crime. Situational crime prevention encompasses a wide range of crime-reduction methods and distinctions are made among measures directed towards (1) the individual victim (e.g., education regarding locking your home); (2) the community (e.g., neighbourhood watch); and (3) the physical environment (e.g., street lighting) (Bennett and Wright, 1984:21).

Attempts to prevent crime by altering the situation are not new. Locks and bars were part of the Roman villa and the medieval castle, and few property-owning cultures have ever left valuable goods completely unprotected. European cities in the Middle Ages were often walled and their gates were shut at night to keep out strangers. The goal of eliminating robbery is a utopian ideal since there is no universally proven method of preventing this crime. Even as we reduce the amount of cash available and improve and increase the security of targets, robbery has not disappeared. Target-hardening may only displace robbery to another victim or location. The goal of robbery prevention is not so much the elimination of robbery, but its reduction, the minimizing of risk of harm to victims, and the increased apprehension of robbers. However, no matter what benefits are derived from a particular scheme, there will always be costs. It is essential that one determine the costs of a particular measure before implementing it.

Situational crime prevention strategies include a range of measures that focus on architectural and target-hardening strategies designed to reduce the opportunities for, and increase the risks of, committing specific kinds of crime (Clarke, 1983). Routine activities theory suggests that if targets are made less vulnerable and guardianship is increased, net reductions in crime may result. Predatory-stranger offences like robbery, depend heavily on place and opportunity where offenders converge with vulnerable victims and low surveillance (Sherman et al., 1989:47). Cash businesses that are open late at night, for example, generate opportunities for robbery, the absence of which could mean fewer robberies. In addition, certain hot spots exist that produce higher incidents of crime by bringing together likely offenders with suitable and unguarded targets. Just as lions look for deer near their watering hole, criminal offenders disproportionately find victims in certain settings or high-risk occupations (Block, Felson, and Block, 1985). Obvious places like underground parking garages that are poorly lit and unguarded leave late-night residents open to muggers. A study in Birmingham, England noted that although pedestrian tunnels in the downtown area accounted for a negligible portion of total public space, they produced 13 percent of criminal attacks on persons (Poyner, 1983:85). Eliminating or hardening these hot spots of crime should result in a reduction in specific types of offences.

Robbery is a crime that may never be eliminated but it is one over which potential victims can have some control. There are many effective strategies that have been developed to deter robbery, minimize the potential loss, prevent violence, and provide the police with information that can assist in the capture and conviction of the offender. These strategies suggest what victims should do (a) before the robbery, (b) during the robbery, and (c) after the robbery.

ROBBERY PREVENTION
FOR CONVENIENCE STORES

Using the robber's perspective, Crow and Bull (1975) have assessed the characteristics of frequently robbed stores and suggested procedures to prevent robberies and avoid violence. The potential robber is assumed to have made a preliminary selection of the target. As he or she approaches, the site characteristics and the employee's behaviour lead the robber to proceed with the robbery, postpone it until conditions become favourable, or abandon the plan and leave. From the robber's perspective, the ideal target is one in which there is a good deal of money, few staff or customers, little or no resistance, an absence of cameras and alarms, a small likelihood of being seen by passersby in the act of robbery, an unimpeded exit from the store, and escape routes out of the area. By using a variety of security devices and implementing certain robbery prevention policies, small businesses can make their establishment unattractive to potential robbers. These countermeasures are meant to inform the robber that there is little money to be had; that he or she can be seen from the street; the likelihood of identification is high; staff are alert and take notice of people; and that escape is not easy. Targets who harden themselves in this way will not make themselves invulnerable, but they will make robbery less lucrative, more risky, and possibly deter or discourage some would-be robbers.

Protection implies costs for the owner. Theft and protection can be analyzed as economic decisions in that choices reflect anticipated benefits and costs to the decision-maker (Ozenne,

1974:19). It can be expensive to set up a security system aimed at discouraging robbery and protecting employees and clients. A recent decision by Toronto's Transit Commission (TTC) to "beef up security" after 13 gunpoint heists is costing millions of dollars. The measures include the installation of security cameras in all 65 subway stops to monitor ticket collectors. The move follows a Saturday-morning heist at 1:40 a.m. in which four of five bandits pulled handguns, taped up a ticket collector and maintenance man, and robbed them of cash receipts. A Hold-Up Squad officer is quoted as saying that word has spread through the criminal underworld that the TTC was an easy hit. A spokesperson for the TTC refused to disclose other new security measures (*Toronto Sun*, June 16/92).

Robbery typically represents the smallest property loss for small businesses, falling significantly below shoplifting, employee theft, fraudulent cheques, and burglary (Post, 1972:49). Because the financial losses of robbery are relatively low, store owners resist taking precautions that are not cost-effective. Fortunately, there are many inexpensive means of implementing prevention strategies before a robbery occurs.

PHYSICAL CHANGES TO THE STORE

Robbery prevention procedures are intended to build into the site those characteristics possessed by stores that are seldom robbed and to eliminate features found in businesses that are frequently held up. Good external lighting and clear windows provide the store with an image that might discourage a potential robber. A large window that is clear of obstructions and a cash register located in a place that can be viewed from outside will give pedestrians and motorists, including passing cruisers, a clear view of the store clerk and the would-be robber. The installation of a highly visible security camera above the till and the exit indicates that all customers are being videotaped or photographed. Signs and/or television screens can be used to warn people that security devices are operational. Cameras are meant to deter offenders by making them aware that they may be identified if they commit the robbery. The installation of height markers near the doors allow staff and/or cameras to accurately determine the height of robbers as they leave.

Some target-hardening methods are aimed at protecting store clerks from possible injury. Counters may be raised, which makes it more difficult for the robber to vault over and attack personnel; doors leading behind the counters or to the cash registers are locked; and the installation of bullet-resistant glass or bandit barriers can be used to protect staff and prevent access to the cash. Some establishments have recently installed electronically controlled entrances into the store to allow staff to deny entry to suspicious-looking persons. These devices also protect employees in another way. Since solo bandits cannot leave without the clerk first pushing the door release, the offender cannot incapacitate, immobilize, or kill store personnel without being trapped inside.

Revolving doors and turnstiles aim to slow the robber's escape and may discourage the robbery of a particular target or increase the probability of capture by giving the robber less time to escape. However, the situation risks a hostage-taking incident if the police arrive too soon and corner the robber within the store. Other means of making escape difficult include the blocking-off of laneways and the use of speed bumps to slow cars in the parking lot. Not all features of escape, however, are subject to manipulation. Easy access to a nearby expressway may attract customers but will also make the store a more vulnerable target by providing an ideal escape route for bandits with a car.

MINIMIZING THE POTENTIAL GAIN

One way to minimize losses and deter robbery is to ensure that only small amounts of cash are kept in the register. The use of exact fares on buses and subways helps to prevent robbery since there is no cash available for the robber. Small businesses cannot operate this way, however, and must maintain some cash to make change for customers. For this reason, all businesses are advised to minimize the level of cash exposure, to make bank deposits often but not regularly or predictably, and to protect valuable merchandise. The amount of cash does not have to be large to tempt some robbers. Staff must be instructed to routinely deposit excess money into a drop-in safe so that a robber's potential take is always small. Signs placed prominently at the entrance and cash register should inform potential bandits that minimal amounts of cash are kept in the till and that employees do not have the keys or combination to the safe. Prospective robbers should be able to see the signs before they initiate the robbery. Typical messages include:

PREMISES UNDER VIDEO SURVEILLANCE

TIME-LOCKS ARE USED ON THESE PREMISES

ROBBERY PREVENTION IN EFFECT

WE KEEP A MINIMUM OF MONEY ON HAND

CLERK CANNOT OPEN THE SAFE

REGISTER HAS LESS THAN $50

ALL $20 AND $50 BILLS ARE PUT IN LOCKED SAFE

Some stores also request the cooperation of customers with signs that state:

WE APPRECIATE EXACT CHANGE

PLEASE PAY WITH THE SMALLEST BILL POSSIBLE

Taken together, the signs communicate the message that a robbery is not financially worthwhile.

STAFF TRAINING AND PREPAREDNESS FOR ROBBERY

Few businesses are immune to robbery. Retail outlets are particularly vulnerable and should therefore realize the possibility, if not the inevitability, of a robbery and develop staff training procedures. Business people need to prepare themselves and their employees by implementing policies and a plan to be followed in the event of a robbery.

Staff behaviour can influence people who enter the store with the intention of robbing it. Sales clerks should be alert and communicate this vigilance to potential robbers. A bell that rings whenever a person enters the store informs the robber that his or her presence has been noted. Greeting customers also tells potential robbers, who presumably wish to be unnoticed, that their presence is known. This gives the impression that the store is less vulnerable to a surprise attack and that the robber is more vulnerable to identification. Noting suspicious-looking persons both inside and outside the store and writing down their descriptions will be helpful to the police if a robbery should occur. Alerting the police to their presence before a robbery happens is also helpful. Other proactive strategies include writing down licence-plate numbers of suspicious persons; training employees on the use of the alarm system; and making advance plans to call the police, record observations, protect evidence at the scene, and detain witnesses. Management should discuss with employees what they must do in the event of a robbery so that they know how to act to prevent violence and assist the police in apprehending the offender.

Other preventive action includes keeping a well-lit store, both inside and outside; maintaining a clear view into the building and not obstructing the window with advertising; recording bait money by serial numbers; ensuring that alarms and cameras are working; avoiding routine procedures that can be observed and exploited by would-be robbers; keeping cash exposure and cash on the premises at the lowest possible level; and separating cheques and credit-card receipts from cash. When making bank deposits, staff should conceal the money, go directly to the bank, never leave deposits unattended in an automobile, vary time and routine of bank trips, and, if possible, only make deposits during the day.

Many establishments have worked out signals with adjoining businesses to inform others that a robbery is in progress. This "buddy system" among neighbourhood merchants also functions to alert one another to suspicious-looking persons lurking about. Local taxi drivers may be encouraged to keep a lookout for potential robbers and robberies in progress and alert the police. Some store owners encourage and attract police presence by offering free coffee to officers who drop by.

Robbery prevention procedures do not involve deception. In fact, they correctly alert potential robbers that there are cameras, alarms, and little money in the till. The practice of lying can become self-defeating over time. Secrets cannot be maintained in an industry in which there are many personnel and a high staff turnover. It is very important to adhere to the practice of not maintaining large amounts of cash in the till—otherwise word may escape to the street. Similarly, clerks can easily tell friends that there are no alarms, cameras are not real, or that staff know the combination to the safe. This deception undermines the deterrent benefit of real alarms and cameras. In addition, it can endanger personnel if an employee cannot open the safe yet the robber believes that he or she can (Crow and Bull, 1975:72).

PREVENTING VIOLENCE DURING THE ROBBERY

The most alarming feature of robbery is the threat to personal safety. An act of robbery is sudden, surprising, and frightening. To prevent employees from reacting in a manner that will jeapordize their lives, they should be clearly instructed on how to act in the event of a holdup. Violence prevention procedures stress cooperation with the robber and are based on the assumption that the offender is armed and capable of committing physical harm. Victims are advised not to act in any way that might jeopardize personal safety; to consider firearms to be loaded; and to activate the silent alarm only when it is safe to do so. Almost universally, police counsel against business persons resisting robbers. They are also opposed to the use of weapons to prevent robbery or apprehend the offender because the average business person is neither adequately trained nor mentally prepared to deal with a would-be robber. Store personnel are advised that their best protection is to take no action that might antagonize or provoke the robber. Instead, they are cautioned to cooperate fully with the robber's wishes, but at the same time, to take note of facts that will be useful to police. Most robberies happen very quickly and victims must follow instructions yet make observations at the same time. Having standardized forms nearby to be filled in immediately following the robbery eases the process and helps to ensure accuracy. When making observations, victims note the offender's physical characteristics including skin colour, age, height, hair colour, complexion, clothing, speech, identifying marks such as tattoos, weapons used, and modus operandi. They should also look for accomplices, the mode of escape, the type of car and licence number, and the direction of travel.

A set of robbery prevention procedures developed by the Western Behavioral Sciences Institute lists a number of instructions to staff in the event that they are robbed (Crow and Bull, 1975: 70).

— Keep it short and smooth. The longer it takes, the more nervous the robber becomes.

— Obey the robber's commands. Offenders almost never hurt anyone who cooperates.

— Don't argue. It's too late for the robber to change his or her mind—but not too late to get angry and harm you.

— Don't fight. The money isn't worth risking your life. To attack an armed robber is foolhardy, not heroic.

— Don't use weapons. Weapons breed violence. The robber's weapon is already one weapon too many.

— Tell the offender about any surprises. If someone is in the backroom, or expected soon, or if you must reach or move in any way, tell the robber what to expect, so he or she won't be startled into shooting. Warning the robber about any surprises that may occur acknowledges that violence sometimes occurs for unanticipated reasons.

— Offer to lie down. This may solve the robber's problem of what to do with you after he or she has the money. Lying down is better than being knocked down or tied up.

— Don't chase or follow offenders. Robbers shoot at pursuers. Also, police may shoot at you, thinking you're one of the robbers.

The principle behind violence prevention procedures is cooperation with the robber. Most robbers have no desire to harm anyone; they want the money quickly, with as little resistance and few surprises as possible. Robberies are safest when things go according to the robber's plan and violence prevention procedures are established to ensure that this happens. Having a plan and following procedures will give staff some control of the situation, which in itself will make them feel less nervous and lessen the possibility that something will go wrong. In addition, victims are better able to make observations if they remain calm during the robbery. The chances of apprehending robbers are considerably enhanced if the victim can give an accurate description of the person or persons involved. The ability of the police to apprehend the robber depends on the speed of notification by the victim and the clarity with which he or she describes the robbery.

AFTER THE ROBBERY

Provisions need to be made for contacting the police immediately after the robbery has occurred. Victims should keep the telephone number of the police station nearby, contact them, and follow their instructions. Robbery victims are also advised not to reveal the amounts stolen to the media since these reports may attract subsequent robbers. Instead, staff should only inform investigating officers about the exact amount stolen. Store personnel should also protect and retain any evidence such as a holdup note; lock the doors of the premises; hold all witnesses until police arrive; and write down all information immediately. Witnesses should not discuss the holdup until the police have had time to question everyone separately.

FRAUDULENT ROBBERIES

A possibility that store owners and the police should keep in mind is the fact that employees have been known to cover up thefts by falsely reporting them as a robbery. One unexpected finding from Kansas City police stakeouts in the 1970s was the discovery of fraudulent robbery reports by retail staff. On several occasions, the police stationed surveillance officers on commercial targets without notifying owners or store clerks. When uniformed officers pulled up in answer to a robbery call, the stakeout officers walked into the store to find out what was going on. A police search of the clerks discovered the stolen money. Stakeouts in Washington, D.C. also revealed falsely reported robberies by store employees (Sherman, 1992:190). To what extent this practice occurs and influences robbery statistics is difficult to determine.

One thing that is certain, however, is that the installation of in-store video cameras should make false robbery claims difficult, if not impossible.

CRIME DISPLACEMENT

Defensive measures can be expected to produce an overall reduction in crime because much robbery is opportunistic. Some offenders, however, are highly motivated and will seek out targets until they find one. Any scheme that succeeds in influencing offender decision-making is likely also to displace crime, which creates an important moral dilemma because crime shifts to other victims. Despite clear evidence that target-hardening strategies and life-style changes limit the victimization of specific targets, critics argue that preventive measures that increase the difficulties of a particular target or crime will merely displace the criminal activity to other targets, times, places, or types of crime (Reppetto, 1976; Gabor, 1981). This criticism partly assumes that some crimes are functionally equivalent, offenders have needs or desires that propel them to act in a criminal manner, and this behaviour can only be deflected but not stopped.

The routine activities and situational approaches to crime prevention, however, suggest that displacement is not inevitable and occurs only under particular conditions. Similarly, rational choice theory (Cornish and Clarke, 1987) assumes that offenders respond selectively to characteristics of particular offences such as opportunities, costs, and benefits, in deciding whether to displace their attentions elsewhere. Crime-control efforts, it is argued, must recognize that offenders seek quick gain with minimal risk. Bank robbers, for instance, choose this crime because it is easy, and requires little effort and skill. Research generally shows that most offenders tend to find the shortest route, spend the least time, and seek the easiest means to accomplish their crimes. Robbers tend to be lazy in their criminal enterprises and choose convenient and obvious targets. Consequently, target-hardening can be expected to deter offenders who do not have the drive, resources, or persistence to tackle more elusive or formidable adversaries. Being frustrated in their desire to commit a particular crime does not compel the offender to seek out another crime or even a noncriminal solution. He or she may simply desist from any further action, rationalizing loss of income in various ways: "It was good while it lasted," or "I would have ended up getting caught." Some argue that the problem of planned reductions in criminal opportunity unintentionally producing displacement of crime has been exaggerated by policy-makers pessimistically resigned to the perseverence of criminals (Sherman et al., 1989:47).

It appears that target-hardening strategies aimed at persons and places can reduce, rather than simply displace, crime by increasing risk, diminishing benefits, and eliminating opportunities. A routine activities criminology of place hypothesizes that crime cannot be displaced merely by displacing motivated offenders; the offenders must also be displaced to other places with suitable targets and weak guardianship (Sherman, 1989: 46). If displacement does occur, it is likely to occur among offences that share similar properties—for example, where the likely cash yield per crime is comparable, where the same skills and resources are required, and where the physical risks are the same.

Empirical research indicates that in some instances, displacement occurs and in other situations, it does not. Whereas a police "crack-down" on subway robberies in New York City displaced robberies to the street (Chaiken, Lawless, and Stevenson, 1974), the security measures introduced by airlines in the early 1970s dramatically reduced airliner hijackings (Wilkinson, 1977). When new cars in Great Britain were fitted with steering-column locks, theft of older, unprotected vehicles increased. The fitting of steering-column locks to all cars in West Germany, however, brought about a 60 percent reduction in car thefts (Mayhew, Clarke, Sturman, and Hough, 1976). It appears that displacement of crime occurs when there is an obvious, equivalent, accessible, alternative target nearby. There may not be an equivalent target for airline hijacking, but there is one for gas-bar holdups. The hardening of gas bars might simply displace robbery to convenience stores if these remain soft and vulnerable targets. It is clear, therefore, that to achieve a total reduction in the crime rate and the rate for specific offences such as robbery, target-hardening strategies must be applied consistently and on the greatest number of possible targets and locations.

Another criticism of target-hardening strategies is that success at deterring offenders and reducing crime is modest. Robbery rates may be reduced and individual targets may be made less attractive, but robbery still occurs and even unattractive, hardened targets are struck. Crow and Bull (1975:55) note, for instance, that robbery prevention procedures implemented in stores that had been frequently robbed reduced, but did not eliminate, robbery. In addition, they found that although overall attractiveness of a store was related to previous robbery frequency, the relationship was significant but low. The low relationship suggests that a large element of chance determines which stores are robbed and/or that additional variables are related to robbery frequency. It also suggests that target-hardening strategies for convenience stores can have dramatic success in some cases but much more limited success in others.

SUMMARY

Little is presently known about offender decision-making in their selection of target victims. Rational choice theory cautions us that we should not assume that offenders will assess targets in a similar way. Different offenders may lack information about police capabilities, may be ignorant of the risks involved, may vary in the degree of risks they are willing to assume or how desperate they are, and may assign particular importance to certain factors such as eschewing the use of violence. This means that target-hardening strategies may work well on some robbers but fail to deter others. Robbery will never be completely eliminated. On the other hand, target-hardening strategies when applied to a variety of targets may prevent some potential robbers from committing the crime. According to rational choice theory, target-hardening strategies will not only influence decisions relating to the selection of a target/victim, but they will also influence various stages of criminal involvement including initial motivation, continuation, and disinvolvement from robbery (Cornish and Clarke, 1987:933).

The Police and Judicial Response to Robbery

THE HOLD-UP SQUAD

Large urban police forces, like all bureaucracies, are organized into areas of specialization. The Major Crimes Section (Special Services) encompasses detective branches that work specific categories of offences such as homicide, drug enforcement, automobile theft, fraud, and robbery. It may also include support services used by all branches of the force including polygraph, swat team, and intelligence. The Hold-Up Squad is a specialized division that investigates robberies. Although homicide is acknowledged as the elite corps of detectives—"the calling" as one officer describes it— the Hold-Up Squad is often regarded as their equal or a close second in ability, dedication, and status. In three cities in this study, Hold-Up and Homicide Squads were housed in adjacent offices in the same buildings. Officers occasionally move within these departments and in one department, the head of Hold-Up had been a former homicide investigator and later became Superintendent of Special Services, overseeing all major crimes.

INVESTIGATING ROBBERY

Holdups can be classified into three categories: (a) robberies of financial institutions such as banks, trust companies, and armoured vehicles; (b) robberies of other commercial establishments such as corner grocery stores, and (c) robberies of individuals (i.e., muggings). In the three Canadian cities in which Hold-Up Squads exist, muggings were handled by detectives in the Criminal Investigation Branches (CIB) of each division. In two police forces, the Hold-Up Squad deals exclusively with robberies of financial institutions and armoured vehicles, leaving muggings, grocery stores, and other robberies to divisional detectives. In another city, the Hold-Up Squad handles robberies of both financial institutions and other commercial establishments but assigns detectives to one type of crime or the other.

The division of labour is based on the police experience that men who rob banks seldom rob grocery stores and vice versa. Muggings are usually committed by offenders who live in the area and these offences are handled by divisional detectives. Although some holdup artists begin their bank robbery career by targeting other commercial establishments, they seldom move backwards since small businesses are usually less profitable than banks. One major function of the Hold-Up Squad, therefore, is to gather information and coordinate investigations across the city, regardless of the area in which the crime was committed. In one city, the decision to specialize in robberies of financial institutions and transfer the investigation of commercial robberies and muggings to the divisions in which they occur has received considerable criticism. An editorial in the city's leading newspaper attributed a decrease in bank robberies to the reorganization but also blamed it for the dramatic increase (displacement) of robberies to other commercial establishments. Commenting on the killing of two robbers by the owner of a variety store, the paper ran an editorial:

> It is regrettable that [the store owner] resorted to the Wild West method of taking justice into his own hands, but it is thoroughly understandable. He had been held up six times…in six months…[There has been] a drop of over 50 percent in armed holdups of financial institutions but armed robbery is rising [in] variety stores, supermarkets and other kinds of stores, big and small. One big reason for this rise is clear. The police have a special squad which today deals with nothing except armed robberies of financial institutions. If a store next door to a bank gets held up, this squad won't bother with it. Criminals know about this crack squad so they practice their trade at relatively defenceless places like Mom and Pop stores. Police at each of the 24 police districts now concern themselves with such holdups along with many kinds of crime, and coordination between these districts leaves much to be desired. The centralized Hold-Up Squad… did deal with all holdups until the big shakeup in police operations…Its old wider mandate should be revived.

After a bank robbery has occurred and the alarm has been pressed, the signal is received by a security firm, which calls the bank to confirm that a robbery has occurred and then contacts the police. A police dispatcher notifies patrol cars in the area that an alarm has been sounded and officers converge on the area. The goal is to secure the area by stationing police at predetermined locations such as subway stops and street corners. Meanwhile, the security firm or bank personnel relays relevant information to the police dispatcher including the number of offenders, physical descriptions, direction of travel, vehicles used, and whether the robbers are known to be armed. In one city, the police prefer that the teller call them directly so that the information can be dispatched more quickly and accurately. Either way, patrol officers are advised to look for particular suspects as they approach the bank and seal off the area. To avoid a hostage-taking situation, the police wish to know whether the robber has indeed left before they approach the bank. Despite such precautions, robbers are occasionally trapped inside the bank, panic, and take staff and customers hostage. This occurred in only one case in this sample and the situation was resolved peacefully through negotiation and the robbers surrendered to the police.

Robbery is a high-priority crime and police respond immediately to calls for assistance. Cruisers race to the scene and usually arrive within minutes of receiving the call. Conklin (1972:125) found that three-fifths of victims estimated that the police arrived in less than ten minutes and one-third said it was less than five minutes. In most cases, the offender has escaped before the police arrive and patrol officers check to see if there are any injuries, call an ambulance if necessary, question witnesses, and seal the premises. The officer will fill in an occurrence sheet, detailing the results of his or her preliminary investigation. The follow-up investigation is handled by Hold-Up Squad officers who arrive shortly thereafter and speak to patrol officers, employees, and customers. All witnesses are kept apart and interviewed separately. An officer explains:

> It's the same principle as any crime. If you want reliable information, you don't let them discuss the events amongst themselves.

The information is then recorded on standard forms, classified, and placed in Hold-Up Squad files. If a robbery suspect is arrested, the offender is also handled by detectives and questioned back at headquarters. He or she will be cautioned, photographed, fingerprinted, and held in police cells before being brought up for a bail hearing. Robbery suspects are normally denied bail because the crime is a threat to community safety.

THE FILES

Hold-Up Squad files help detectives determine which crimes are being committed by the same offender(s) and clear cases after he or she (they) has been caught. Occasionally the data contained in the files will assist in identifying and apprehending the culprits. A variety of data are gathered: the name and address of the bank; the date and time of the offence; amount of money stolen; serial numbers of marked bills; photographs; fingerprints; descriptions of the weapons and vehicles used; language spoken; and a detailed description of the suspect(s) including gender, age, race, height, eye colour, and other distinguishing features such as acne or tattoos. Any notes left behind are checked for fingerprints and compared to notes in Hold-Up Squad files. A file of bank-robbery notes is maintained and a handwriting specialist compares wording, writing styles, and searches for unusual or telltale signs that indicate that the same individual is responsible for a series of robberies. One bank robber, for example, may use a withdrawal slip to rob banks and fill in the exact amount requested while others will make the same spelling errors in each note.

Police collect and compare holdup notes to link offenders to their robberies. Note the similarities in the above notes. *Courtesy Metro Toronto Police Hold-Up Squad.*

The most important information usually relates to the physical descriptions and the modus operandi used by the robber(s), including the number of offenders, disguises, and actions such as the use of a note, jumping the counter, verbal instructions, threats, or the use of a weapon. Bank robbery is a crime that is often repeated in the same way. One officer explains:

We categorize bank robberies according to M.O. I believe in it. You don't see it in homicide because you don't have the repetition. In Hold-Up, we see repetition and use it to catch them or at least connect them to a large number of robberies after they're caught.

There are normally several characteristics of a bank robber's appearance or M.O. that remain the same for each robbery. Occurrences are studied and compared to identify distinguishing features that indicate a particular offender or crew may be responsible for various holdups. In each Hold-Up Squad, an officer known as the analyst is responsible for maintaining the files. This official or semi-official position is assigned to someone with several years' experience in robbery investigations. Besides updating and organizing information, the analyst helps other detectives to use the file system. In one department, the analyst also maintains radio contact with detectives on the road and relays information to the scene of the crime. An example of how the forms are organized and used is explained by this analyst:

In this occurrence, there's two robbers, one spoke French and the other didn't speak. They robbed the bank in the East End in a French area so I'll assume they're both French. Both have sunglasses, they used plastic bags and their behaviour was normal—nothing aggressive. So we use a numerical system 2 (2 suspects) F (French) 7 (sunglasses) 1 (normal behaviour) 1 (plastic bag) 3 (pistol)—2F7 113. Now I go to the central files and look under 2F7 and I find three other forms in that file. Here's a file 2F7 143 and you can see that there are 2 French males, both white, about the same age and weight. One's described as having short hair and the other's hair is black. They both have moustaches. By putting these files together we have a better description of our suspects if they're the same. Checking out their M.O., one suspect stays outside and the other walks in alone, goes around the counter, empties two tills and says "Merci Beaucoup." If witnesses see one suspect, there may also be another outside so we'll check our files with one suspect as well. Once we get photos, we have a lot more to go on.

When a holdup occurs, the case is assigned to a pair of detectives and if a similar-style robbery is committed later, it too will be passed on to the same investigating officers. Over a period of weeks and months, the offender(s) may commit several robberies using the same M.O. and each occurrence is analyzed and assigned to the same officers. Hold-Up Squads will usually assign each robber or crew a name that reflects some aspect of their appearance or their modus operandi. For example, a 25-year-old white male robbed a number of banks by passing the teller a note demanding money. The description of the robber was similar in all instances and the distinguishing feature of each offence was his wording of the note, which always began with the word "relax," mispelled as "relaxe" or "relaxes." In prison, he expressed amazement that the police knew so much about his robberies.

The "Relaxe" bandit was convicted of 13 bank robberies. In each of his hold-ups, he passed a note with the word "relaxe" or "relaxes." In several incidents, he left the note behind. He has a past criminal record for break and enter and was sentenced to six years for his robberies. *Courtesy Metro Toronto Police Hold-Up Squad.*

In another case, a pair of young men were named the "Back Back Gang" because of their verbal instructions to staff and customers: "Back! Back! Back against the wall!" In addition, the descriptions of their M.O. matched in each case—one stood at the door with a gun while the other leaped the counter and rifled the tills. The "Dime Bandit" always asked tellers for a roll of dimes before passing his holdup note; "The Greek" looked like a Greek—dark hair, tanned, with a moustache; and the "Crown Royal Bandit" handed tellers a Seagrams Crown Royal whisky bag and ordered them to fill it with large bills. Similarly, robbers are frequently identified by the day or area of the city they strike, e.g., "The Downtown Bandit," "The East End Gang," "The West End Gang," "The Borderland Gang," "The Friday Afternoon Bandit," and "The 401 Gang." Examples of other names attached to bank robbers by Hold-Up Squad detectives include the following:

The Dirty Tricks Gang: set cars on fire as a diversion and threw slices of nail-embedded hoses over the road as they left the bank.

The Polite Bandit: dressed the same each time and politely requested and thanked tellers for the money.

The Gentleman Bandit: wore a suit and passed a politely worded note.

The Expo Bandit: wore a Montreal Expo cap in his robberies.

The Swamp Gang: given the name because one of them stated in the bank, "We've just come from the swamp."

The Subway Bandit: robbed banks along the subway line and close to subway stops.

The Wig Bandit: wore make-up and long wigs during hold-ups.

The Chrysler Gang: stole Chryslers or other large North American cars and left them running outside the bank.

The Stopwatch Gang: the doorman wore a stopwatch upside down from his neck to time their heists.

The Pot-Belly Bandit: named for obvious reasons.

The American Express Gang: besides emptying the tills, always stole American Express travellers cheques.

The John Denver Bandit: looked like John Denver.

Filou: a French term used to describe a bank robber who committed a daring robbery and escaped.

The Crowbar Gang: smashed the bank window with a crowbar as tellers emptied the night deposit safe. Later discovered to be the Chrysler Gang.

The Bible Bandit: for unknown reasons, carried a bible as he robbed banks.

The Motorcycle Bandit: wore a helmet and made his getaway on a motorcycle.

The Punk Rocker: had a punk-rock hairstyle.

Most bank robbers are arrested by patrol officers or detectives in other branches of the police force and transferred to the Hold-Up Squad for questioning. In many instances, the offender is suspected of additional robberies and Hold-Up officers must now build a case. They begin by comparing the robber's M.O. with occurrences in the files and questioning him or her about similar crimes. When more than one suspect is apprehended, they are separated upon arrest and questioned individually. In many instances, the police suspect a link with other robberies but lack sufficient evidence to ensure a conviction in criminal court. Every effort is thus made to obtain a signed confession and the files assist police in their efforts.

Cases "cleared by arrest" are those in which police believe they have apprehended the persons responsible but lack the evidence to obtain a conviction. Since a small number of bandits may be responsible for a large number of robberies, clearance rates may increase dramatically with the arrest of a few culprits. This occurred in one city when two bandits were found to be responsible for 78 of the 112 banks that had been robbed in a single year.

The use of the files helps to clear large numbers of cases and they can be dramatically effective in questioning suspects. By confronting offenders with a list of their crimes, detectives often shock astonished bank robbers into making a confession. As one suspect explains:

> After my arrest, these guys walked in and laid it on me. They knew everything! There was no point denying it.

This bank robber's reaction is exactly what is intended by the use of occurrence sheets. The offender believes that the police have sufficient evidence to obtain convictions, so why resist? After his or her arrest, the offender is often frightened and confused. Many are also uninformed about police practices and the requirements of the criminal court system. Add to this the shock of discovering that police "know" about other robberies and any resolve to stand on their rights and refuse to implicate themselves may quickly dissolve. The police, of course, utilize standard interrogation techniques, act confident in their "knowledge," and attempt to convince the culprit that there is nothing to be gained by lying or being uncooperative. If more than one suspect is in custody, the police will play one against the other, by telling each that the other has confessed. This, too, is disarming and may lead the suspect into an admission of guilt.

Hold-Up Squad detectives report that accused persons are often cooperative and willingly confess to their crimes. In some instances, offenders may have committed so many robberies that they cannot recall all of them. Files are used to stimulate their memory but the police will also drive them around the city to locate the banks they have robbed and provide details of each crime. This helps in the recollection of offences and strengthens the police case with evidence corroborating a confession that may later be disputed in court.

SURVEILLANCE CAMERA PHOTOS

Photographs taken by bank and other business surveillance cameras greatly assist the police to identify robbers. Investigating officers first pass the photos among themselves, then distribute them to other divisions. Offenders are often identified by officers who have had previous contact with them. The police will also make use of the local media to assist in identifying culprits. Occasionally information will be placed in "Crime Stoppers" and rewards will be offered. In cities in which there are frequent robberies, photos of robbers taken by security cameras are published in local newspapers. The media cooperate as a public service and the Canadian Bankers' Association offers a financial reward for information leading to an arrest. A senior Hold-Up Squad officer explains their procedure:

> We make a bulletin with six photos and send copies to different newspapers each week. We give them the name of the bank, the address, and the date. The banks offer a $500 reward for information. We try to choose good pictures. It's effective. Look here, on this page we have six arrests for six cases, here four for six, and here five for six... Here we published a picture of a guy on October 25 and you can see it's quite blurry. Then he did another robbery and we got a better picture so we published it October 31 and got an arrest.

In a sample of 353 photos published in one city over the course of a year, 262 were identified and arrested: 152 of these identifications were made by police officers and 110 by citizens. In one case, a man was photographed leaving the bank after robbing a teller by passing her a note and displaying a handgun. The picture was published in a local newspaper and identified by a hotel reception clerk who informed detectives that the suspect had stayed at the hotel days earlier but had since checked out. The man's address turned out to be a parking lot but one of the investigators recognized the street number as the same address as a well-known homosexual steam bath one street over. Since many criminals have a long history of incarceration including juvenile detention, bisexuality is not uncommon. The arresting officer explains:

> A lot of these guys swing both ways. That's why we thought it was worth our time to check the steam bath. Besides, he looks gay from the photo—short hair, neat, tailored appearance... Just his look made us decide it was worth checking.

The steam-bath attendant identified the suspect as a frequent customer and agreed to alert the police the next time the man arrived. He did so less than two hours later and the suspect was arrested the same afternoon. A search of his clothing revealed a subway locker key that held the robber's .45 magnum replica gun. The offender readily admitted robbing four banks.

OFFENDER SURVEILLANCE

The police occasionally suspect an individual of robbery but do not have sufficient evidence for an arrest and/or a conviction. Often the tip is provided by informants who are reluctant to testify or whose testimony alone would not convict. Under these circumstances, suspected holdup artists may be placed under surveillance. A suspect who is under surveillance may be arrested before a holdup but typically the arrest is made immediately afterwards. The police do not attempt to make the arrest during the robbery because of the possibility of a shootout or hostage-taking situation. One officer explains:

> Often we can't arrest him before the crime because we might not have the evidence. What if he's only casing the joint and he's not carrying a gun? The thing to do is get him afterwards and get him in his car if possible. The car is a box and prevents innocent bystanders from getting hurt.

MUG SHOTS, LINEUPS, AND VICTIM IDENTIFICATION

Victims and witnesses may also assist in a robbery investigation by examining mug shots and identifying suspects. Police usually limit the photos to offenders with previous robbery offences since the number of photos in police files would otherwise be overwhelming. This strategy is based on the assumption that offenders tend to specialize in their offences and that robbers have high recidivist rates—assumptions that are often borne out in practice. Although it did not occur in any of the 101 incidents in our sample, witness identification of mug shots occasionally leads to an arrest. More frequently, the police will use a photo spread or a lineup after the arrest. Identifications by victims and witnesses then strengthen the case for prosecution.

Occasionally, the victim can identify the offender because he or she knows him (only one case in our sample). When the victim and offender know one another and are engaged in illegal or disreputable acts such as a sexual or drug transaction, identifications can be made. Conklin (1972:145) notes that in such cases the offender assumes that the victim will not report the crime, since the victim has also violated a law and may be subject to embarrassment. When the crime is reported, however, an arrest is often made, since the offender usually remains in the place where he or she committed the crime.

THE STAKEOUT

Sometimes the police will attempt to apprehend robbers by stationing police officers inside and/or near banks or commercial establishments so that they can respond immediately to a holdup. This proactive approach is taken when a robber is working a specific area of the city; or to target areas where there has been an increase in the number of robberies. This method involves positioning plain-clothed and patrol officers in and around specific targets or target areas. The police will use this technique only if they believe that there is a high probability that robberies will occur at a particular time and place. This assessment is based on information provided by an informant, by an evaluation of a robber or robbers' modus operandi, or by the frequency of robberies at a particular location or specified area.

Stakeouts rely on the reoccurrence of robberies following the pattern that has been established in prior weeks. Because the personnel involved can be enormous, this is an expensive undertaking for a police department. It is also prone to failure and thus not used very frequently. In one city, for example, several stakeouts were undertaken in response to an increase in bank robberies. In one day, however, two robbers escaped when plain-clothed police officers assigned to stakeouts within the bank were negligent in their duties: one left the bank to purchase a battery for his wristwatch; and the other was so engrossed in his magazine that he failed to notice the teller's signal that a robbery was in progress. Both men were disciplined but not dismissed.

In one large urban centre in which bank robberies were investigated by the Criminal Investigations Branch of each district, a Divisional Commander established a task force in response to the occurrence of four bank robberies that occurred in quick succession in the same area. The description of the suspect in each case led the police to believe that the same person was responsible for all four holdups. Permission was granted to position plain-clothed officers in a number of banks and police supervisors consulted with bank security officials in developing law-enforcement strategy. The task force was composed of 40 officers and operated five days a week for seven consecutive weeks.

Individual officers were stationed inside 20 banks and unmarked patrol cars containing two plain-clothed officers were positioned halfway between two closely situated targets. Officers reported to Divisional Headquarters each morning for a daily briefing and those inside the bank were instructed to alert police stationed in cars in the event of a holdup and assist in the arrest. No attempt was to be made to apprehend the robber in the bank, to minimize potential risk to customers and bank employees.

Inside the bank, police dressed and acted like employees but positioned themselves to view the action of tellers and customers. Tellers would use a predetermined signal to inform them that a robbery was in progress. In one bank, for example, a teller would drop her keys if a customer handed her a holdup note. To remain inconspicuous, officers did filing and auditing, and made credit checks on customers. Their assistance was warmly received and bank employees showed their appreciation by organizing a dinner in honour of the task force after the project ended.

The seven-week stakeout was unsuccessful. No banks were robbed in the area over that period but one man was arrested for attempting to pass a stolen cheque. Even though officers and bank employees were cautioned against talking to friends and family about the stakeouts, a local radio station learned of the project and announced it over the air. The Divisional Commander in charge of the operation telephoned the station news director and demanded an explanation. The officer complained that the radio station had not only jeopardized a carefully planned and expensive operation—an expense supported by public taxes—but it had also increased the danger for the public and the police. The station director argued that the public has the right to know and the media have an obligation and a right to report the news. The Divisional Commander criticized this justification as shallow and accused the station of irresponsible journalism. The news director refused to apologize for the announcement. The stakeout was discontinued the following day.

In the United States, stakeout units have been criticized as inefficient in their consumption of police time and also for the high rate of shootouts with and deaths of robbers that they produced (Milton et al., 1977). No shootouts occurred on stakeouts in the present study but two bank robbers under police surveillance were wounded; one had a partner wounded; and two had partners killed. No police officers were injured in these incidents.

Overall, the police response to the menace of armed robbery is reactive as patrol cars respond to calls for assistance. Proactive measures, such as surveillance of suspected offenders and stakeouts of vulnerable targets, are used relatively infrequently to apprehend offenders. The police also advise merchants and financial institutions on how to train staff and implement security measures. In addition, the police use their influence to ensure that long prison sentences are imposed on robbers to deter the potential robbers and incapacitate convicted offenders.

How Bank Robbers Get Caught

"I just didn't know when to stop."

—A typical statement by a bank robber

The present study indicates that bank robbers generally fail to consider the possibility of being caught and sent to prison. Overall, offenders believe that bank robbery is a low-risk activity, even after they have been caught. Many believe that they pushed their luck too far or that bad luck is the only reason they're behind bars. Only a few robbers admit retrospectively that serial bank robbery is indeed a high-risk crime.

Several men in this study were apprehended and convicted more than once—one man was arrested for bank robbery four times. Because of this, our sample of 80 bank robbers includes 101 arrests. In some instances, bank robbers were unsure or unaware of the reasons for their downfall and this information was obtained from the police. Offender accounts of how they were caught were checked against investigating officers' accounts. The following discussion differentiates between factors that lead to an offender being caught versus factors that assist in his conviction. The discussion of informants, for instance, includes only cases in which the offender's identity became known to the police through an informant. There are many instances in which both partners have already been caught and give statements to the police implicating one another. The information may assist in the investigation but since the offenders are already in custody, the information does not lead to their capture. The 15 categories listed below include factors that are directly responsible for the bank robber's arrest. Some cases appear in more than one category because two or three factors are significant. For example, police may receive information about a suspect, place him under surveillance, and make the arrest as he leaves the bank. This case would be classified under #1 Informants and #6 Police Surveillance since both factors were instrumental in the offender's capture.

1. Informants

> I used to believe you go to jail because you're a man. You can flush that philosophy down the toilet.
>
> — *Police informant*

Informants play a part in the capture of bank robbers in 32/101 cases (31.7 percent). Information is frequently developed through police questioning of friends, acquaintances, and criminal associates. Fourteen informants are men who were arrested and revealed their partner's identity. Two other robbers backed out of a holdup, turned themselves in, and informed on their partners. Six men were informed upon by criminal associates, seven by acquaintances and friends, and three by ex-girlfriends. In 11 instances, the informant provides information that leads directly to the bandit's capture. In the other 21 cases, however, the information is used with other techniques (e.g., surveillance) to capture the offender.

2. Licence-plate Numbers and Car Descriptions

In 20/101 cases (19.8 percent), bank employees or customers provided a licence-plate number and/or description of the getaway car that led directly to an arrest.

3. Being Chased or Followed

In 11/101 cases (10.9%), a bank robber was arrested when either bank employees or customers chased and accosted him (five cases), or when they followed the offender and directed the police to his place of hiding (six cases). The following case example describes the events that preceded the arrest of two bank robbers with the assistance of conscientious citizens.

CASE EXAMPLE

Caught in Traffic

This 22-year-old man is serving three years for one count of robbery and an additional one-year term for the use of a firearm in the commission of an indictable offence. He has a high-school education and comes from a middle-class background. He also has a previous record for break and enter.

I did some B & E's when I was 18 and for that I served six months in jail. Before the robbery, I was working but I was reading the newspapers and read about it all the time. "Record high bank robberies this year. Less people being apprehended." Then I was laid off and things were slow. I was pretty loose at that time and I was capable of foolish things. I met Bobby who I used to know and who had been in jail for a robbery. He told me what he had done. I told him, "If I don't find a job in a couple of weeks, I'll speak to you then." Later I gave him a call and said, "Let's get together and talk." So he tells me that he has a friend who has a gun and all I have to do is jump over the counter. So the next day we three took a bus downtown, Tom, he was the one who had the gun, Bobby, and me. Bobby wanted to be the one holding the gun—he told me that he didn't know Tom all that well and he didn't trust him with the gun—so they made the switch. So we were walking around, walking around, walking around. I was getting all hyper and sweaty figuring everyone was watching me. We go inside this huge building and there's a bank on the ground level just inside the door. I'm thinking I'm not into it but I need the money. Instead of having to go to my mother and father to borrow another $300 for food during the month, I'm not into that.

We took a quick look to see if we could spot any police cars on the street. There was no police. So we went back to the bank, we pulled open the door. "Let's go!" Bobby took the gun out of the duffle bag, went into the bank, and screamed that it was a holdup, and pointed the gun into the air. People were all shocked. No one bothered to move. I pulled down the full-headed mask and jumped over the counter. Tom and I started taking money and throwing it into the bag. It was a big bank, sixteen teller drawers. We

both took money from three drawers and Bobby starts yelling, "Let's go! Let's go!" No names obviously. I leaped over the counter and took off. During all the commotion and whatever, Tom slipped away some place because when we came out of the bank, there was just me and Bobby. Tom had flown the coop.

We came out and we ran a very short downtown block to the left. The masks were off the moment we came out the door. Even before we hit the door the mask was off. So we ran down the corridor, through the revolving doors, up one slight block and there was a cab right there. So he says, "Let's jump in the cab." What we don't know at this time is that three women coming into the building saw us chuck the masks and looked to see where we were going. The cab pulls out, makes a turn, and comes back towards the bank and stops at a red light! Then we get another red light! Traffic was all backed up. Clogged. We had to wait. We start to go again and we drive past the bank and it looks like we're going to make the next light and "Bingo!", the guy stops at a yellow! Oh, I was sweating. But I'm making casual conversation like I'm coming from work and I can't wait to get home to take a shower. Meanwhile these women are following us. And I see this cop, this lone rookie cop up ahead on the street and I seen him grab his walkie talkie—just getting the call that moment. It took them a minute-and-a-half to get the call out on the air. So we could see he was listening. Like there's a bank robbery just down the street from where he's at. So we see him put it back in and look down the street. My friend's in a nice $350 suit and I'm dressed not too badly, nice pair of corduroys, nice shirt, clean cut, well shaven. We didn't look like bums. People you hear about doing bank robberies you expect to be wearing patches, uncombed hair, you know. We don't look like that. It's to my advantage if people cast a stereotype. So he's in front of us looking down the street behind us to see if a car was booting away or someone running. But he didn't figure we were that close. We're close, three cars down. He looks right by us but it doesn't even click in his head that it could be possible. But the women have followed us and they start pointing at the cab. Then I see the cops' eyes bulge, bulge, bulge!

So the light turns green and the cab starts to go and the cop puts his hand out, "Stop." The cabbie doesn't know what's going on. I'm going to myself, "Oh my God, I'm going to jail! I'm going to jail!" So the cop's gun goes through the open window right into the side of my head and he says, "Keep your hands where I can see them." "You too!", he says to my buddy. So I put my hands up and by now he's pulled the gun back out of the window. He says to me, "With one hand, open the door and come out." As soon as we come out I said, "Listen, you got no right. We're just coming from work. What do you think this is? What the hell is going on?" I didn't know that these women had pointed us out. I figured I was going to bluff. What the hell do I have to lose? I'm just going to give him a piece of my mind like he just stopped me from going to an orgy and I wanna get there. But rookie or no rookie, he knew how to react to the situation. He knew how to handle himself. He wasn't bluffed. So he says, "Up against the wall."

They arrested us and took us down to the station. Tom escaped and because we didn't know his last name, he was never arrested. He escaped with $3,800 and we had $3,300 on us. Not worth going to jail for. We weren't treated too badly by the cops. They were verbally abusive obviously but they were very fair. They weren't too thrilled with the weapon. It turned out to be an automatic, sawed off rifle with a 30-shot clip that had 27 bullets in it. No, they weren't too thrilled about that.

---

4. Caught in the Police Dragnet

In 21/101 cases (20.8 percent), the police's quick response results in an arrest in the vicinity of the bank. Offenders are typically apprehended in roadblocks, on the subway, walking along the street, or in other getaway vehicles such as buses or taxis. One man was observed in his car counting the money a few blocks from the scene and was arrested following a brief car chase.

5. Caught Inside the Bank

Police wish to avoid a confrontation with the offender inside the bank because they fear that staff or customers may be injured.

Nonetheless, three arrests (2.97 percent) occurred within the bank. The quick response of a patrol officer resulted in a temporary hostage-taking incident that was settled through negotiation and without injury. In another instance, a plain-clothed detective slipped into the bank and arrested a solo bandit who was holding a bank manager hostage with a fake bomb. In the third case, five uniformed police entered the bank and arrested an armed man who was waiting in line to rob a bank he had robbed one week earlier.

2ND HEIST AT BANK FLOPS
BRAZEN BANDIT CAUGHT IN ACT

A brazen bandit ran out of luck when he tried to rob the same bank branch twice in one week.

Police said he was spotted about 5 p.m. Friday in a teller's lineup at the Bank of Nova Scotia branch at 1464 Queen St. W. at Lansdowne Ave. he had robbed Aug. 12.

"One of the citizens who was in the bank last Friday (Aug.12) spotted the man and told a teller," said Sgt. Roly Semprie of 14 Division. "The teller informed the manager who called police while she locked the door."

By the time the man arrived at another teller's wicket and produced a note demanding cash and indicating he was armed, police were on the way.

The teller stalled the man long enough for police to arrive and arrest him.

"He did eventually catch on to what was going on," Semprie added, but what he said wasn't fit to print.

No one was hurt during either holdup.

Police said the man had tried to rob the Boots Drug Store at 1476 Queen St. West about two hours earlier Friday, but he fled when the cashier refused to hand over any money.

Charged with three counts of robbery is [name deleted], 56, of 1387 Queen St. W.

Reprinted by permission of The Toronto Sun.

6. Police Surveillance

In 13/101 cases (12.87 percent), police surveillance is employed to apprehend culprits. Seven of these men came to the attention of the police through informants. Surveillance is used when police lack sufficient evidence to make an immediate arrest. Eleven bandits were observed robbing the bank and arrested immediately afterwards. In the other two instances, police retrieved bait money that helped to convict the accused.

7. Bank Camera Photos

Photos taken of bank robbers during a holdup resulted in the capture of 10/101 culprits (9.9 percent). In six instances, citizens identified photos that were printed in newspapers. The other four were recognized by police officers from photographs circulated/posted in divisional offices.

This bank robber was identified to the police by an ex-girlfriend who spotted his photograph in the newspaper. The offender spent several years in penitentiary, was later paroled, and was re-arrested in 1992 when he robbed the same bank branch using the same modus operandi. *Photo courtesy Metro Toronto Police Hold-Up Squad.*

MAN JAILED FOR 3 BANK HEISTS

BY WENDY DARROCH

A laid-off Toronto tool and dye maker said he was so desperate to get rent money that he turned to robbing banks because other people seemed to get away with it.

But [name deleted] of Phyra Ave. was caught after his third heist and was jailed yesterday for six years by County Court Judge Hugh Locke.

"Tragically, in his mid-30s, this man has turned to a very serious crime. He says he was desperate and didn't want to hurt anyone," Locke noted. "This city is cursed with people who rob banks and convenience stores."

[The offender] told police when he was arrested a month ago that he had been laid off work since last Christmas and had a part-time seasonal job with an ice cream company.

He told them he was kicked out of the place where he had been living because he couldn't pay the rent. "I had read about all the bank holdups in the city and thought if those guys were getting away with it, it must be easy," he told police.

During the first heist the robbery was filmed by the bank's security cameras.

Source: Toronto Star *(22 October 1983). Reprinted with permission—The Toronto Star Syndicate.*

This bank robber was named "The Wig Bandit" because of his disguise. He operated as a solo gunman for five years but changed his modus operandi and began using partners. Police received information on his activities, placed him under surveillance, and arrested three men as they emerged from having robbed a bank. A gun batttle occurred in which one of the robbers was wounded. *Photos courtesy Metro Toronto Police Hold-Up Squad.*

8. Other Criminal Investigations

Police investigations of other crimes led to information that resulted in the arrest of four (3.96 percent) culprits. These are not cases in which an associate informs but rather instances in which the police serendipitously trip over a bank robber. In one case, for example, a police investigation of a suspected drug dealer led them to one of the dealer's clients. A search of his apartment uncovered a make-up kit, machine guns, and bullet-proof vests. The follow-up investigation led to the conviction of a criminal who had been robbing banks for ten years.

9. Turning Oneself In

Five bank robbers (4.95 percent) voluntarily turned themselves over to the police and admitted their crimes. In one instance, the bandit's photo appeared in the newspapers and was recognized by family members, who convinced the suspect to contact the police. In another case, the suspect had robbed the bank while he was drunk and recognized the seriousness of his crime the next morning. He visited a lawyer, who notified the police on his behalf. A third culprit turned himself in because he felt remorseful and believed that he needed psychiatric assistance. The fourth bank robber grew apprehensive over a planned robbery and turned both himself and his partners over to the police. The fifth robber left the province when he learned that the police had arrested a partner and were now searching for him. He later hired a lawyer and turned himself in.

10. Suspicious Behaviour Before or After the Robbery

In 8/101 cases (7.9 percent), the offenders' behaviour outside the bank (either before or after the crime) results in their arrest. In one case, a passing mail carrier jotted down the licence-plate number of a car containing two suspicious-looking men casing a bank. When the bank was later robbed, the licence number was passed on to the police, who placed the crew under surveillance and arrested them following a bank holdup. Two other bank robbers were identified by 9 suspicious passersby; two more were stopped and arrested in a taxi 320 km from the city limits; another was pulled over by an officer because of his erratic driving; another was arrested by drug officers at a bus depot; and the final culprit was apprehended after he returned his rental car with a sawed-off shotgun and balaclava in the trunk.

11. Fingerprints

Three men (2.97 percent) were identified through fingerprints—two men left their prints on bank robbery notes and one even signed his name to the withdrawal slip that he used as the holdup note. In the third instance, an armoured-vehicle robbery was solved when police recovered a thumbprint from a nearby pay telephone. The suspect was placed under surveillance and arrested in possession of marked bills.

SAVINGS ACCOUNT CASH WITHDRAWAL RECEIPT
NOT NEGOTIABLE OUTSIDE THIS OFFICE

Nov. 19*82*

RECEIVED FROM **THE TORONTO-DOMINION BANK** $ *10,000.00*

Bank - Robbery - Gun - Partner DOLLARS

M. Forester

(Please sign in presence of Teller)

GREEN CARD BRANCH NO. 13206

SAVINGS ACCOUNT NO. *123*

This offender used a withdrawal form to commit his robbery but inadvertently signed his name to the note. *Courtesy Metro Toronto Police Hold-Up Squad.*

12. Police Stakeouts

If the city is experiencing a crime wave of bank robberies or the police are targeting a particular bank robber (or crew) who is operating in a defined geographical area, they will sometimes place a number of banks under surveillance. Three men (2.97 percent) (in separate incidents) were arrested when they robbed banks that were being watched by the police.

13. Eyewitness Identification

Eyewitness identification of a suspect usually occurs after the arrest. In four cases (4/80 3.9 percent), however, teller/victim identification of the offender led to his apprehension. In one instance, the teller spotted a man putting on a mask before entering and robbing the bank. She recognized him as a former high-school classmate. Another teller was having lunch at a nearby restaurant when she spotted the bandit who had robbed her a few weeks earlier. A third teller/victim similarly recognized the man who had robbed her when he returned to the bank to rob it again a week later. He was arrested while patiently waiting his turn in line. The fourth robber who was identified by bank staff disguised himself slightly, robbed the bank where he kept his accounts, and wore a hockey sweater with his name on the back. Police were waiting when he arrived home minutes later with the loot.

14. Through Other Crimes

Only three bank robbers (2.97 percent) were arrested while committing other crimes: one man attempted to pass travellers' cheques taken from an earlier holdup; another was jumped by customers as he held up a grocery store; and the third man robbed a jewellery store and was arrested in a police dragnet. All three admitted to committing a number of bank robberies.

15. Bait Money
Like eyewitness identification, bait money normally helps to convict but not capture offenders. In one case (.99 percent), however, the culprit was caught because he deposited stolen foreign currency to his own account within days of the holdup.

The fact that one-half (51/101) of all cases in this sample were solved with direct public assistance illustrates the importance of this variable. In 31/101 (30.7 percent) cases, bank employees and other public citizens assisted the police in the arrest of bank robbers by providing licence-plate numbers or vehicle descriptions and direction of travel. The public also assisted in instances in which culprits were identified through informants (seven by friends and acquaintances), published photos (six cases), reporting suspicious behaviour (four cases), and eyewitness identification (three cases). Conklin similarly found that 19.7 percent of clearances result from information furnished by the victim or witness of a robbery. This includes cases in which the victim knows the identity of the robber (rare), has apprehended the robber and holds him or her until the police arrive, or follows the culprit and reveals his or her hiding place (Conklin, 1972:143).

The quick reaction and sharp eye of uniformed patrol officers resulted in two arrests inside the bank, 21 in the immediate area, and another three some time later when offenders were acting in a suspicious manner. More than three-quarters of all arrests in this sample of bank robbers were made with the assistance of bank employees and customers (50.5 percent) and the good work of uniformed patrol officers (26.7 percent).

The important role of informants is evident by the fact that almost one-third (31.7 percent) of arrests result directly from the information provided by partners, criminal associates, friends, and acquaintances. Haran and Martin (1984:51) found that 22 percent of robbery suspects were identified and ultimately arrested on information supplied by their co-defendants. This information can also be used to question the accused and build a case against him or her. Although some informants come forward because they are civil-minded citizens, most are offenders themselves who implicate others. Some provide the information in exchange for lenient treatment in the courts but most informants in this study received no rewards for their cooperation.

This study, like others (Gabor and Normandeau, 1989), indicates that robbers are usually identified and arrested with information furnished by victims, witnesses, and informants and the assistance of other police branches. The role of the Hold-Up Squad detective does not fit the movie image of a sleuth unearthing and analyzing clues until suspects are identified and located. In only a very few cases do investigators begin with clues (e.g., a fingerprint) to discover the identity of the suspect. Detective work does not move from clues to criminals, rather it moves from known suspects to corroborating evidence (Ericson, 1981:85; Reiss, 1971:108; Sanders, 1977:81). In most cases, detectives take over a case once a suspect is known (or captured) and bring it to a successful conclusion by making an arrest (if the offender is not already in custody), building the case, and obtaining a conviction and appropriate sentence on all or most of the robberies that the bandit has committed. In this capacity, they are extremely effective.

CAUGHT AT THE SCENE: OTHER STUDIES

In a study of 500 bank robbers in the United States, Haran and Martin (1984:51) found that 21 percent were caught at the scene or later the same day. Ciale and Leroux's (1983) study of armed robbery in Ottawa indicates that of 108 offenders apprehended, 11 percent were arrested at the scene of the crime. In their sample of 1,266 cases, Gabor and Normandeau (1989:203–4) note that one-third of robbery arrests are made on the day of the offence— many presumably as the offenders attempt to escape. Conklin (1972:136) similarly found that 38 percent of all clearances result from an officer making an arrest at or near the scene of the crime soon after the offence is committed. These findings suggest that the speed of response and the police methods used to patrol and cordon off an area significantly influence the number of robbers caught at or near the scene of the crime. Gabor and Normandeau (1989:203) note that the police typically respond to the scene of an armed robbery in under three minutes but that it takes almost twice as long for some victims or witnesses to place the call. In fact, people often telephone their spouses or employers before phoning the police. Shortening the time that elapses between the incident and the arrival of the police therefore requires a faster reaction by victims and witnesses.

The increased public usage of cellular telephones has helped the police to respond quickly to crimes in progress. People witnessing a robbery will frequently call the police, describe the suspect(s) and getaway vehicle, and even follow the offender(s) and provide directions to his or her whereabouts. Similarly, taxi drivers and courier services often provide immediate information about crimes in progress.

Although solving cases is partly a function of good police work, public assistance greatly enhances criminal investigations. The more detailed the descriptions of the suspects given by the victims and/or bystanders, the more likely it was that a case would be solved (Gabor and Normandeau, 1989:203–4). The fact that one-half (51/101 50.5 percent) of all cases in the present study were solved with direct public assistance illustrates the importance of this variable.

INTERROGATION AND THE USE OF FORCE

The image of the Hold-Up Squad both inside and outside police departments differs considerably from that of Homicide. Whereas Homicide is perceived as crafty and sophisticated, Hold-Up is seen as crafty and fierce. Historically, Hold-Up Squads in Canada have been criticized for their alleged use of force (Henshel, 1983:43–46). This reputation has led some departments to decide against forming a special squad to deal with armed robberies. The Chief of Police in a large urban centre explains why he resisted establishing a Hold-Up Squad:

> Robberies are handled by the Criminal Investigation Branches in each of our divisions and they're doing the job. If the number of holdups increased dramatically in our area or if our clearance rates dropped to an unacceptable level, then I'd consider forming a Hold-Up Squad. I'd be reluctant to do so because I don't want our officers becoming overly specialized and I don't like the reputation that Hold-Up Squads have. They're not good for a police force's image.

How does this group of men (there were no female Hold-Up officers at the time this study was conducted) get their reputation? Robbery itself is violent because it involves the threat or use of force and Hold-Up Squads respond in kind. "You fight fire with fire!" is the defiant response of one senior officer to critics of the Hold-Up Squad's retaliatory law-enforcement policy.

Whereas attempts are made to downplay their image in public, the Hold-Up Squad promotes this notoriety among criminals as an effective deterrent in their city. This reputation for violence is also effective in gaining the cooperation of culprits. For example, a divisional detective who had unsuccessfully interrogated two suspects, later stood aside and watched in frustration as the suspects confessed to Hold-Up Squad officers.

> I questioned those guys for over an hour and they stonewalled me. Then Hold-Up comes in and it didn't take them 10

minutes before they get the whole story. And I know why too, you just mention Hold-Up Squad and these guys are scared.

The Hold-Up Squad's reputation is spread effectively by the criminals themselves, particularly in prison. Most bank robbers acknowledge this squad's reputation for violence even though most have not been personally subjected to police brutality. According to some inmates, however, the infamy of the Hold-Up Squad is greatly exaggerated.

> A lot of guys will tell you how brutal Hold-Up is because it makes them look good. They claim they stood up to torture and didn't admit anything. But if they talk or rat on friends, this is their justification.

Four middle-class men in their early twenties were spotted running from the scene of a bank robbery by a patrol officer making his rounds. Three escaped but the fourth was captured in a footchase. Later, he implicated his partners—one of whom was his brother. In prison, a partner expressed his feelings about being informed upon:

> We talked about getting caught and we agreed that we wouldn't squeal on one another. I pulled my end of the bargain but my partner didn't think that way when he was caught and just signed away. In a place like this [prison], that's murder material but I don't hold any grudges. I was mad at him but that's past. We're on okay terms...I think the cops really frightened him. They fired a shot at him and they treated him pretty rough when he was questioned. That brought him back to reality.

This man is willing to excuse his partner's betrayal because he believes his accounts of police brutality. The investigating officer presents a different version of events:

> He was more than willing to talk. He had a big ego and we appealed to it. "You guys had us on the run for over a year. How the hell did you ever do that?" He sold them down the drain. His attitude seemed to be, "If I'm caught, they're going with me."

In many instances, offenders admit to having committed a number of robberies and provide signed statements detailing their involvement. In Conklin's study, 17.9 percent of clearances result from statements or confessions by offenders in custody who admit to other crimes and were rarely penalized for their confessions: "The suspect usually understands that if he confesses to the other crimes, he will not be charged with these offences and may even receive more lenient treatment in the court. The police may question suspects about other cases, but do not seem to get upset if the suspects refuse to confess" (1972:147–48). Conklin's observations are dramatically different from the present study in which statements are used to prosecute suspects on additional charges and obtain higher sentences, and investigators are extremely frustrated when offenders refuse to cooperate.

In the sample of 80 convicted bank robbers, 31 allege they were physically abused by the police. Two men complain of rough treatment at arrest; one alleges that he was forced to lie on the pavement in the rain for 45 minutes; the other was punched by an officer who was angry because he was wearing a bullet-proof vest. A third man complained that he was punched by police officers who escorted him back to jail after being acquitted of a bank-robbery charge: "That really bugged them that I beat the beef." The remaining 28 subjects complained that they were physically assaulted during their interrogation. Of these, 10/28 received minor forms of abuse and the remaining 18/28 report more serious beatings. Physical abuse is described as "minor" if it is brief and does not result in injury. "Serious" physical abuse involves sustained beatings that sometimes result in injury. Minor physical abuse usually involves "slaps" and "punches" and tends to be accepted by bank robbers as "part of the game." Most define these assaults as minor and express no bitterness:

> I got slapped around a bit but nothing too serious. You expect that.

> They try to be intimidating...There were three of them but they were fairly decent. I was a bit roughed up but I ignored it. It goes with the trade.

> They had pictures, man, and they looked really good. He shows me a picture of my partner, "Do you know this guy?" "Never seen him before." Slap across the face! They're fucking rough. They will slap you around but if you stick to your story, that's the end of it.

An analysis of allegations of serious beatings reveals several patterns: (a) all 18 have previous criminal records with 15/18 convicted of robbery; (b) 15/18 were armed; (c) 15/18 operated with a partner or in crews; (d) 5/18 discharged a gun; (e) 7/18 were from another city; and (f) 16/18 initially refused to cooperate with the police during the interrogation. The two men who did cooperate admitted to some crimes but not to others and refused to name their partners who had escaped. In addition, no one who was allegedly beaten claims that the police attempted to force them to admit to holdups that they did not commit. To place these allegations of police misconduct in a proper perspective, most of the interviews for this study were conducted during the early 1980s and the majority of incidents had occurred in the 1970s. Several older bandits describe incidents of police brutality experienced as far back as the 1960s.

The police appear to be harshest with repeat offenders who are uncooperative, work in heavily armed crews, and are from out of town. Hold-Up Squads in all cities seek, achieve, and publicize higher sentences for out-of-town criminals since their robberies require more premeditation and planning. "Out-of-towners" are also targeted as a deterrent. This can be effective as revealed by a 21-year-old speed addict:

> Wow! Coppers there don't fuck around. Those coppers will beat your brains in...I had been in town for 36 hours and they arrested me for an armed robbery. I was guilty as sin but they couldn't pin it on me. No, but I got a good beating. Oh! I seriously believed these guys were going to dump me. Like "Pow pow," and throw me in the lake and I'm gone. Holy fuck! They frightened me. Oh fuck! You wouldn't have recognized me if you had seen me two days later. I was in bad shape. It was wild stuff. The guy knocked me out four times! They told me, "Don't hang around in this city." Oh yeah, fuck. "See you. I'm gone. Catch you later." Fuck that shit. I took the bus...

Another robber was scouting armoured vehicles as possible targets for his heavily armed crew when he was picked up by the police.

> The Hold-Up Squad really came down on me. If their purpose is to keep me from going back to their city, they've done their job. I've never gone back. If I have to change planes at the airport, I'm worried. They are vicious policemen. They told me they'd kill me if I came back and I think they will. I know they do it. I was three days with them and they beat me half to death.

This man, like others, reports differential treatment from police in different cities. The most vicious beatings, however, happen to those who venture to another city to commit a robbery. Deterrence does not work in all cases. "Police violence is not a deterrence," says one robber, "It's a pitfall, that's all. I'll just be more careful the next time." Another states, "My frame of mind was such that if I had to rob a bank, I'd rob it regardless."

Several bank robbers believe that the police in major cities attempt to limit bank robbery to the unarmed note-pusher and are harshest with armed robbers. The message they wish to communicate to criminals: "If you're going to rob banks, don't use guns." Others suggest that police brutality results because Hold-Up Squad officers are sick or evil and enjoy "power-tripping."

> They are just brutal. The Hold-Up Squad are stone-cold killers. I know by the look in their eyes. They are evil.

> They stuck a broom up my ass and beat my head, my chest, and my testicles. They're a gang, a clique. They're all sadists. They kill people. They're worse than me. I don't use violence.

Although some bandits suggest that Hold-Up Squad officers are sadistic, the primary motive behind their use of force is clearly to gain information, evidence, and admissions of guilt. To the extent that it occurs, Hold-Up Squad violence is not a tit-for-tat, knee-jerk reaction. On the contrary, it appears to be a rational and discretionary strategy used to obtain convictions, deter others, ensure that justice (retribution) occurs in sentencing, and identify partners who are still at large. Hold-Up Squad violence expedites the process. Suspects who cooperate are not harmed and those who are "roughed up" report that the abuse ceases when they begin to talk. Suspects who cooperate describe their interrogators as polite and friendly: "They treated me all right. They got kind of rough when they wanted statements but after that there was pity in their eyes." Many bank robbers who refuse to make a statement express surprise when they escape their interrogation unharmed. In retrospect, most explain that the police already had sufficient evidence and did not need a statement to convict.

Unarmed bandits appear to be exempt from physical assault even when they refuse to talk. Uncooperativeness is a necessary, but not usually a sufficient, condition provoking the police's use of force. The need for information, combined with a suspect who is uncooperative and perceived to be violent, are the main factors behind serious police violence. Of the 18 men who claim they were seriously beaten, five signed statements that implicated them in bank robberies. Two of the five contested the statements in court, arguing that they had been extracted through the use of force. The statements were admitted as evidence, however, and juries convicted both men.

Although many of the eighty bank robbers interviewed were critical of the police, only one man claimed to have been convicted of a crime he did not commit. Pursued by staff and customers, he was arrested by patrol officers two blocks from the bank. He claims to have found the stolen and baited money that was in his possession and that no one believed him because he was on parole for previous bank robberies. Apart from this very implausible denial, all other inmates admit to their guilt but some are nonetheless bitter about the way in which police obtained convictions. Some even harbour vengeful feelings but state they will probably never act upon them.

> You think about doing something after it happens and you go to jail but by the time you get out, you're thinking about getting money.

> I'm pretty rational. Right now I wouldn't go after them 'cause it's not worth the trouble. I'd rather pursue a different avenue... If I was ever in a state of mind or at a point where I didn't care anymore, I know exactly who the guys are and they'd wish they'd never... They're going to do it to the wrong guy some day.

Two victims of serious abuse express some understanding. One man, whose partner was killed in what he calls a police ambush and who also claims to have been beaten, expresses no bitterness.

> They wanted to finish the job by shooting me. No paper work [Laughs]. I can laugh now. I thought about it a lot of times. If you put me in their shoes, I'd do the same fucking thing.

An armoured-vehicle robber who was also beaten attempts to understand the police's reasons for brutality.

> I guess they have their own justifications for why they do what they do. They think it's a dirty vicious game and they think in terms of a bunch of women tellers and heroin addicts holding them up. And they think in terms of their fellow officers being shot. I'm sure they have a whole moral structure that they work within. I'm sure it's righteous but they are in my mind a lot more evil than most bank robbers I know. They are capable of a lot more evil.

Although this man is angry and condemns Hold-Up officers as evil, he too says that he would not bother to seek revenge. Like most bank robbers who claim to have been beaten, he prefers not to think about it and refers to the beatings as humiliating.

Why are statements necessary? In some cases, the police act on information from informants and arrest the suspect long after the robbery has occurred. They may have evidence to convict the person on some holdups yet have insufficient evidence to press charges on others. In addition, a suspect's partners may still be at large. In such situations, police are likely to pressure the culprit to admit involvement and/or reveal the identity of partners. A more common scenario arises when the suspect is caught committing a robbery but is also believed to be guilty of others. To clear cases and obtain an appropriate sentence, the police try to obtain information on all previous robberies. High clearance rates and heavy sentences are viewed as evidence of a job well done and are also used as measures of the Hold-Up Squad's effectiveness.

A common situation arises when police obtain a statement from a suspect's partner that implicates them both in a series of robberies. Offenders who are inexperienced with the law and unaware that police also need their partner's testimony to obtain a conviction, often mistakenly believe they are finished when police produce this statement. In the face of this "evidence," many confess. However, the statement by one partner implicating another is not sufficient to obtain a conviction unless the "informant" also testifies against his or her partner. Partners are unlikely to testify, particularly if they were coerced or tricked into providing statements in the first place. In one case, the driver for two young bank robbers was arrested on the basis of statements that his partners made to the police. He denied all involvement and was later acquitted when his partners refused to testify against him in court. Experienced criminals are usually aware that a partner's statement is insufficient to convict without his or her corroborating testimony and will refuse to incriminate themselves during the interrogation.

Offenders who have made statements implicating their partners often refuse to testify because they have nothing to gain and everything to lose by taking the stand. Testifying in court immediately labels one as an informant and could endanger his life in prison and on the street upon his release. At the very least, it guarantees that his time in prison will be spent in protective custody—a situation he may wish to avoid. Once a suspect is in jail, police find it difficult to persuade him to testify without offering considerable incentives. The offender is out of their custody, in no physical danger from them, and has undoubtedly been charged with robbery. The only bargaining chip for the police is a deal involving a reduction in charges and/or sentence—something they may be unwilling to make in their pursuit of an appropriate sentence.

The prosecutor can subpoena a robber, question him or her about the partner's involvement, and attempt to introduce his or her statement as evidence. This is risky, however, since the witness may now deny the statement and/or contend that it was obtained under duress. In fact, perjuring oneself and denying that one's partner was involved helps to atone for making the statement in the first place. Most bank robbers do not hold a grudge against partners who made statements to the police implicating them in crimes if their admissions were made under pain and threat of death. Taking the stand in exchange for a reduced sentence, however, is unforgiveable. Although partners commonly implicate one another in their statement, it is relatively uncommon to see them testify against one another. In only four cases in this study did a partner take the stand against another: one for religious reasons; and the other three because they had been offered a considerable reduction in sentence, with two of these also seeking revenge for having been double-crossed.

The police also use other methods to force robbery suspects to cooperate. Common tactics include trickery and a variety of perils or incentives including (1) the laying of charges against an offender's wife (girlfriend) and agreeing to drop the charges if the subject gives a statement and/or pleads guilty; (2) a reduction in charges and/or sentence in exchange for a guilty plea; (3) the threat of additional future charges if new evidence arises and the suspect has not "cleaned the slate"; and (4) the presentation of "evidence" from police files, witnesses, and a partner's statement.

CLEARANCE RATES

Like other formal organizations, the police attempt to evaluate the competence and efficiency of their officers and departments. The measure of effectiveness generally used to evaluate detective investigative abilities is known as the clearance rate. The term "clearance" refers to the process by which a crime is solved. Although detectives attempt to obtain convictions for all robberies they believe that an offender has committed, convictions are not required to classify a case as cleared. Many cases are "cleared by arrest," which means that investigators are convinced that the suspect in custody is responsible for several crimes based on victim or witness descriptions and/or the similarity of M.O. Although corroborating evidence such as a confession or an eyewitness identification is preferred, it is not necessary to close the file and define the case as cleared. Even if the suspect is acquitted in court, the case will still be considered cleared and will not be reopened for investigation.

Some researchers are concerned that clearance rates are calculated by the police themselves, instead of an independent source. This means that detectives are, in effect, measuring their own success, which makes the rates a suspect method of judging the competence of individual officers, their division, or their department (Skolnick, 1967; Gabor and Normandeau, 1989). Some critics believe that these figures may be manipulated and used to create a positive public image of the police. Consequently, some researchers have suggested that the conviction rate might be a better measure of police effectiveness (Conklin, 1972:133).

In his study of detectives, Skolnick (1967:174) found that officers' concern with clearance rates in burglary cases led them to offer incentives to offenders who were in custody for one offence to admit to having committed other break and enters. The favourable treatment that detectives exchanged in return for the defendant's cooperation included a reduction of charges and counts, concealment of criminality, and freedom from further investigation of prior offences. Skolnick (1967:176) observed that serious criminals who confessed to a large number of crimes were treated more leniently than those who are in fact less culpable— thus undermining standards of justice.

Ericson's study (1981:53) of detectives in a Canadian police department reports that there was no apparent pressure on investigators to produce high rates of clearances. Instead, collective cooperation was emphasized rather than individual productivity and quality rather than quantity of charges and arrests was the goal. Ericson concludes that detectives in his study were not primarily oriented to producing statistics to impress various groups. Interviews with Hold-Up Squad detectives and other armed-robbery investigators in this study indicate that clearance rates are used with other criteria to evaluate individual or group performance. The ability to obtain signed statements, prepare cases for court, obtain guilty pleas, avoid trials, and gain hefty sentences are all important dimensions of the job. Unlike Skolnick's study, Hold-Up officers are not overly concerned with clearance rates nor are they inclined to use incentives to gain suspect cooperation. Instead, investigators treat offenders harshly, charge them with numerous offences, and pursue heavy sentences in the courts. Although concessions in charges and sentences were used in a few instances to entice suspects to inform on their partners, there were very few cases of lenient treatment for bank robbers in exchange for self-incrimination.

When a person is arrested for robbery, Hold-Up Squad investigators automatically assume that he or she has committed multiple robberies—a valid assumption in most instances. Incidents based on the similarity of M.O. are analyzed to determine which cases can be linked to the offender. The existence of centralized Hold-Up Squads that record city-wide robberies and the modus operandi of various bandits, help to clear many robberies. The failure to share information among divisions or cities makes it more difficult to link offenders to their crimes and clear cases. In Canada, investigating officers in various cities routinely share information and intelligence on bank robberies, resulting in high clearance rates for these types of offences throughout the country.

Since many cases are cleared in part because of the similarity of M.O., offenders who change their M.O. are unlikely to be linked to prior robberies. Although few bank robbers in our study used more than one M.O., those who did change their holdup style report that they were not questioned about earlier robberies committed using a different M.O. These cases, presumably, are never cleared from the books even though the offender is in custody on other charges.

CONFLICT THEORY AND ROBBERY

Bank robbery has an exceptionally high clearance rate compared to other types of crime and other types of robberies in particular. Haran and Martin (1984:47) report that U.S. clearance rates show that over 80 percent of bank robbers are identified and arrested. The conviction rate is also exceptionally high, averaging 88.8 percent. In contrast to the high clearance rates for bank robbery, only 25 percent of other robbery offences reported to law-enforcement agencies were cleared during the same period. The police calculated the clearance rate for all robberies in Conklin's (1972:150) sample to be 35.8 percent. He emphasizes, however, that only 22.9 percent of the cases produced an arrest and prosecution and even fewer robberies produced convictions. Similarly, while Hold-Up Squads in Canada routinely report regional clearance rates of 70 to 80 percent for bank robbery, the national clearance rate for all robberies is 33.7 percent (Statistics Canada, 1992:34).

Every day, the media report incidents in which cab drivers, ordinary citizens, and convenience-store clerks have been robbed, assaulted, tied up, stabbed, shot, and even killed. Several researchers have also noted that muggings and convenience-store robberies are more violent and more frequent than bank robberies—a crime that seldom results in injuries to victims (Gabor and Normandeau, 1989; Conklin, 1972). Paradoxically, however, bank robbery is given a higher priority by the police and is treated as a more serious offence than other types of robbery by the criminal-justice system. Conklin (1972:149) suggests that detectives probably work harder to develop evidence in commercial robberies since they involve more money and carry more prestige if solved. In their study of robbery in Montreal, Gabor and Normandeau (1989) similarly note that bank robberies are viewed more seriously than other robberies by the police and prosecutors. Bank robbers were more likely than other robbers to be apprehended; to have more charges laid against them; to be detained before trial; and to receive longer prison sentences. Much of this differential treatment was due to the formation of the Montreal Bank Robbery Squad, consisting of experienced detectives who investigate bank robbery cases only. In addition, a special prosecutorial unit focuses on case preparation and attempts to lay the most serious charges possible in bank robbery cases. Both units have superior resources than those available to investigate and prosecute other crimes. They have succeeded in increasing, by about two years, the prison sentences received by bank robbers. Furthermore, solution rates have significantly increased and the number of bank robberies has been reduced significantly over the past decade. In view of the resources provided to combat this particular crime, Gabor and Normandeau (1989:200) conclude that the interests of the banks take precedence over the welfare of other commercial establishments and mugging victims.

A similar phenomenon occurs in the United States, where bank robbery has a special status as both a state and a federal offence. The FBI treats bank robbery as a high-priority crime and has created special units in all of its main offices to cope with this problem. Due to their organization and the resources assigned to bank robbery cases, the FBI is able to identify and arrest bank robbers in 80 percent of the cases falling within their jurisdiction. With the cooperation of the U.S. Attorney's office, they also achieve a very high conviction rate for those charged with this crime. Haran and Martin (1977:29) note that both organizations consider bank robbery a serious offence and consistently seek and achieve lengthy prison sentences.

Conflict theory can be used to explain the differential distribution of police resources to bank robbery compared to other types of robberies by pointing to the fact that the banking community is a wealthy and powerful organization that acts as an influential lobby group within the criminal justice system. Consequently, the police and courts are pressured to solve bank holdups and give them the highest priority. The Canadian Bankers' Association also maintains favourable relations and cooperates with Hold-Up Squads across Canada. In addition, the Canadian Bankers' Association Corporate Security Branch sponsors and participates in robbery seminars with armed-robbery detectives. Bank security officials are normally ex-police officers with criminal investigative experience and thus understand the values and problems of police work. Bank security personnel keep communication channels open and aid the police in any way they can. Significantly, the banks ensure that teller/victims assist the police in their investigations, by providing staff with time off work to help identify and testify against suspected bank robbers. Victims of other robberies may be less motivated because they have lost little money in the robbery, have difficulty getting the time off work or away from their business, and/or cannot afford the time to view photos, offender lineups, or attend court and testify. Thus the resources of the banking community help to ensure that the police devote the time and energy necessary to investigate and prosecute bank robbery cases.

PLEA BARGAINING AND THE POLICE

Hold-Up Squad detectives are responsible for gathering evidence and preparing the case for court. The Crown attorney is responsible for presenting evidence in court, questioning and cross-examining witnesses, and making a submission with respect to sentence. Most bank robbery cases in this study, however, are resolved through guilty pleas and many of these happen through pre-trial negotiations between the defendant and his/her counsel on one side and the police and prosecuting attorney on the other. The defendant usually agrees to plead guilty to certain offences if (a) other charges are dropped or lowered and/or (b) the Crown agrees to a particular sentence or a range of sentences or to leave unopposed the defence's submission for sentence. Although judges are not normally informed of plea bargains or bound by them in determining sentence, they recognize this as a standard practice and usually acquiesce.

The discretionary authority allowed the Crown attorney permits him or her to make these exchanges but is rarely done without prior consultation with the police. In fact, the bargain is often struck between the defence attorney who initiates the proceedings, and the investigating officers. For example, an interview with Hold-Up Squad officers was interrupted by a phone call from an attorney who offered to have his client plead guilty to several bank robberies in exchange for a four-year sentence. The officer who received the call explained that he would have to discuss the matter with his partner and would call the attorney back in ten minutes. The following conversation ensued:

1st officer:	[Hanging up the phone] That was [lawyer], the attorney representing [Jones]. He's offering to plead if we'll accept four years.
2nd officer:	Four years. What did [Smith] get?
1st officer:	Six.
2nd officer:	Yah, that sounds okay. Smith did a dozen banks and Jones has about eight. What do you think?
1st officer:	Smith had a larger sheet [criminal record]. [John Doe] was sentenced last month and he got four. Jones' case is almost the same.
2nd officer:	We wouldn't get much more if we went to trial— six at the most but more likely four or five. Four is fair.
1st officer:	Should I call [the attorney] back and tell him it's a deal?
2nd officer:	Do that and give the Crown [attorney] a call too.

In this case, the deal was struck between the defence attorney and the investigating officers. The detectives discussed the fairness of the proposed sentence by comparing it to the prison terms given to other bank robbers and decided that it was equitable. The agreement depends on the consent of the Crown attorney but both officers explained that they did not expect any objection. The Judge was also expected to consent to the deal.

The police work closely with Crown attorneys, who are responsible for preventing a backlog of cases from developing in court. The police and Crown attorney attempt to avoid lengthy trials that tie up courts, judges, police officers, prosecuting attorneys, and witnesses. Success in obtaining a statement from the accused solidifies their case, allows the police to bargain from a position of strength, and pressures the suspect to seek a deal in sentencing. Defendants and their attorneys are less likely to contest a case and more willing to negotiate if the prosecution's case is strong. A statement admitting guilt, particularly if it is corroborated by other evidence that the police have obtained, undermines the defence. Once a confession is given, lawyers can do little to assist their defendants in trial and are likely to seek a deal regarding sentence. In such cases, the defence may challenge the statement's validity in court but this strategy is problematic and unlikely to succeed. A more plausible course of action is to plead guilty in exchange for a reduction in the charges and/or an agreement regarding sentence.

Psyched Out and on the Run

This 24-year-old male stripper avoids arrest temporarily but eventually turns himself into the police and confesses to each of his robberies.

We had done a bank that day and we had a problem. There were some kids playing when I came out of the bank and as we took off they guessed something was going down and they took the plate number down. It was a stolen plate but we got pulled over an hour later on the other side of the city for a traffic offence and had the same plate. The cop gives me a ticket and lets me go. Later I'm at a certain party's place and someone phones and says the cops were here looking for you. "Ten cops!" Ten cops, not one, ten! The heat was on. I didn't bother with who, what, where, I got this friend to drive me out of town but the cops picked my partner up and he spilled the beans. Meantime I catch a train and I went to California. But while I'm doing this, this cop, Sergeant Boot, he's playing "Mr. Tough Guy" with his guns. Everywhere he went he was flashing his guns, telling people he was gonna get me—playing the real bad guy. He was going to blow me apart. He's telling everybody that he doesn't want me to turn myself in, he wants to get me. He was literally going into my friends' places with guns out, "Where the hell is he?" He was going under couches, going into bedrooms. They cocked the guns at my parents' place and my father couldn't believe it—I got two younger sisters at home. I heard this in Vancouver and I started hitch-hiking from Vancouver along the coast of California. I'd phone from California and I still got the same story. He's at my parents' house waving his gun—and at my sister's too. My parents would open the door and there he is with three other officers with shotguns and he has his handgun out, "Where is your son? We want to search this place." This went on three nights a week. My parents wouldn't let him in but he played this role and so naturally I got the impression he's out to get me.

I'm travelling and having a good time and when I got to Texas, I had had enough. In two months of running, I've already spent my money. I'm getting desperate and I'm in a very deep depression as well because I realize that when I do get caught, I'm looking at a lot of time. A lot of things built up, a lot of things at once and I came pretty close to being suicidal. I talked myself out of it and I phoned a girlfriend and told her to phone this guy that's after me, Sergeant Boot, and tell him I'm turning myself in and to lay off. She calls him up, gets back to me and says, "They're surprised and they don't believe you." So I says to her, "Okay, give them this date and this time and I'll be in town then."

I showed up on that date and I got my lawyer together and we phoned Boot and he was a completely different person. Completely! My lawyer says: "Where is this bad guy? It's as if I'm talking to a friend." This guy was nice, super nice. He even granted me, get this, he even granted me two days. I said, "I'm here, I'm willing to turn myself in but I'd like to see my family first and a couple of friends and then we'll do it." He granted me those two extra days and said, "Just make sure you're here in two days."

I went to see him in two days and it was completely different. I was the strong man. I said to him: "Who the fuck do you think you are scaring my family and friends like that?" "Oh no, no," he says, "You'll hear a lot of stories but I had no idea what kind of guy you were." This is where he amazed me. I still have it in my mind, "Okay you piece of shit, you're playing double boat with me." But he didn't, at least I see now that he didn't because he actually helped me through this.

When I got to the police station, my lawyer's standing up for me and telling them I'm not giving a statement. So Boot realizes this and he says, "Well I just want to tell you something, I have a list of eight banks that you're being charged with. We'll go over each of them and you don't have to say a thing if you don't want to but I think you will in the end." So we go through the charges and he's showing me the statements and these are pretty serious statements from the two guys who drove the car. And he has statements from four other guys on the street that I know. Just with the statements alone they have a conviction. So as we're talking he gets me a hamburger, fries, and a coke and he's being a nice guy. I can't figure it out because he's not going to get a statement from me. I expected a beating and he's not beating me. I had experience with the police before and I know what they are capable of which is really hurting you. So I was prepared for this and I guess it showed. I was sort of expecting them to do something and I guess maybe he detected that. The guy totally amazed me because he's supposed to be this hard cop. I noticed that things were getting really touchy and I said to my lawyer, "Shall I give a statement?" He said, "No." But I thought it was best and it turned out best. I asked my lawyer to leave and I gave Boot a full statement that I did them and that I did them alone—nobody else was there. This is what really killed me. I give him a statement and I don't implicate anybody. I say to my lawyer, "Was it a good idea that I give him that?" "No," he says, "we can't fight it now." So he tries to make a deal with Boot but now Boot doesn't want to make a deal. He says, "Cop a plea for six bank robberies, we'll drop two and give you fifteen years." My lawyer came back to me with that—I was in jail at that point and I said, "Come on!" So he goes back and two months later Boot approaches us and says, "We'll give him a year on each—eight years. It's now or never." So I took that. Boot is very strange when he gives me that, he comes up and shakes my hand and says, "You got a break, kid." Amazing! This guy Boot is amazing.

This case illustrates how the investigating officer successfully convinced this offender to turn himself in and make an incriminating statement. The officer also avoided a trial by offering an eight-year sentence in exchange for a guilty plea.

A plea bargain in which the accused pleads guilty and receives an adequate sentence is a measure of competence for detectives. It saves court time and indicates that the evidence is strong and the case is well prepared—a weak case is more likely to be challenged in court or result in an unsatisfactory sentence evolving out of pre-trial negotiations. Plea bargaining has an additional benefit to detectives: it maintains what Ericson (1981:17) terms the "low visibility" of criminal investigators. The process by which detectives conduct investigations, interview witnesses, interrogate suspects, and otherwise gather evidence and prepare cases is not visible to other social control agencies or to the public. The Crown attorney and criminal court judges depend upon police accounts of events and the manner in which investigations are conducted. A courtroom trial may challenge police accounts, open them to accusations of wrongdoing, and bring into public scrutiny police investigative practices. A guilty plea avoids this situation and maintains the low visibility of Hold-Up Squad investigations—another reason, perhaps, to negotiate guilty pleas.

Several Hold-Up Squad detectives suggest that bank robbers are more willing to make a deal and plead guilty than other types of criminals. One officer comments:

> I'd say 7 of 10 plead guilty. I don't know if they're afraid of court or a heavy sentence. I think with holdup artists, it builds and they want to get rid of it. Fraud guys are more cool and expect to beat it. They try to con their way out. Even when they have a lawyer, bandits plead guilty.

One reason for pleading guilty may be that the evidence is often conclusive and damaging. No judge is likely to be sympathetic when photographs of terrified tellers and customers are introduced as evidence.

In their study of robbery in Montreal, Gabor and Normandeau found considerable evidence of plea bargaining. Most cases were resolved through guilty pleas and only eight percent were tried before a judge and jury (Gabor and Normandeau, 1989:204).

THE CHANCES OF GETTING AWAY

What are the chances of getting away with robbery? How effective are the police in catching this type of criminal? Gabor and Normandeau suggest that the chance of getting caught for robbery is low for a number of reasons: many robberies go unreported; even if charges are laid, a conviction is not guaranteed; and only one of several perpetrators may be charged while their partners evade arrest. Consequently, they argue that the chances of conviction for a typical robbery are substantially less than one in ten. They also argue that since robbers usually succeed in leaving the scene with some cash. which they often use to achieve short-term goals (e.g., buy drugs), then even some of those who are eventually caught have already achieved a measure of success. "If we apply a very tight definition of failure—robberies in which perpetrators are caught and convicted without achieving even short-term goals, then the failure rate is extremely miniscule, maybe one in twenty or one in thirty" (Gabor and Normandeau, 1989:203).

One problem with this argument is that the clearance rates for robberies nationwide are around 33 percent (Statistics Canada, 1992:33), which is not low. This means that police usually have solved a third of all robberies in Canada by arresting a suspected offender. In addition, because the process of solving crime is often time-consuming, a criminal incident may take months or even years before it is cleared and is not therefore recorded on the Statistics Canada Uniform Crime Report Survey. Another problem with their argument is that although the risk of getting caught on a single robbery might be low, the chances of getting caught increase significantly as one engages in subsequent holdups. Because the amount of money obtained in a single robbery is small, anyone who wishes to support himself or herself this way has to rob repeatedly. Given that police respond immediately and professionally to a robbery, the odds against anyone surviving in this career for long are not great. As one bank robber said, "The police have time on their hands. All you have to do is make one mistake and you're going to do time." Evidence indicates that most offenders do not commit a single robbery and then retire. Instead, they engage in a series of holdups and stop only when they have been caught. Thus, serial robbery is a high-risk activity.

This high risk is evidenced by the fact that the Hold-Up Squad typically clears over 70 percent of all bank robberies. Furthermore, the 30 percent of unsolved cases do not represent the proportion of men who succeed without being arrested. Several bank robbers in this study commit holdups for which they are never suspect. The crime may go unsolved but the culprit does not go unpunished since he or she is convicted and serves time for other robberies. The career of most robbers seldom lasts more than a few months. Haran and Martin, for instance, report that 52 percent of 500 bank robbers were arrested within 30 days and only 7 percent remained free for over a year (Haran and Martin, 1984:51). It is impossible to estimate the percentage of robbers who get away with it. Evidence indicates, however, that the numbers are small and include only those few who quit in the early stages of their career. Most bandits will push their luck until it runs out.

Sentencing and Plea Bargaining with 80 Bank Robbers

Sentencing for a criminal offence is strongly related to the seriousness of the crime and the person's past criminal record. Since robbery and armed robbery are considered serious offences and since most bank robbers in this study have lengthy criminal records, it is not surprising to find that the average prison term for the 80 men in this sample is 9.37 years. Only one person received probation, two others received provincial time (less than two years), and the remaining 77 men received federal penitentiary sentences. Three offenders were given life sentences and one of these was sentenced to 10 life sentences. The average number of convictions in their most recent court appearance was 6.1 bank robberies and the average number of bank holdups they were charged with and/or admitted committing was 17.8 robberies. On the one hand, this figure is high because it includes a small number of offenders with a large number of robbery offences. On the other hand, the figure underestimates the total number of bank robberies committed by these men since some offenders refused to comment on holdups for which they were not charged and others were not charged with all the offences that they had committed. The sample includes one man (Case Example "Prolific", Chapter Four) who robbed 300 banks and one of his partners who committed over 100 bank robberies and a dozen armoured-vehicle holdups. In addition, three others admit to having committed 50 or more bank holdups. Only two of these men were convicted of over 50 bank holdups and they pleaded guilty to 80 bank robberies. The median number of total convictions (including present and past offences) for bank holdups in this sample was 10. A total of 21/80 (26.25 percent) were convicted of one to five bank robberies; 19/80 (22.5 percent) with six to 10 holdups; 20/80 (25 percent) on 11 to 20; and 20/80 (25 percent) had more than 20 bank robbery convictions.

CRIMINAL BACKGROUND

Most offenders in this sample had lengthy and varied criminal backgrounds. Only five men had no previous criminal convictions and two others had only minor convictions for possession of marijuana. The remaining 73/80 had serious criminal records, including 45 men with robbery offences. Twenty-five (25/45) had previous convictions for bank robbery and 16 of these had other robbery convictions. An additional 20/80 offenders had been convicted for robberies of convenience stores, grocery stores, gas stations, drug stores, liquor outlets, and individuals. The remaining

28 offenders report a variety of offences that include convictions for car theft, assault, break and enters (B & E), possession of narcotics, trafficking in narcotics, shoplifting, possession of offensive weapons, theft, possession of stolen property, fraud, escape from lawful custody, violation of terms of probation, wounding, abduction, kidnapping, murder (one case), attempted murder (one case), and manslaughter (one case). The typical combination of offences included robbery, B & E's, drug offences, and crimes involving theft (car theft, shoplifting, and possession of stolen property). Most had served time in prison and some offenders were serving their third and fourth penitentiary terms.

In their latest criminal escapade, 17 offenders were on parole; 11 were on mandatory supervision (now called statutory release); 15 were illegally at large after escaping from prison or walking away from a halfway house; four were on bail awaiting other charges; and four were on probation from other criminal convictions. A total of 51/80 in this sample, therefore, were already before the court on criminal charges or under sentence from the court when they committed their present offences.

As this cartoon illustrates, robberies are often poorly planned and executed. Three offenders in this study robbed their own banks. The cartoon also jokes that the offender is on a day pass when he commits the robbery. Hold-Up Squad officers find little humour in the fact that so many robberies are committed by offenders on parole or some other form of release from custody. In the present study of 80 bank robbers, 17 were on parole when they were arrested for bank robbery, 11 were on statutory release, 15 were illegally at large, 4 were on bail awaiting other charges, and 4 were on probation from previous criminal convictions.

Another aggravating factor for sentencing purposes is the fact that 46/80 were armed and another 11/80 used replica firearms in their recent bank robberies. Given the large number of robberies committed, the use of weapons, past criminal records, and the fact that so many were illegally at large or recently released on bail, probation, parole, or mandatory supervision, it is understandable that judges are inclined to hand out lengthy penitentiary sentences.

PLEA BARGAINING

In 46/80 cases in this study, offenders were offered no concessions for guilty pleas. The majority of these made no attempt to strike a deal and the rest report that the police and/or Crown attorney refused to plea bargain. In several cases, the police and Crown threatened the offender with a lengthy prison term if he decided to proceed to trial. Ten of these cases went to trial anyway and one man won an acquittal. In another case, the offender asked the Crown for a 10-year sentence and was offered 16 years. He refused the offer and elected a trial by judge and jury. He was found guilty and sentenced to 16 years. In two other cases, the Crown had sentences increased from five to seven years and from four to six years on appeal. One offender won a reduction in his sentence from 10 to eight years on appeal.

A total of 34 cases were resolved through guilty pleas that involved concessions from the Crown and/or the police. In 16 cases, the Crown/police promised a particular sentence in exchange for the offender pleading guilty to the charges. In most cases, the Crown and defence made joint or similar submissions to the judge concerning the sentence and the judge concurred. In one instance, however, the judge refused a suggested 4.5-year term and sentenced the offender to 5.5 years in prison. In four of these cases, additional concessions were included: robbery charges were dropped in two instances; in another case, robbery charges were dropped and the police also agreed not to proceed with charges against the offender's girlfriend; and in a fourth case, agreement was made between investigators in several cities to allow the accused to plead to charges in one trial only.

One man who testified against former partners (see Case Example, Prolific) also pleaded guilty to 95 bank robberies. He was given a two-year prison term, however, in exchange for his plea and testimony against 13 men involved in a series of bank and armoured-vehicle robberies across the country. In two other cases, offenders were offered substantially reduced prison terms if they would identify partners who had escaped arrest. Both refused and received lengthy prison terms.

In 11/80 cases, the accused was offered a reduction in the number of charges. This typically involved the withdrawal of a few robbery offences in exchange for an agreement on the part of the accused to plead guilty to the remaining charges. The Crown and police typically dropped weaker cases and proceeded with the remaining charges. There were no promises regarding sentence and the Crown often requested and received lengthy penitentiary terms. In only three instances were firearm offences withdrawn as part of the deal. The police and Crown seemed determined to secure separate convictions and sentences for the use of firearms during a robbery. One case also included an agreement by the Crown/police to not publicize the case to protect the reputation of the offender's father—a prominent lawyer in the city.

In four other cases, offenders had committed their robberies in different cities and faced several prosecutions. They agreed to plead guilty to all charges, providing they were tried and sentenced only once. This agreement contained no promise regarding sentence and required and received the consent of the Crown in the cities where the robberies occurred. In one of these cases, the Crown and police also agreed to withdraw charges against the offender's girlfriend.

In the final 3/80 cases, offenders agreed to plead guilty to all charges on the condition that their girlfriend or wife not be prosecuted. In two instances, the women were originally charged as accomplices and in the other case, the police had threatened to charge the offender's wife with possession of stolen property.

SUMMARY

In most cases (87.5 percent), the offender foregoes his right to a trial and pleads guilty. Furthermore, in the majority of these cases (54/70 77 percent), he pleads guilty without any concessions regarding the sentence that the court will impose. Many explained that their reason for not fighting the charges was their desire to "get the thing over with" and begin serving their sentence. Some wished to avoid spending time in jail awaiting trial ("dead time" that may not be counted towards their sentence). Five subjects expressed relief at having their crime spree end before they committed more robberies and received an even harsher sentence.

Some suspects avoided a trial because they had already given statements admitting guilt and/or believed that the police had sufficient evidence to convict. Others believed that a trial might result in a more severe sentence if aggravating factors were introduced as evidence. Some suspects realized that a trial on charges over which they were obviously guilty might provoke the judge to impose a particularly harsh sentence.

Those who accepted a reduction in the number of charges against them in exchange for a guilty plea simply hoped that their sentence would be more lenient than what it might otherwise have been. Offenders report that the Crown frequently referred to robbery statistics in their city and asked the judge for deterrent sentences. This was particularly true in cases where offenders had travelled from another city to commit the crime. Although some were satisfied with the time imposed, most thought that the period of incarceration was excessive. These feelings were exacerbated in prison where inmates pointed to the disparity in their sentences versus those of men convicted of manslaughter (defined by inmates as murder) and/or sex offences. A cynical view of sentencing priorities expressed by several bank robbers goes like this: "You can molest children or kill somebody in this country and get a slap on the wrist. But don't you dare steal our money or we'll put you in prison and throw away the key."

A final criticism of the sentencing process was aimed at defence lawyers who—in the inmates' view—did nothing to help their cause. Several accused their lawyer of having been in league with the Crown and of "selling them out." Others simply viewed their attorney as incompetent or unmotivated. Since most bank robbers rely on legal aid, respondents recognize that they may not be getting the most talented, experienced, and motivated defence counsel. A few of the older and more accomplished career criminals confided that they arranged to pay their legal aid lawyer an extra fee (usually $1,000 to $2,000) to ensure a proper defence: "They work a lot harder for you if you make it worth their while."

There is little evidence that offenders in this study considered the sentence they might receive for their crimes prior to their arrest. The vast majority of subjects planned to stop robbing banks in the immediate future and/or did not believe they would get caught. A few robbers (only three) stated that they did not use a weapon in part because of the sentencing ramifications. Most subjects only began to think seriously about sentencing after they had been apprehended and jailed. About a dozen inmates report that they began to scour the newspapers on the sentences handed out to other holdup artists and a few used media reports as a guide in their plea bargaining. Two men report seeking out a particular judge who they read had given what they considered a favourable sentence to someone with a criminal background similar to theirs.

Crime Prevention and Social Policy

No Deal

This 28-year-old man's name was obtained from a newspaper article that also featured a picture of him wearing a bullet-proof vest. The subject was initially cautious about being interviewed and refused to allow me to use a tape recorder. He also asked to see my identification and stated that he had consulted the head of the inmate committee for information about me prior to agreeing to be interviewed.

This is my second time in the penitentiary system. The first was because of a jewellery robbery. In both cases, the jewellery and the bank robbery, there were extraordinary circumstances that made me do it. I'm a very impulsive person. I'm not an aggressive type of person even though I used guns in both cases. This last time, my wife was pregnant and not working. I wasn't working and we had bills to pay. I've been on welfare before and I'd rather steal. After losing my job, I was depressed. I know a lot of criminals not because I associate with them but because I was raised in the area. Just about any bar I go into, I know guys who are into crime. It was I who had gone to them to ask if they had a score for some good money. Not a

Mac's Milk or a taxi. I'm a family man myself and I know what it's like to have to work for a living and pay bills. These were acquaintances. I knew these guys from what you might call "le milieu." They mentioned they were planning to do a bank and I said, "Okay." They supplied the gun and the bullet-proof vest.

The police offered me a deal if I would tell them the names of my accomplices. They said if I cooperated, I would get a two- or three-year sentence. I asked them who was going to protect my family and they said they would. I just laughed at them. The police would throw me to the dogs afterwards. I have no faith in the police or the justice system. I got an exemplary sentence because I wouldn't cooperate and because I was from out of town. The police charged me with other banks and they questioned me about a Brinks. The other charges were thrown out at the preliminary hearing. The bullet-proof vest really blew their minds. That and the 9 millimetre pistol. The arresting officer found that I was wearing a vest and he put his gun to my head and cocked the trigger and said,

"You bastard. That's cheating! I should just blow your fucking head off right here."

From the time of my arrest to the sentence was only six weeks. I wanted to get everything over with quickly so I could start my sentence. If I had a chance to beat the charge I would have fought it. But I was guilty as hell and they had all the evidence they needed. There was no deal. The Deputy Chief of Police came to my trial and read off the armed-robbery statistics for the past three years. There had been a big increase. He really made the point. It doesn't look too good for me when the Deputy Chief comes to the trial to read off the stats. They were looking for a deterrence sentence.

The ten-year sentence shocked me. I hate prison. Ninety percent of the guys in here are crud. Prisons don't do anything for any-body. It's simply to punish the inmate and to protect the public. There is no such thing as rehabilitation. I love my freedom but I can accept being in prison. I know what I did was wrong and I did it with premeditation. Most guys deny what they did. What I cannot accept are the injustices in sentencing. I got ten years for robbing a bank and the same week three guys got nine months for rape and another guy got two years for beating up his little daughter. You can rape women and beat children but don't steal our money. I understand that I had a gun but there was no violence, no threats, and no shots were fired.

I wanted to divorce my wife but happily she talked me out of it. She said she was willing to wait. She's very patient and sensitive and I'm very lucky to have her.

A SUMMARY OF THEORY AND RESEARCH

This chapter deals with issues of social policy with respect to crime in general and robbery in particular. Sociological theory typically adopts the perspective that crime is linked to a number of social problems that are partly caused by the structure and distribution of economic and social opportunities. Before examining suggestions for societal reform, this chapter begins with a summary of what theory and research tell us about robbery. The goal of the book has been to introduce readers to the crime of robbery, characteristics of the offence and offenders, variables associated with the crime, and theories that shed light on this behaviour. While the text has discussed individual components of robbery, it has also emphasized how social variables such as gender, poverty, race and ethnicity, and opportunity strongly influence criminal conduct. As discussed throughout the various chapters, robbery is a crime that is motivated in large part by money, but at the same time, it is an offence in which culprits confront and control victims using force or the threat of violence. The behaviour included in this criminal category ranges from the mugging of individuals to convenience-store robberies, to financial institution and armoured-vehicle holdups. Whereas most commercial robberies are reported to the police, self-report studies tell us that many individuals fail to report incidents of victimization.

Robbery in Canada is a serious offence punishable by a maximum sentence of life imprisonment. Holdups are also associated with other crimes including weapons offences, assault, and occasionally even murder. While sociological theories emphasize financial motives, the police, courts, and other agencies of social control perceive robbery as a crime of violence because of the trauma and injuries that are inflicted on victims. Laws prohibiting robbery are based on consensus since they protect the welfare and reflect the interests of citizens of all social and economic backgrounds.

Research indicates that robbery is typically a high-risk, low-reward, and somewhat opportunistic offence that is frequently committed by young males who live in the vicinity and who put little thought or effort into the planning and execution of the score. Even though bank robbery pays more than other holdups, the money obtained is still modest considering the risks involved. Official statistics reveal that the United States has a robbery rate that is two to three times that of Canada, and that Quebec has the highest rate among all provinces. Although robbery incidents have increased over the past decade, the rate for robbery with firearms had remained relatively stable. Most holdups occur in large urban centres, which can be explained in part through social inequality, opportunity, and routine activities theories. The age-crime curve indicates that involvement in crime increases from adolescence to late teenage years and then declines rapidly throughout life. Social control theory attempts to explain this phenomenon by suggesting that young adolescent urban males drift beyond the control of conforming adults and their families and are influenced by their peers, many of whom are delinquent. Other versions of control theory aim to explain the higher male/ female ratio for robbery, which averages about 10 or 15 to one.

French Canadians in Quebec and blacks throughout the United States have the highest rates of robbery in their respective countries. Several authors evoke anomie, opportunity, and conflict theory to suggest that the over-representation of both groups can be understood in terms of the underprivileged position that each has occupied in their home countries. Individuals in the lower socioeconomic classes have limited economic resources, few job prospects, criminal role models and associates, a fatalistic mentality, and access to weapons. Theories based on illegitimate opportunity, socialization, and differential association help to clarify the drift into robbery.

Although illicit drug usage is linked to crime, the causal connection is complex. Research supports both the drug-addiction hypothesis that suggests that drug usage leads offenders to crime to support their habits, and the criminalization hypothesis that contends that criminal associations precede and give rise to drug abuse. Regardless of which comes first, it is clear that increasing drug usage often leads to greater criminality. Although persons involved in street crimes are disproportionately over-represented among the unemployed, there is no clear causal connection between unemployment and crime. Findings are inconsistent and the unemployment-crime relationship is neither simple nor is it fully understood. Economic conditions such as recessions and high rates of unemployment appear to be only remotely and indirectly related to criminal behaviour and crime rates.

A discussion of offender typologies suggests that although such categories are valuable for distinguishing patterns and similarities among offenders and crime categories, they must be used cautiously because they oversimplify reality and fail to demonstrate the rich diversity that exists in the criminal world. In particular, any portrayal of offenders must recognize that criminals engage in a variety of offences and few specialize in one type of crime throughout their criminal career. Research also shows that a small proportion of career criminals are hardened recidivists who are responsible for a high proportion of street crimes such as robbery.

Even though people may be affected by criminogenic forces such as poverty, relative deprivation, discrimination, blocked opportunities, dysfunctional families, communities that are crime-ridden and socially disorganized, and delinquent and criminal associates, individuals can still make decisions about crime. Rational choice theory examines the decision-making processes of robbers, portrays criminal behaviour as the outcome of choices, and assumes that the decisions made by offenders exhibit limited or bounded rationality. Although criminals operate with incomplete knowledge and are subject to various constraints and criminal influences, their actions still contain elements of rationality, given the contingencies they must face and the subjective way in which they view their world.

A review of the literature on robbery emphasizes how the money motive takes precedence but secondary motives include excitement, status, power, and a mood of fatalism. An analysis of the motivation of 80 bank robbers indicates that the attraction to bank robbery is based on the cash available along with the perceived ease of committing the crime. About one-third of bank robbers in the sample originate the idea to rob a bank from media reports/portrayals of this crime. Note-pushers in particular are attracted to bank robbery because they perceive it to be nonviolent, impersonal, fast, easy, and a low-risk means of solving financial problems. The media appear to influence motivation indirectly through portrayals of bank robbers as glamorous and daring adventurers. Media reports are also found to influence the planning and modus operandi of the majority of these men. Consistent with differential association theory, half the bandits in this study are initiated into bank robbery through criminal associates who also provide the rationale, partners, and knowledge about modus operandi. Interactions that bandits maintain in their daily lives are important in making criminal associations and this is influenced by the social and economic environments in which they live. Although most offenders are out of work prior to committing their first robbery, they already have a history of criminal involvement, few are looking for work, and few blame unemployment for their drift into robbery. Bandits report instead that they choose to rob in part because they wish to maintain or regain their financial independence. Bank robbery is viewed as a risk worth taking since they believe that the variables are known and can be controlled. The motivation to continue is related to increasing self-confidence due to initial success combined with extravagant spending habits. Most bandits spend quickly and foolishly on hedonistic pursuits that include alcohol, drugs, gambling, and partying. The reason for robbing again is frequently a desire to continue the lifestyle. Research indicates that for career criminals, the decision to eventually leave crime relates to the fear of further incarceration along with increasing involvement in conventional activities and relationships.

Modus operandi involves selecting a target, planning the score, confronting the victim, controlling resistance, acquiring the money, and making one's getaway. Most offenders develop and maintain the same modus operandi throughout their usually brief robbery escapade. Significant decisions include whether to use a weapon; to do it alone or with partners; and to commit the holdup discreetly or use a commando-style attack. A significant concern is the risk of getting caught and the possibility of resistance and violence. Most robbers have no wish to harm anyone but some have clearly demonstrated a willingness to use whatever force is required to obtain the money. Almost all subjects in the present study are willing to use violence against bystanders who would attempt to stop them. Chapter Four provides detailed descriptions of the M.O. of note-pushers, bank robbery crews, solo gunmen, and men who rob armoured vehicles and armed guards.

Lifestyle-exposure and routine activities theories attempt to explain how certain lifestyles and daily routines bring individuals into situations, places, and contacts with potential offenders that increase the risk of victimization. Ecological theories of crime discuss "hot spots" of criminal victimization and shed light on the high rate of robberies in specific locales and experienced by certain commercial establishments. Research largely supports the common-sense belief that it is wise to cooperate with armed bandits and not resist their attempts to steal. Although the emotional trauma to victims of robbery is easily observable, there have been few studies that document the extent to which long-term disability results. Chapter Five includes a discussion of practical steps that can be taken by commercial and retail outlets to harden themselves against would-be robbers, deter holdups, and prevent injuries to staff and customers.

Chapter Six, Police and Judicial Response, describes how robberies come to the attention of the police, the convergence of patrol officers on the scene, and the follow-up investigation. Most holdups are handled by detectives in the criminal investigation branch or the Hold-Up Squad of larger cities. Since robbery is a crime that is frequently repeated using the same modus opearndi, files are used to organize robberies according to M.O. and link offenders to their crimes once they have been arrested. The present study found that bank robbers are most often caught through informants, police dragnets, and the assistance of bank camera photos, victims, and witnesses. Proactive policing includes surveillance of suspected offenders and bank stakeouts and resulted in about 15 percent of the arrests. The fact that half of all arrests occurred through direct victim/witness assistance and a third through informants testifies to the significance of these variables. The present study reports on the forceful reputation of Hold-Up Squads among robbers and their attempts to deter violent robberies, out-of-town robbers, and to gain evidence that will convict and incarcerate offenders. The study also reveals the role of the police in pre-trial negotiations, the limited gains that bandits obtain from plea bargaining, and the lengthy sentences imposed by the courts.

CRIME, ROBBERY, AND SOCIAL POLICY

It is not unreasonable to ask whether a high level of crime is inevitable and a necessary price for a society that promotes individualism, competition, and financial success. It appears quite obvious that Robert Merton (1938) was correct when he observed that the ruthless pursuit of profits creates a criminogenic society. When society's value system glorifies wealth, when people are exposed daily to opulent lifestyles through the media, when government policy encourages everyone to concern themselves with making money, is society not creating pressures on people to use illegitimate means to obtain wealth if they cannot do so legitimately? Should we be surprised when citizens turn to crime as a shortcut or as their only avenue to material success? The theories discussed in this text suggest that a certain degree of crime is normal and inevitable. These same theories also suggest, however, that social policies can diminish crime and lessen its impact on victims. Given what we know about the factors that influence robbery behaviour, what can we do about it? Suggestions for dealing with robbery include the following: limiting opportunities through target-hardening; declare a war on illicit drugs; ameliorate societal conditions that are linked to crimes of theft and violence; limit criminal access to guns; enhance the security of public places; provide more proactive policing; add greater resources to those vulnerable to robbery; and deter and incapacitate offenders through lengthy prison terms.

As discussed in Chapter Five, opportunity theory suggests that a direct way of deterring robbery is through the use of target-hardening techniques that reduce possible gains and increase the risks of apprehension. One approach to crime prevention is to assist potential victims of robbery to reduce their vulnerability. Targeting the routine activities of citizens and business persons that are potentially hazardous can remove the opportunity for crime. This might be done with police assistance through organizations that already exist among commercial and financial establishments, through insurance firms that cover losses due to robbery, and with the assistance of the media and public educational institutions.

A common proposal for crime prevention is to reduce some of the correlates of robberies such as alcohol and drug addiction. Alcohol is clearly related to a variety of social problems and violent events including murder and robbery (Silverman and Kennedy, 1993). Yet when we acknowledge the carnage that occurs on our roads due to alcohol-related motor-vehicle accidents, it is clear that society is unwilling to substantially restrict alcohol use or its tax revenues because some persons abuse it. The use of illicit drugs is also linked directly and indirectly to other criminal activity and any success in diminishing the availability and consumption of drugs is likely to affect the robbery rate. Many theories suggest, however, that an attack on illicit drugs requires an attack on the social conditions that give rise to drug abuse and other crimes.

Two broad and conflicting positions exist with respect to policies dealing with crime control. Some view the root cause of crime as the economic and social conditions that create a disadvantaged underclass. Liberal criminologists believe that crime occurs as a result of social and economic conditions that frustrate, demoralize, and embitter people. Their approach to crime prevention requires that society confront and ameliorate the negative social conditions that affect potential offenders such as racism and discrimination, inadequate educational and job opportunities, poverty, social disorganization, dysfunctional families, and poor housing and living conditions. Conservative theorists, on the other hand, argue that social policy initiatives cannot alter crime since criminal conduct is a result of individual characteristics or stems from the decline in personal morality rather than from flaws in the economic and social structure. Offenders are seen as responsible for their actions and deserving of harsh punishment that itself serves as a means of protecting society by deterring others.

Theorists who advocate the mobilization and redistribution of resources to potential offenders point to social conditions that give rise to crime and assume that criminal conduct can be prevented. In advocating an interventionist social policy for crime prevention, Elliot Currie writes:

> If we are serious about attacking the roots [of crime]... we must build a society that is less unequal, less depriving, less insecure, less disruptive of community ties, less corrosive of cooperative values. In short, we must begin to take on the enormous task of creating the conditions of community life in which individuals can live together in compassionate and cooperative ways (1985:225–26).

Despite their differences, both anomie and conflict theories suggest that policies that reduce structural inequality will reduce crime. Liberal theorists advocate broadly based changes to the social structure that decrease the gap between rich and poor and increase economic opportunities for the less privileged members of society. Also advocated are generous social welfare benefits to those in need, better housing, an improved schooling system, and neighbourhood and community improvements. Social control theory also suggests that policies that strengthen family and community bonds and alleviate social disorder should reduce crime. Basic institutions such as the economy, family, schools, and religion, are the primary crime control forces in society. The impact of the police on crime is seen as marginal in relation to these more fundamental institutions. Thornberry (1987), for instance, argues that delinquent behaviour causes a deterioration in attachment and commitment to family and school, which further erodes the restraints on delinquency. Family interventions that improve attachments to parents should also indirectly improve commitment to school, thereby making the efforts of teachers more effective. He suggests that family interventions should start early since parental control of children weakens as they become adolescents. In addition, schools should attempt to make the classroom experience during the early years enjoyable, to diminish feelings of alienation and to reduce peer control of adolescents before they drift into delinquency (Thornberry et al., 1991). Efforts to improve economic conditions and alleviate social disorder will not be easy, inexpensive, nor do they promise immediate results. The lessons to be learned from sociological theory and research, however, tell us that governments cannot combat crime effectively by ignoring the social and economic conditions that lead to violence in general and robbery in particular.

Another approach to dealing with robbery and other crimes of violence is to legislate the ownership and use of firearms. The argument in favour of gun control is that it reduces the opportunity of potential offenders to obtain access to lethal weapons. Research, however, has found no direct correlation between legislative change and use of weapons. Mundt (1990), for example, found that restrictive Canadian gun control legislation passed in 1977 has had little effect on the overall rates of violence. Despite this finding, Mundt speculates that the legislation may have at least slowed the rise of violence that might have happened in its absence. Restrictive gun laws also have an educational function since they symbolize society's stand against violence and emphasize how gun ownership is potentially dangerous.

Some theorists suggest that community settings have a powerful influence on behaviour and that crime prevention can be achieved through environmental design of residential and public places that deter crime by creating "defensible space" (Newman, 1973; Stark, 1987). Housing designed to allow residents to notice and identify strangers and encourage neighbours to interact has been found to reduce crime in English public-housing areas (Baldwin, 1979). Public transportation systems have also been designed to reduce criminal victimization. A study of Hong Kong's Mass Transit Railway (MTR) (Gaylord and Galliher, 1991) describes how architects consulted with the police and MTR security to incorporate crime-proofing features. Subway stations have mirrors and closed-circuit television, and were built with few alcoves, columns, and other possible hiding places for potential assailants. Glass partitions in subway cars allow passengers to observe what is happening throughout the train and to use the alarms to call for assistance; train operators maintain contact with security; and security officers can quickly seal exits to prevent offenders from escaping. Besides their potential for reducing victimization, environmental and ecological approaches to crime prevention are likely to produce additional dividends by reducing fear of crime and promoting a sense of personal safety within the community.

HEIST DEATH RE-OPENS GUN DEBATE

TORONTO (CP)—The gun-control controversy is raging anew in the wake of this week's slaying of Roger Pardy, co-owner of a sporting-goods store in Oshawa.

David Tomlinson, president of the National Firearms Association, said four people have been killed in gunstore robberies in the last year in Canada—two in a British Columbia holdup, one in Edmonton, and, now, 43-year-old Pardy.

"And what the hell do you expect? What the government does with its gun-control law is give a criminal an absolute guarantee of his personal safety while he is robbing and murdering," Tomlinson said from Edmonton.

Gun-control advocates were appalled by Tomlinson's remarks.

Dr. Perry Kendall, Toronto's chief public-health official, said it's ridiculous for gun lobbyists to suggest the solution to violent crime is to arm shopkeepers "so they can blow (robbers) away."

Pardy was killed and three others injured when two armed robbers entered Pardy's store, Gagnon Sports, and told the 12 people inside that it was a holdup.

A few moments later, the two men opened fire, hitting four victims. They stole some guns and ran from the store, Durham Region police said.

A sign outside Gagnon Sports bears the message: Crime Control/No Gun Control.

"When you actually need protection, there is not going to be a cop around," said Tomlinson.

His views disturb Wendy Cukier, a professor at Ryerson University and president of the Coalition for Gun Control.

"One of the concerns I have is that the National Firearms Association is saying what we need is for everyone to have a gun in their store, so robbers won't dare come in," Cukier said.

"We have a sizable number of robberies, but robbers do not generally kill their victims," Cukier said. "But if they, the robbers, anticipate that people will be armed, they will just shoot and ask questions later."

She said cameras would be a more effective deterrent than armed shopkeepers.

The role of the police in combatting crime is clearly significant. One crime-fighting strategy involves the police focusing on "hot spots" of crime where robberies and other acts of violence regularly occur. Police maintain a visible presence in the area, stopping and questioning suspicious persons, targeting local criminal gangs, gathering information and intelligence on suspected offenders, using stakeouts on high-risk targets, working with government and community organizations to install lighting, cut down underbrush, or make other physical changes to the setting that make locations less vulnerable to surprise attacks and robbery. Research indicates that police resources deployed on "hot spots" can be successful and do not necessarily displace potential offenders to other locations (Sherman et al., 1989). There is also evidence to show that aggressive and proactive policing can affect robbery rates citywide. From 1976 to 1981, for example, bank holdups in Montreal averaged 600 to 700 incidents a year on some 600 bank branches. At that time, Montreal was known as the bank robbery capital of North America. In 1982, however, a reorganized Hold-Up Squad, along with the assistance of bank security personnel devoted greater resources to the problem, staked out robbery-prone banks, placed suspected offenders under surveillance, and pressured the courts for harsh sentences. Bank robberies dropped by almost half in one year, from 648 in 1981 to 336 in 1982 and maintained low levels through 1983 (365 incidents) and 1984 (270 bank holdups) (Ballard, 1985). These results indicate that a combination of specialized and proactive policing in cooperation with organizations that are targeted by robberies, along with harsh, deterrent and incapacitative prison sentences can significantly reduce holdups.

A more recent attempt by the police to combat crime involves a cooperative and consultative approach with the community. Community-based policing aims to enlist citizens and local organizations to assist in their own protection. Community-based policing asks for citizen assistance in crime prevention, educates individuals and groups on steps they can take to better protect themselves and their neighbours, and creates positive relationships with the police that pay dividends in citizen cooperation with investigations and the prosecutions of offenders.

What does sociology have to say about the efforts made by psychiatrists, psychologists, and social workers to rehabilitate offenders through counselling and therapy? A sociological orientation would argue that psychologically based theories will never be adequate as a basis for social policy since social work and psychological models tend to ignore factors external to individuals, families, and groups. Counselling is not likely to significantly affect offenders who have been raised in criminogenic conditions, influenced by criminal and delinquent associates, subjected to alienating and frustrating school experiences, and who have few social or family bonds, job skills, or employment opportunities. Although some prison programs may help individuals to deal with problems such as substance abuse and addictions, unless factors that influence the structure of society can be modified, efforts at a psychological level are not likely to be effective.

Principles of Sentencing
in Robbery Cases

One of the most significant and visible approaches to dealing with crime is through the sentencing of convicted offenders in our criminal courts. Three major principles of sentencing are discussed including rehabilitation, deterrence, and incapacitation.

REHABILITATION

Rehabilitative sentences are generally lenient, allow offenders to remain in the community, and aim to help criminals terminate their involvement in crime. Absolute and conditional discharges and probation are rehabilitative sentences and are usually reserved for first offenders who do not represent a serious threat to the community. Persons who commit robbery are not often considered for rehabilitative sentences because most have past criminal records and their crime is considered serious and threatening. The protection of the community is given priority. A prison sentence is not considered rehabilitative because it requires effective programs for modifying the behaviour of individual offenders, a task that has proved difficult to achieve (Lipton et al., 1975; Martinson, 1974). Only one bank robber in this sample avoided a prison sentence. His case was exceptional in that the crime was spontaneous, alcohol was involved, there was no violence, he turned himself in, expressed deep remorse for his actions, did not have a prior criminal record, and perhaps received sympathy from the sentencing judge since he suffered from physical disabilities.

DETERRENCE THEORY

There has been much debate about the usefulness of various forms of punishment and their severity in deterring crime. Discussions have often focused on the use of the law and criminal-justice system to diminish robbery and limit the potential for violence through harsh sentences. Deterrence involves efforts to change people's behaviours through the use of legal penalties handed out by the courts. Deterrence theory views the offender as a rational person who will be deterred from committing crime by a rational assessment of the risks and costs of legal sanctions.

Since research has cast serious doubt on the rehabilitative aspirations and goals of the criminal justice system over the past few decades, the argument for punishment as a way of deterring crime has gained increasing prominence. Though crime rates continue to rise, it is nonetheless assumed that many criminals are deterred by the threat of criminal sanctions. Even though lengthy prison sentences are routinely imposed and justified by our courts as a deterrent to future crime, some critics are unconvinced that long sentences deter offenders (Fattah, 1976; Fattah, 1982). The experience of the United States is often cited as proof of the failure of a deterrence policy. The rise in violent crime there has led to a "get tough" position on crime yet rates of violent crime continue to climb regardless of tough sentencing policies.

The punishments meted out by the courts should deter if they are judged by their severity. In Canada and the United States, robbery is punishable by life imprisonment and 20 years respectively. Gabor and Normandeau (1989:203) note that about 90 percent of those convicted for robbery in Canada receive a prison sentence. Haran and Martin (1977:29) similarly note that 25 percent of federal prisoners are convicted bank robbers and that about 80 percent of men convicted of bank robbery received prison sentences and 80 percent of these received prison sentences of five years or more. Bank robbers in the present study also received harsh penitentiary sentences averaging approximately nine years each. It appears, therefore, that upon conviction, the certainty of a stiff response by the courts is quite high. Long prison sentences for robbery are the norm and are frequently justified in part by the need to protect the community through deterrence. The sentencing judge has few alternatives to heavy prison sentences for robbery since the crime is defined as a serious offence and a grave danger to the community. Deterrent sentencing has two components: specific deterrence sends a message to the convicted offender—commit further crimes and you'll spend many more years in prison; general deterrence is a harsh sentence given to one offender but meant as a message to other would-be criminals to think twice before embarking on a robbery career. Deterrent sentences are frequently criticized as unjust since they impose a heavy penalty on one person to deter another. Bank robbers in this study, for instance, define their crimes less seriously than our Canadian courts and see themselves as undeserving of the heavy jail sentences they received. The harsh treatment is unexpected and criticized by offenders who cry foul when they compare the time they're serving against that imposed on other criminals. A man serving 10 life sentences on his third conviction for bank robbery asks the question:

> I know I've done wrong but what did I do wrong? Ten life sentences! That's a long time. For what? The way I rob a bank, it's so simple that, you know, I wouldn't even consider myself a criminal. I'm not robbing an everyday guy on the street.

Haran and Martin (1984) similarly note that bank robbers in their study frequently express a sense of injustice over their prison sentences in comparison with the time being served by other offenders for a variety of crimes.

Deterrent sentences operate on at least two basic assumptions: (1) offenders will recognize the risk of serving long periods of incarceration; and (2) they will refrain from these crimes because they fear the consequences. But how do offenders become aware of the risks and does this deter them from involvement in robbery? The effectiveness of deterrence sentences is difficult to research and is highly controversial. Haran and Martin's study of bank robbers (1977:29–30) indicates that offenders seem unaware of the odds and unconcerned about the risks and penalties. There is an enormous gap between the beliefs and assumptions under which robbers operate and the punitive philosophy of the criminal justice system. Most are surprisingly oblivious to the fact that robbery can land them behind bars for years. They suggest that there is little that can be done to reach the potential bank robber because such persons constitute such a random group as to be almost unreachable: youthful males, unattached, blacks, lower social class, unemployed, high-school dropouts, with no vocational skills, and a third of them addicted to opiate drugs. "As a group they have moved beyond the influence of such socialization agencies as family, school, and religion. They represent the offshoot of a structural societal problem which is far beyond the ability of the courts or the correctional components of the criminal justice system to handle" (1984:53). Despite such reservations, Haran and Martin suggest that in some respects, deterrence appears to work. The number of bank robberies across the United States remains relatively small and old-time professional criminals have moved away from robbing banks because it is too hazardous. "The pros are deterred from robbing banks because they know they will end up in prison for many years with little chance of parole. Current bank robbers appear to be a new breed that hasn't gotten the word" (1977:30). In Canada too, serious criminals have moved away from this crime and been replaced in large part by the relatively amateurish note-pusher. Whether this is because of deterrence, however, is questionable. Bank robbery is no longer the lucrative crime it once was, whereas drug dealing offers far better opportunities for career criminals.

Research findings on the decision-making process of robbers have implications for deterrent sentences. The fact that even the most active holdup artists do relatively little planning and rarely think about getting caught clearly weakens the argument that deterrence is an appropriate strategy for controlling robbery. Steep penalties are unlikely to deter those who believe they will not be caught. It is still possible, however, that the fear of severe penalties may deter some would-be robbers but not others. The fact that some offenders leave the bullets out of their guns because of the possible penalties, Feeney suggests, is evidence that they do worry about penalties (1986:70). It is widely recognized that as offenders age, they eventually desist in their criminal involvement. This might indicate that older offenders who have done time develop a fear of a lengthy prison sentence. Deterrence may work on persons who have served many years while at the same time be ineffective for youthful and inexperienced criminals.

Offenders' source of beliefs about getting caught is important in the study of deterrence because it gives some indication of the ways in which the probability of capture is communicated. As discussed in Chapter Three on motivation, offenders view robbery as a low-risk crime. Thus, the possibility of getting caught and receiving a heavy prison term is not part of the equation when offenders consider committing a robbery. It seems apparent that for deterrent sentences to work, potential robbers need to be informed of the realities of the crime with its small proceeds, high arrest rates, and long jail sentences. Perhaps an extensive media campaign that advertises the high risk and harsh penalties attached to robbery might deter some offenders. Effective deterrence might be achieved by advertising just how many robbers actually get caught and how high the risk of robbery actually is. A strategy of publicizing the high risk and harsh sentences for robbery will have little deterrent effect, however, if the message does not reach or is ignored by potential offenders. How do you get the message across to the population of young, lower socioeconomic-class males who commit most robberies? Even if the message reaches the desired audience, the self-destructive attitude of many recidivists effectively neutralizes any deterrence that the threat of arrest and imprisonment may have. Many offenders are down and out, have low self-concepts, few job prospects or job skills, minimal work experience, and little motivation. They simply drift into robbery as the route of least resistance. A despairing, defeatist attitude is common in inmates who were recently released from prison and is particularly evident with offenders who are on the run. In addition, many bank robbers say the deterrent effect of imprisonment is substantially diminished once it has been experienced. Arrest and imprisonment are not feared—partly because they have served time before and they know they can handle it. Prison is viewed as nothing more than an employment hazard and many are undeterred by the risk.

It is clear from this discussion that the deterrence value of court sentences is highly questionable. Yet it is also clear that there are limits on what types of behaviours society can tolerate. It would be foolishly naive to assume that any modern society could operate without criminal law, a criminal justice system, and legal sanctions on criminal conduct. Although we may disagree on the punishment for particular crimes, there is nonetheless agreement that the threat of arrest and imprisonment does deter some, but not all potential robbers. The validity of this assumption is best illustrated by the dramatic increase in crime whenever the police go on strike. A 17-day strike by 86 percent of the police force in Finland in February 1976 resulted in a 50 percent increase in some robberies (Makinen and Takala, 1980). Similarly, a 17-hour Montreal police strike in October 1969 resulted in 50 times the normal hourly rate of bank robberies along with widespread looting (Clark, 1969).

INCAPACITATION

While there is no definitive answer to the efficacy of deterrent sentences, what is certain is that offenders are incapacitated by imprisonment. In the 1980s, the Rand Corporation study claimed that the U.S. crime rate could be significantly reduced if a small proportion of highly active criminals were incapacitated through incarceration. The Chaikens (1984) extended the Rand Corporation study by identifying a subset of offenders whom they called "violent predators." These men represented 15 percent of their sample and had committed a combination of robberies, assaults, and drug offences. "Violent predators" averaged less than 23 years of age when first incarcerated; had been committing serious and violent crimes for at least six years; and had significantly more arrests than other offenders. Moreover, they had spent considerable time in juvenile facilities; were likely to have had their parole revoked; and were unlikely to have been regularly employed, married, or to have family obligations. Both the Rand Corporation and the Chaikens' study demonstrate how a small proportion of the criminal population is responsible for a very large portion of the total amount of crimes committed.

The policy implications from this are clear: if we can identify and incarcerate high-risk offenders, we could substantially reduce crime and increase the protection of the public. Even if lengthy jail sentences do not deter, they certainly incapacitate offenders during their stay. The argument can be made that since holdups are committed by a very small number of persons, lengthy prison sentences will have a marked reduction in the robbery rate. The concept of a career criminal supports incapacitative sentences since it assumes that certain criminals are frequent offenders, engage in crime for many years, and commit serious offences. The effectiveness of selective incapacitation assumes that there is continuity in criminal careers and that by incarcerating high-risk offenders for years, there will be a significant reduction of crimes in the community. The benefits of an incapacitation policy are measured in terms of crimes averted. The important research question from the viewpoint of policy, Blumstein et al. (1988:23) argue, is whether violent predators can be identified in the early stages of their careers before they have committed large numbers of crimes. Greenberg (1991) argues that we cannot accurately identify serious offenders until late in their career—a time at which they may have already decided to withdraw from crime. To the degree that desistence occurs and is unpredictable, a policy of preventive detention will have questionable effectiveness. Gottfredson and Hirschi (1986) are also sceptical that career criminals can be identified, and especially identified early enough to be useful for policy purposes. They argue that past criminal record is an imperfect predictor of future criminal record and that criminality declines more or less uniformly with age. This means that many offenders will be "over the hill" by the time they are old enough to be plausible candidates for preventive detention. The social and economic costs must also be considered. Lengthy sentences applied to all robbery offenders punish those who would re-offend along with those who may have learned their lesson. Thus if a criminal career ends early, the efficacy of incarceration in preventing crime is reduced.

Nevertheless, selective use of imprisonment as a sentencing philosophy has a certain appeal because of its apparent simplicity. The case for incapacitation is strengthened by the argument that incarceration controls both impulsive and calculating robbers (Feeney, 1986:70). Whereas specific deterrrence and rehabilitation programs attempt to intervene in ongoing criminal careers to achieve sustained behavioural changes in offenders, incapacitation, by contrast, reduces crime by simply isolating the offender from the community and thereby suspending the normal progress of his or her career (Blumstein et al., 1988:24). Incapacitation policies are targeted narrowly on identified offenders and do not require effective programs for modifying the behaviour of individual offenders. This distinguishes them from more broadly based and often multipurpose social, economic, and environmental policies directed at the larger general population, which have crime reduction as one of their aims. The narrow focus of incapacitation policies on removing offenders from the community makes them potentially easier to manage and control, and easier to evaluate (Blumstein et al., 1988:25).

Data from the present study support those who call for incapacitative sentences and other measures. It appears that the robbery rate could be reduced by restricting the number of offenders on mandatory supervision, parole, or free on bail while awaiting trial on other criminal charges. In addition, tighter security and improved correctional classification systems might help identify high-risk offenders who escape or walk away from prisons and halfway houses, or fail to return from temporary absences. As noted in Chapter Six, the present study found that at the time of their last arrest for robbery, 51/80 bandits were before the court on criminal charges or under sentence from previous offences. These data support the Hold-Up Squad's repeated claim that better control of these offenders would significantly reduce the robbery rate.

Despite the moral dilemmas and unproven efficacy of deterrent and incapacitative sentences, the police, criminal courts, victims of robbery, and a large segment of the public believe that lengthy prison terms are needed to reduce crime and protect society. Members of the Hold-Up Squad routinely attempt to obtain the longest sentences possible for robbery to deter and incapacitate offenders and thereby protect the public. In addition, the police seek to keep culprits in prison as long as possible and they oppose parole and other early-release programs for inmates. The National Parole Board is frequently criticized for undermining the benefits of incapacitative sentences by allowing hardened criminals into the community before having completed their sentences. Hold-Up Squad detectives cynically recount cases in which the offender was on parole or mandatory supervision when he committed his most recent robberies. In addition, the high number of repeat offenders is frequently cited as evidence that lengthy prison sentences are needed and justified to deter and incapacitate criminals and provide some measure of protection for the public. Hold-Up Squad officers have little faith in rehabilitative sentences for robbers.

CONCLUSION

Having described the variables associated with robbery, motivational components, and the theories that shed light on this activity, it has been possible to make some suggestions on how government policy-makers, the police, and individuals can work to reduce the robbery rate and personal vulnerability. Not addressed, however, are the social and financial costs of implementing robbery prevention procedures. Financial resources are significant considerations for government and taxpayers who must fund expensive social welfare and crime prevention programs. Given the limited budgets of public-sector organizations, decisions on how to allocate taxpayers' money are likely to occur in a political environment in which various interest groups compete. Governments, police, businesses, and social agencies have many priorities to consider besides the problem of robbery, which often pales in comparison to other social problems. Thus strategies and policies for the prevention and deterrence of robberies will be restricted by costs and competition by other social problems that require police and government resources. Costs are also relevant considerations to commercial and financial institutions. The banking community, for instance, could no doubt make their branches less vulnerable to robberies with armed guards, bullet-resistant glass, and controlled entrances, but they believe that a move to a fortress concept is unwarranted, costly, and presents a poor image to the public.

Suggestions about social policy based on sociological theories of crime should be examined cautiously and critically. Criminological research can show us correlations between robbery and various aspects of social structure but criminological theory cannot attribute cause directly to specific variables. Nor can we say with much confidence that policies suggested by sociological theories will have a major impact on crime. After all, sociologists themselves cannot agree on which factors are most significantly criminogenic and which policies are best. In addition, some of the broadly based changes advocated in the social and economic structure of society are difficult and expensive to produce and may not be politically feasible. And finally, even if society had the resources and the will to reduce the criminogenic pressures that arise from disparities in income and economic opportunities, there would still be crime. Disadvantaged social conditions are not the only factors contributing to crime, as is evident by the existence of corporate violations (Snider, 1993), employee theft, embezzlement, tax evasion, and other offences of the middle and upper classes.

REFERENCES

Abell, Peter Ed. 1991. *Rational Choice Theory*. Cambridge, MA.: University Press.

Akman, D.D., A. Normandeau, and S. Turner. 1967. "The Measurement of Delinquency in Canada." *The Journal of Criminal Law, Criminology, and Police Science* 58:330–37.

Baldwin, John. 1979. "Ecological and Areal Studies in Great Britain and the United States." In Norval Morris and Michael Tonry (eds.), *Crime and Justice: An Annual Review of Research*, Vol. 1. Chicago: University of Chicago Press.

Balkin, Steven. 1979. "Victimization Rate, Safety, and Fear of Crime." *Social Problems* 26:343–58.

Ball, John C., Lawrence Rosen, John A. Flueck, and David Nurco. 1981. "The Criminality of Heroin Addicts when Addicted and when off Opiates." In James A. Inciardi, ed. *The Drugs–Crime Connection*. Beverly Hills, California: Sage Publications.

Ball, John C., and Carl D. Chambers. 1970. *The Epidemiology of Heroin Use in the United States*. Springfield, IL: Charles C. Thomas.

Ballard, Michael. 1985. "On the Safe Side: Bank Robber 1984." *Canadian Banker*. April:36–37.

———. 1992. "Bank Robbery 1991." *Canadian Banker*. May–June:28–30.

———. 1993. "The Bad Guys Take a Break." *Canadian Banker*. May-June: 40–41.

———. 1994. "Holdup Review 1993." Canadian Banker's Association. Unpublished.

Becker, Gary S. 1968. "Crime and punishment: an economic approach." *Journal of Political Economy* 76(2):169–217.

Becker, Howard S. 1963. *Outsiders: Studies in the Sociology of Deviance*. New York: The Free Press.

Bennett, Trevor, and Richard Wright. 1984a. *Burglars on Burglary*. Brookfield, VT: Gower Publishing.

———. 1984b. "Constraints to Burglary: The Offender's Perspective." In Ronald Clarke and Tim Hope, eds. *Coping with Burglary*. Boston: Kluwer-Nijhoff Publishing.

Bernard, T.J. 1981. "The Distinction Between Conflict and Radical Criminology." *Journal of Criminal Law and Criminology* 71:362–79.

Biderman, A. 1967. "Surveys of Population Samples for Estimating Crime Incidence." *Annals of the American Academy of Political and Social Science* 374:16–33.

Blau, J.R., and P.M. Blau. 1982. "The Cost of Inequality: Metropolitan Structure and Violent Crime." *American Sociological Review* 47:114–29.

Block, Richard, Marcus Felson, and Carolyn R. Block. 1985. "Crime victimization rates for incumbents of 246 occupations." *Sociology and Social Research* 69:442–51.

Block, Richard. 1977. *Violent Crime*. Lexington, MA: Lexington Books.

———. 1989. "Victim-Offender Dynamics in Stranger to Stranger Violence: Robbery and Rape." In Ezzat A. Fattah, ed. *The Plight of Crime Victims in Modern Society*. London: The MacMillan Press.

Blumstein, Alfred, Jacqueline Cohen, and David P. Farrington. 1988. "Criminal Career Research: Its Value for Criminology." *Criminology* 26, no. 1:1–35.

Blumstein, Alfred, Jacqueline Cohen, and Paul Hsieh. 1982. *The Duration of Adult Criminal Careers*. Washington, D.C.: U.S. Department of Justice.

Blumstein, Alfred, Jacqueline Cohen, Jeffrey Roth, and Christy A. Visher (eds.). 1986. "Criminal Careers and Career Criminals," Vol. I. Report of the Panel on Research on Criminal Careers, National Research Council. Washington, D.C.: National Academy Press.

Boyd, Neil. 1995. *Canadian Law: An Introduction*. Toronto: Harcourt Brace & Company Canada.

Brantingham, Paul, and Patricia Brantingham. 1984. *Patterns in Crime*. New York: MacMillan.

Brown, Claude. 1965. *Manchild in the Promised Land*. New York: The Macmillan Company.

Bursik, Robert J., Jr. 1988. "Social Disorganization and Theories of Crime and Delinquency: Problems and Prospects." *Criminology* 26:519–52.

Burt, M.R., and B.L. Katz. 1985. "Rape, Robbery, and Burglary: Responses to Actual and Feared Victimization, with Special Focus on Women and the Elderly." *Victimology* 10:325–58.

Camp, George Mallery. 1968. *Nothing to Lose: A Study of Bank Robbery in America*. Ann Arbor, Michigan: Yale University Ph.D. Dissertation.

Cantor, David, and Kenneth C. Land. 1985. "Unemployment and Crime Rates in Post-World War II United States: A Theoretical and Empirical Analysis." *American Sociological Review* 50:317–32.

Caron, Roger. 1978. *Go Boy*. Toronto: McGraw-Hill Ryerson. 1985. *Bingo*. Agincourt: Methuen.

Carroll, John, and Frances Weaver. 1986. "Shoplifters' Perceptions of Crime Opportunities: A Process-Tracing Study." In Derek B. Cornish and Ronald V. Clarke, eds. *The Reasoning Criminal: Rational Choice Perspectives on Offending*. New York: Springer-Verlag.

Caroll, Leo, and Pamela Irving Jackson. 1983. "Inequality, Opportunity, and Crime Rates in Central Cities." *Criminology* 21:179.

Carter, C.L. 1978. "Is Your Bank a Soft Target?" *Security Management* 22:6–8.

Chaiken, Jan M., Michael W. Lawless, and Keith Stevenson. 1974. "Impact on Police Activity on Crime: Robberies on the New York City Subway System." Report No. R–1424–N.Y.C. Santa Monica, CA: Rand Corporation.

Chaiken, Marcia R., and Jan M. Chaiken. 1982. *Varieties of Criminal Behavior.* Santa Monica, Calif: Rand Corporation.

——. 1984. "Offender Types and Public Policy." *Crime and Delinquency* 30(2) (April):195–226.

——. 1990. "Drugs and Predatory Crime." In Michael Tonry and James Q. Wilson, eds. *Drugs and Crime* 13. Chicago: The University of Chicago Press.

Chambers, Carl D. 1974. "Narcotic addiction and crime: an empirical overview." In James A. Inciardi and Carl D. Chambers, eds., *Drugs and the Criminal Justice System.* Beverly Hills, CA: Sage Publications.

Chiricos, Theodore G. 1987. "Rates of Crime and Unemployment: An Analysis of Aggregate Research Evidence." *Social Problems* 34:187–207.

Ciale, Justin, and Jean-Pierre Leroux. 1983. "Armed Robbery in Ottawa: A Descriptive Case Study for Prevention." University of Ottawa: Department of Criminology.

Clark, Gerald. 1969. "What Happens When the Police Strike." *New York Times Magazine* (November 16), sec. 6: 45, 176–85, 187, 194–95.

Clarke, R.V., and G. McGrath. 1992. "Newspaper Reports of Bank Robberies and the Copycat Phenomenon." *Australian and New Zealand Journal of Criminology* 25:83–88.

Clarke, R., and D. Cornish. 1985. "Modelling offender's decisions: a framework for research and policy." In Michael Tonry and Norval Morris, eds. *Crime and Justice: An Annual Review of Research* 6, Chicago: University of Chicago Press.

Clarke, R.V.G. 1980. "Situational Crime Prevention: Theory and Practice." *British Journal of Criminology* 20:136–47.

Clarke, Ronald V. 1983. "Situational crime prevention: Its theoretical basis and practical scope." In Michael Tonry and Norval Morris, eds. *Crime and Justice* 4, Chicago: University of Chicago Press.

Clemente, Frank and Michael B. Kleiman. 1977. "Fear of Crime in the United States: A Multivariate Analysis." *Social Forces* 56:519–31.

Cohen, Lawrence E., and Marcus Felson. 1979. "Social change and crime rate trends: A routine activity approach." *American Sociological Review* 44:588–608.

Cohen, L.E., Kluegel, J.R., and Land, K.C. 1981. "Social Inequality and Predatory Criminal Victimization: An Exposition and Test of a Formal Theory." *American Sociological Review* 46:505–24.

Conklin, John E. 1972. *Robbery and the Criminal Justice System.* New York: J.B. Lippincott Company.

Cook, Philip J. 1976. "A strategic choice analysis of robbery." In Wesley G. Skogan, ed., *Sample Surveys of the Victims of Crime*. Cambridge, MA: Ballinger.

——. 1983. *Robbery in the United States: An Analysis of Recent Trends and Patterns*. Washington: U.S. Department of Justice.

——. 1986a. "Criminal Incapacitation Effects Considered in an Adaptive Choice Framework." In Derek B. Cornish and Ronald V. Clarke, eds. *The Reasoning Criminal: Rational Choice Perspectives on Offending*. New York: Springer-Verlag.

——. 1986b. "The Demand and Supply of Criminal Opportunities." In Michael Tonry and Norval Morris, eds. *Crime and Justice: An Annual Review of Research* 7, Chicago: University of Chicago Press.

Cornish, Derek B., and Ronald V. Clarke. 1986. *The Reasoning Criminal: Rational Choice Perspectives on Offending*. New York: Springer-Verlag.

——. 1987. "Understanding Crime Displacement: An Application of Rational Choice Theory." *Criminology* 25:933–47.

Criminal Code of Canada. 1994. *Martins Annual Criminal Code*. Aurora: Canada Law Books.

Crow, Wayman, J., and James L. Bull. 1975. *Robbery Deterrence: An Applied Behavioral Science Demonstration*. La Jolla, California: Western Behavioral Sciences Institute.

Currie, Elliot. 1985. *Confronting Crime*. New York: Pantheon Books.

Cusson, Maurice, and Pierre Pinsonneault. 1986. "The Decision To Give Up Crime." In Derek B. Cornish and Ronald V. Clarke, eds. *The Reasoning Criminal: Rational Choice Perspectives on Offending*. New York: Springer-Verlag.

DeBaun, E. 1950. *"The Heist: The Theory and Practice of Armed Robbery."* *Harpers* 200–69.

Downes, D., and P. Rock. 1988. *Understanding Deviance*, 2nd ed. Oxford: Clarendon Press.

Duffala, Dennis C. 1976. "Convenience Stores, Armed Robbery and Physical Environmental Features." *American Behavioural Scientist*.

Durkheim, Emile. 1933. *The Division of Labor in Society*. New York: The Free Press.

——. 1951. *Suicide*. New York: The Free Press.

Einstadter, Werner J. 1969. "The Social Organization of Armed Robbery." *Social Problems* 17:64–83.

Elliott, Delbert S., David Huizinga, and Suzanne S. Ageton. 1985. *Explaining Delinquency and Drug Use*. Beverly Hills, Calif.: Sage Publications.

Emerson, Joan P. 1970. "Nothing Unusual is Happening." In Tamotsu Shibutani, ed. *Human Nature and Collective Behavior*. Englewood Cliffs, N.J.: Prentice-Hall.

Ericson, Richard V. 1981. *Making Crime: A Study of Detective Work*. Toronto: Butterworth & Co.

Evans, John, and Alexander Himelfarb. 1992. "Counting Crime." In Rick Linden, ed. *Criminology*. Toronto: Harcourt Brace Jovanovich.

Farrington, David P. 1986. "Age and Crime" In Michael Tonry and Norval Morris, eds. *Crime and Justice: An Annual Review of Research* 7, Chicago: University of Chicago Press.

Fattah, Ezzat A. 1976. *Fear of Punishment: Deterrence*. Ottawa: Ministry of Supply and Services.

———. 1982. "Making the Punishment Fit the Crime: The Case of Imprisonment as a Retributative Sanction." *American Journal of Criminology* 24:1–11.

———. 1991. *Understanding Criminal Victimization*. Scarborough: Prentice-Hall.

Faupel, Charles E., and Carl B. Klockars. 1987. "Drug-Crime Connections: Elaborations from the Life Histories of Hard-Core Heroin Addicts." *Social Problems* 34:54–68.

Federal Bureau of Investigation. 1985. *Uniform Crime Reports—1962–1989*. Washington, D.C.: U.S. Department of Justice.

Feeney, Floyd, and Adrianne Weir. 1975. "The Prevention and Control of Robbery." *Criminology* 13:102–105.

Feeney, Floyd. 1986. "Robbers as Decision-Makers." In Derek B. Cornish and Ronald V. Clarke, eds. *The Reasoning Criminal: Rational Choice Perspectives on Offending*. New York: Springer-Verlag.

Felson, Marcus. 1986. "Linking Criminal Choices, Routine Activities, Informal Control and Criminal Outcomes." In Derek B. Cornish and Ronald V. Clarke, eds. *The Reasoning Criminal: Rational Choice Perspectives on Offending*. New York: Springer-Verlag.

———. 1987. "Routine Activities and Crime Prevention in the Developing Metropolis." *Criminology* 25, no. 4:911–32.

Fields, Allen, and James M. Walters. 1985. "Hustling: supporting a heroin habit." In Bill Hanson, George Beschner, James M. Walters and Elliott Bovelle, eds., *Life with Heroin: Voices from the Inner City*. Lexington, MA: Lexington Books.

Fox, James A. 1978. *Forecasting Crime Data*. Lexington, MA: Lexington Books.

Freeman, L. 1966. "No Response for the Cry of Help." In J. Ratcliffe, ed. *The Good Samaritan and the Law*. Garden City, N.Y.: Anchor Books.

Gabor, Thomas. 1981. "The crime-displacement hypothesis: An empirical examination." *Crime and Delinquency* 26:390–404.

Gabor, Thomas, and Andre Normandeau. 1989. "Armed Robbery: Highlights of a Canadian Study." *Canadian Police College Journal* 13(4):273–82.

Gabor, Thomas, Micheline Baril, Maurice Cusson, Daniel Elie, Marc Leb-
lanc, and Andre Normadeau. 1987. *Armed Robbery: Cops, Robbers, and
Victims*. Springfield Illinois: Charles C. Thomas Publisher.

Gardner, Carol Brooks. 1990. "Safe Conduct, Women, Crime, and Self in
Public Places." *Social Problems* 37:311–28.

Garofalo, J. 1986. "Lifestyles and Victimization: An Update." In E.A. Fattah, ed. *From Crime Policy to Victim Policy: Reorienting the Justice
System*. London: Macmillan.

Gaylord, Mark S., and John F. Galliher. 1991. "Riding the Underground
Dragon: Crime Control and Public Order on Hong Kong's Mass Transit
Railway." *British Journal of Criminology* 31:15–26.

Gibbons, Don C. 1979. *The Criminology Enterprise*. Englewood Cliffs, N.J.:
Prentice-Hall.

——. 1992. *Society, Crime, and Criminal Behaviour*, 6th ed. Englewood
Cliffs, N.J.: Prentice-Hall.

Goff, C., and N. Nason-Clark. 1989. "The Seriousness of Crime in Frederic-
ton, New Brunswick: Perceptions Toward White-Collar Crime."
Canadian Journal of Criminology 31(1):19–34.

Goffman, Erving. 1961. *Asylums*. Garden City, N.Y.: Anchor Books.

——. 1971. *Relations in Public*. New York: Harper & Row.

Gomme, Ian McDermid. 1993. *The Shadow Line: Deviance and Crime in
Canada*. Toronto: Harcourt Brace Jovanovich.

Gottfredson, Michael, and Travis Hirschi. 1986. "The True Value of
Lambda Would Appear To Be Zero: An Essay On Career Criminals,
Criminal Careers, Selective Incapacitation, Cohort Studies, And
Related Topics." *Criminology* 24, no. 2:212–33.

Gottfredson, M.R., and D. Gottfredson. 1988. *Decisionmaking in Criminal
Justice*, 2nd ed., New York: Plenum.

Green, Edward. 1970. "Race, Social Status, and Criminal Arrests." *American Sociological Review* 35:476–90.

Green, Gary S. 1987. "Citizen Gun Ownership and Criminal Deterrence:
Theory, Research, and Policy." *Criminology* 25, no. 1:63–81.

Greenberg, David F. 1979. "Delinquency and the Age Structure of Society."
In Sheldon Messinger and Egon Bittner, eds. *Criminology Review Year-
book*. Beverly Hills, Calif.: Sage Publications.

——. 1983. "Age and Crime." In Sanford H. Kadish, ed. *Encyclopedia of
Crime and Justice*. New York: Macmillan.

Greenberg, David F. 1991. "Modeling Criminal Careers." *Criminology* 29,
no. 1:17–44.

Hackler, James C. 1994. *Crime and Canadian Public Policy*. Scarborough:
Prentice-Hall.

Hagan, John. 1975. "Setting the Record Straight: Toward the Reformulation of an Interactionist Perspective in Deviance." *Criminology* 13:421–23.

———. 1985. *Modern Criminology: Crime, Criminal Behavior, and Its Control.* New York: McGraw Hill.

———. 1991. *The Disreputable Pleasures: Crime and Deviance in Canada,* 3rd ed., Toronto: McGraw-Hill Ryerson.

Hagan, John, A.R. Gillis, and J. Simpson. 1985. "The Class Structure of Gender and Delinquency: Toward a Power-Control Theory of Common Delinquent Behavior." *American Journal of Sociology* 90(6): 1151–78.

Hagan, John, J.H. Simpson, and A.R. Gillis. 1979. "The Sexual Stratification of Social Control: A Gender Based Perspective." *British Journal of Sociology* 30:25–38.

———. 1987. "Class in the Household: Deprivation, Liberation and a Power-Control Theory of Gender and Delinquency." *American Journal of Sociology* 92(4):788–816.

———. 1988. "Feminist Scholarship, Relational and Instrumental Control, and a Power-Control Theory of Gender and Delinquency." *British Journal of Sociology* 39(3):301–36.

Hansel, M.K. 1987. "Citizen Crime Stereotypes—Normative Consensus Revisited." *Criminology* 25:455–86.

Haran, James F., and John M. Martin. 1977. "The Imprisonment of Bank Robbers: The Issue of Deterrence." *Federal Probation* 41, no. 3:27–30.

———. 1984. "The Armed Urban Bank Robber: A Profile" *Federal Probation* 48:47–53.

Hartnagel, Timothy F. 1992. "Correlates of Criminal Behaviour." In Rick Linden, ed. *Criminology.* Toronto: Harcourt Brace Jovanovich.

Hartnagel, Timothy F., and G. Won Lee. 1990. "Urban Crime in Canada." *Canadian Journal of Criminology.* 32:591–606.

Hepburn, John R. 1977. "Social Control and the Legal Order: Legitimate Repression in a Capitalist State." *Contemporary Crises* 1(1):77–90.

Henshel, Richard L. 1983. "Police Misconduct in Metropolitan Toronto: A Study of Formal Complaints." Toronto: LaMarsh Research Program on Violence, York University.

Higgins, George V. 1971. *The Friends of Eddie Coyle.* New York: Alfred A. Knofp, Inc.

Hindelang, Michael J., Michael R. Gottfredson, and James Garofalo. 1978. *Victims of Personal Crime: An Empirical Foundation for a Theory of Personal Victimization.* Cambridge, MA: Ballinger Publishing Company.

Hindelang, Michael J. 1978. "Race and Involvement in Common Law Personal Crimes." *American Sociological Review* 43:93–109.

———. 1979. "Sex Differences in Criminal Activity." *Social Problems* 27:144–56.

Hirschi, Travis. 1969. *Causes of Delinquency.* Berkeley: University of California Press.

——. 1983. "Age and the Explanation of Crime." *American Journal of Sociology* 89:552–84.

——. 1985. "Age and Crime, Logic and Scholarship: Comment on Greenberg." *American Journal of Sociology* 9:22–27.

——. 1986. "On the Compatibility of Rational Choice and Social Control Theories of Crime." In Derek B. Cornish and Ronald V. Clarke, eds. *The Reasoning Criminal: Rational Choice Perspectives on Offending.* New York: Springer-Verlag.

Hough, J.M., and P. Mayhew. 1983. *The British Crime Survey: First Report* London: Home Office Research Study No. 76.

Inciardi, James A. 1979. "Heroin use and street crime." *Crime and Delinquency* 25:335–46.

Inciardi, James A. (Ed.). 1981. *The Drug-Crime Connection.* Beverly Hills: Sage Publications.

Irwin, John. 1970. *The Felon.* Englewood Cliffs, N.J.: Prentice-Hall.

Jacobs, Jerry, and Leslie Dopkeen. 1990. "Risking the Qualitative Study of Risk." *Qualitative Sociology* 13, no. 2:169–81.

Jacoby, Joseph E., Neil A. Weiner, Terence P. Thornberry, and Marvin E. Wolfgang. 1973. "Drug Use in a Birth Cohort." In *National Commission on Marijuana and Drug Abuse, Drug Use in America: Problem in Perspective.* Washington. D.C.: U.S. Government Printing Office.

Johnson, Eric, and John Payne. 1986. "The Decision to Commit a Crime: An Information-Processing Analysis. In Derek B. Cornish and Ronald V. Clarke, eds. *The Reasoning Criminal: Rational Choice Perspectives on Offending.* New York: Springer-Verlag.

Katz, Jack. 1988. *Seductions of Crime: Moral and Sensual Attractions in Doing Evil.* New York: Basic Books, Inc.

——. 1991. "The Motivation of the Persistent Robber." In Michael Tonry, ed. *Crime and Justice: A Review of Research* 14, Chicago: The University of Chicago Press.

Kempf, Kimberley L. 1987. "Specialization and the Criminal Career." *Criminology* 25, no. 2:399–420.

Kempf, Kimberley. 1986. "Offense Specialization: Does It Exist?" In Derek B. Cornish and Ronald V. Clarke, eds. *The Reasoning Criminal: Rational Choice Perspectives on Offending.* New York: Springer-Verlag.

Kennedy, L.W., and D.R. Forde. 1992. "Routine Activities and Crime: An Analysis of Victimization in Canada." *Criminology* 28(1):101–15.

Kilpatrick, D. 1985. "Survey Analysis Responses of Female Sex Assault Victims." *Crime Victims Digest* February: 9.

Kleck, Gary. 1988. "Crime Control Through the Private Use of Armed Forces." *Social Problems* 35:1–21.

Koenig, Daniel J. 1992. "Conventional Crime." In Rick Linden, ed. *Criminology.* Toronto: Harcourt Brace Jovanovich.

Kohfeld, Carol W., and John Sprague. 1988. "Urban Unemployment Drives Urban Crime." *Urban Affairs Quarterly* 24:215–44.

Lejeune, Robert, and Nicholas Alex. 1973. "On Being Mugged: The Event and its Aftermath." *Urban Life and Culture* 2:258–87.

Lejeune, Robert. 1977. "The Management of a Mugging." *Urban Life* 6:123–48.

Lemert, Edwin. 1951. *Social Pathology: A Systematic Approach to the Study of Sociopathic Behaviour.* New York: McGraw-Hill.

———. 1971. *Human Deviance, Social Problems, and Social Control,* 2nd ed. Englewood Cliffs, N.J.: Prentice-Hall.

Letkemann, Peter. 1973. *Crime as Work.* Englewood Cliffs, N.J.: Prentice-Hall, Inc.

Linden, Rick. 1992. "Social Control Theory." In Rick Linden, ed. *Criminology.* Toronto: Harcourt Brace Jovanovich.

Lipman, Ira J. 1975. *How to Protect Yourself from Crime.* New York: Atheneum.

Lipton, Douglas, Robert Martinson, and Judith Wilks. 1975. *The Effectiveness of Correctional Treatment: A Survey of Treatment Evaluation Studies.* New York: Praeger.

Liska, Allen E., and William Baccaglini. 1990. "Feeling Safe by Comparison: Crime in the Newspapers." *Social Problems* 37:360–74.

Loeber, Rolf, and Thomas Dishion. 1983. "Early Predictors of Male Delinquency: A Review." *Psychological Bulletin* 94:68–99.

Long, Sharon K., and Ann D. Witte. 1981. "Current economic trends: implications for crime and criminal justice." In Kevin N. Wright, ed. *Crime and Criminal Justice in a Declining Economy.* Cambridge, MA: Oelgeschlager, Gunn and Hain.

Luckenbill, David F. 1980. "Patterns of Force in Robbery." *Deviant Behavior: An Interdisciplinary Journal.* 1:361–378.

———. 1981. "Generating Compliance: The Case of Robbery." *Urban Life* 10:25–46.

MacDonald, John M. 1975. *Armed Robbery: Offenders and their Victims.* Springfield, Ill.: Charles C. Thomas.

Maguire, M., and T. Bennett. 1982. *Burglary in a Dwelling.* London: Heinemann.

Maguire, Mike. 1984. "Meeting the Needs of Burglary Victims." In Ronald Clarke and Tim Hope, eds. *Coping with Burglary.* Boston: Kluwer Nijhoff Publishing.

Maguire, Mike, and John Pointing eds. 1988. *Victims of Crime: A New Deal?* Philadelphia: Open University Press.

Makinen, Tuija, and Hannu Takala. 1980. "The 1976 Police Strike in Finland." *Scandinavian Studies in Criminology* 7:87–106.

Martinson, Robert. 1974. "What Works? Questions and Answers about Prison Reform." *Public Interest* 35:22–54.

Maurer, D.W. 1964. *Whiz Mob*. New Haven, Conn.: College and University Press.

Maxfield, M.G. 1987. "Lifestyle and Routine Activity Theories of Crime: Empirical Studies of Victimization, Delinquency and Offender Decision-Making." *Journal of Quantitative Crimonology* 3:275–82.

Mayhew, Patricia M. and Ronald V. Clarke, Andrew Sturman, and J.M. Hough. 1976. "Crime as Opportunity." *Home Office Research Study* 34. London: HMSO.

McClintock, F.H., and Evelyn Gibson. 1961. *Robbery in London*. London: MacMillan and Co., Ltd.

McDowall, David, and Colin Loftin. 1985. "Collective Security and Fatal Firearm Accidents." *Criminology* 23:401–16.

Merton, Robert K. 1938. "Social Structure and Anomie." *American Sociological Review* 3:672–82.

Meisenhelder, Thomas N. 1977. "An Exploratory Study of Exiting From Criminal Careers." *Criminology* 15:319–34.

Miethe, Terance. 1982. "Public Consensus on Crime Seriousness: Normative Structure or Methodological Artifact." *Criminology* 20:515–26.

Miethe, T.D., M.C. Stafford, and J.S. Long. 1987. "Social Differentiation in Criminal Victimization: A Test of Routine Activities/Lifestyle Theories." *American Sociological Review*.

Milton, Catherine H., Jeanne Halleck, James Lardner, and Gary Abrecht. 1977. *Police Use of Deadly Force*. Washington, D.C.: Police Foundation.

Misner, G., and W. McDonald. 1970. "The Scope of the Crime Problem and Its Resolution." Volume II of *Reduction of Robberies and Assaults of Bus Drivers*. Berkeley, CA: Stanford Research Institute and University of California.

Moffatt, R.E. 1983. "Crime Prevention Through Environmental Design: A Management Perspective." *Canadian Journal of Criminology*. 25:19–31.

Morris, Richard W. 1985. "Not the cause, nor the cure: self-image and control among inner city black male heroin users." In Bill Hanson, George Beschner, James M. Walters and Elliott Bovelle, eds. *Life with Heroin: Voices from the Inner City*. Lexington, MA: Lexington Books.

Mulvihill, J., M.M. Tumin, and L.A. Curtis. 1969. *Crimes of Violence*. Washington, D.C.: Government Printing Office.

Mundt, R.J. 1990. "Gun Control and Dates of Firearm Violence in Canada and the United States." *Canadian Journal of Criminology* 32(1):137–54.

Newman, Oscar. 1973. Architectural Design for Crime Prevention. Washington, D.C.: U.S. Government Printing Office.

Newman, O. 1972. *Crime Prevention Through Urban Design: Defensible Space*. New York: Macmillan.

——. 1980. *Community of Interest*. Garden City, N.Y.: Anchor Press/Doubleday.

Normandeau, Andre. 1966. "The Measurement of Delinquency in Montreal." *The Journal of Criminal Law, Criminology, and Police Science*. 57:172–77.

——. 1968. *Trends and Patterns in Crimes of Robbery*. Ph.D. Dissertation, Philadelphia: University of Pennsylvania.

——. 1972. "Violence and Robbery: A Case Study." *Acta Criminologica* 5:13–93.

O'Donnell, John A. 1966. "Narcotic addiction and crime." *Social Problems* 13:374–85.

Orsagh, Thomas. 1980. "Unemployment and crime: an objection to professor Brenner's view." *Journal of Criminal Law and Criminology* 71:181–83.

Ozenne, Tim. 1974. "The Economics of Bank Robbery." *Journal of Legal Studies* 3:19–51.

Parton, David, and John Stratton. 1984. *Components of Seriousness*. Paper Presented at the Annual Meetings of the Midwest Sociological Society (as referenced in Hansel, 1987).

Petersilia, Joan, Peter W. Greenwood, and Marvin Lavin. 1978. *Criminal Careers of Habitual Felons*. Washington, D.C.: U.S. Government Printing Office: Rand Corporation.

Petersilia, Joan. 1980. "Criminal Career Research: A Review of Recent Evidence." In Norval Morris and Michael Tonry, eds. *Crime and Justice: An Annual Review of Research* 2:321–79. Chicago: University of Chicago Press.

Phillips, David P. 1974. "The influence of Suggestion on Suicide: Substantive and Theoretical Implications of the Werther Effect." *American Sociological Review* 39:340–54.

——. 1979. "Suicide, Motor Vehicle Fatalities, and the Mass Media: Evidence Toward a Theory of Suggestion." *American Journal of Sociology* 84:1150–74.

——. 1983. "The Impact of Mass Media Violence on U.S. Homicides." *American Sociological Review* 88:560–68.

Post, Richard. 1972. *Combating Crime Against Small Business*. Springfield: Charles C. Thomas Publisher.

Poyner, Barry. 1983. *Design Against Crime: Beyond Defensible Space*. London: Butterworth.

Radford, Jill. 1987. "Policing Male Violence—Policing Women." In Jalna Hammer and Mary Maynard, eds., *Women, Violence and Social Control*. Atlantic Highlands N.J.:Humanities.

Radzinowicz, Leon, and Joan King. 1977. *The Growth of Crime: The International Experience*. London: Cox and Wyman.

Reid, Stephen. 1986. *Jackrabbit Parole*. Toronto: McClelland and Stewart-Bantam Limited.

Reiss, Albert J., Jr. 1988. "Co-offending and Criminal Careers." In Michael Tonry and Norval Morris *Crime and Justice: A Review of Research*. Chicago: University of Chicago Press.

Reiss, A. 1971. *The Police and the Public*. New Haven: Yale University Press.

Reiss, A. J., and M. Tonry. 1986. *Communities and Crime*. Chicago: University of Chicago Press.

Repetto, Thomas A. 1976. "Crime Prevention and the Displacement Phenomenon." *Crime and Delinquency* 22:166–77.

Riger, Stephanie, and Margaret T. Gordon. 1981. "The Fear of Rape: A Study in Social Control." *Journal of Social Issues* 37:71–92.

Robins, Lee N., and George E. Murphy. 1967. "Drug use in a normal population of young Negro men." *American Journal of Public Health* 570:1580–96.

Roebuck, J.B. 1967. *Criminal Typology*. Springfield: Thomas.

Rossi, P.H., E. Waite, C. Bose, and R.E. Berk. 1974. "The Seriousness of Crimes: Normative and Individual Differences." *American Sociological Review* 39:224–37.

Sacco, Vincent F., and Holly Johnson. 1990. *Patterns of Criminal Victimization in Canada*. Ottawa: Statistics Canada (Housing, Family and Social Statistics Division), Minister of Supply and Services Canada.

Sacco, Vincent F. 1988. *Deviance: Conformity and Control in Canadian Society*. Scarborough: Prentice-Hall.

Sacco, Vincent F., and Leslie W. Kennedy. 1995. *The Criminal Event*. Scarborough: Nelson Canada.

Sanders, W. 1977. *Detective Work*. New York: Free Press.

Sellin, Thorsten, and Marvin W. Wolfgang. 1964. *The Measuring of Delinquency*. New York: John Wiley & Sons.

Shapland, J., J. Willmore, and P. Duff. 1985. *Victims in the Criminal Justice System*. Aldershot: Gower.

Shaw, Clifford R. 1930. *The Jack-Roller*. Chicago: The University of Chicago Press.

Sherman, L.W., P. Gartin, and M.E. Buerger. 1989. "Hot Spots of Predatory Crime: Routine Activities and the Sociology of Place." *Criminology* 27:27–55.

Sherman, Lawrence W. 1992. "Attacking Crime: Police and Crime Control." In Michael Tonry and Norval Morris, eds. Chicago: University of Chicago Press. *Modern Policing: Crime and Justice Review* 15: 159–230.

Short, James, and Fred Strodbeck. 1965. *Group Process and Gang Delinquency.* Chicago: University of Chicago Press.

Shover, Neil. 1989. "The Later Stages of Ordinary Property Offender Careers." In Delos H. Kelly, ed. *Deviant Behavior: A Text-Reader in the Sociology of Deviance*, 3rd ed. New York: St. Martin's Press.

Shrager, Laura, and James Short. 1980. "How Serious is Crime? Perceptions of Organizational and Common Crime." In Gilber Geis and Erza Stotland, eds. *White-Collar Crime: Theory and Research.* Beverly Hills: Sage.

Silberman, Charles E. 1978. *Criminal Violence, Criminal Justice.* New York: Vintage.

Silverman, Robert A., James J. Teevan, and Vincent F. Sacco, eds. 1991. *Crime in Canadian Society.* Markham: Butterworths Canada.

Silverman, Robert A., and Leslie Kennedy. 1993. *Deadly Deeds: Murder in Canada.* Scarborough: Nelson Canada.

Simon, Herbert A. 1957. *Models of Man.* New York: Wiley.

Skogan, Wesley G. 1978. "Weapon Use in Robbery." In James A. Inciardi and Anne Pottieger, eds. *Violent Crime: Historical and Contemporary Issues.* London: Sage Publications.

———. 1984. "Reporting Crimes to the Police: The Status of World Research." *Journal of Research in Crime and Delinquency* 21:113–37.

Skolnick, Jerome H. 1967. "Justice Without Trial: Law Enforcement in Democratic Society." New York: John Wiley & Sons, Inc.

Snider, Laureen. 1993. *Bad Business: Corporate Crime in Canada.* Scarborough: Nelson Canada.

Solicitor General of Canada. 1982. *Criminal Investigations.* Ottawa: Supply and Services Canada.

———. 1983. *Canadian Urban Victimization Survey Bulletin: Victims of Crime.* Ottawa: Supply and Services Canada.

———. 1984a. *Canadian Urban Victimization Survey Bulletin 2: Reported and Unreported Crime.* Ottawa: Programs Branch/Research and Statistics Group.

———. 1984b. *Selected Trends in Canadian Criminal Justice.* Ottawa: Supply and Services Canada.

———. 1987. *Canadian Urban Victimization Survey Bulletin 8: Patterns in Violent Crime.* Ottawa: Programs Branch/Research and Statistics Group.

Sparks, R.F., Genn, H.G., and Dodd, D.J. 1977. *Surveying Victims.* New York: John Wiley and Sons.

Stark, Rodney. 1987. "Deviant Places: A Theory of the Ecology of Crime." *Criminology* 25:893–909.

Statistics Canada. 1962–1993. *Canadian Crime Statistics*. Ottawa: Supply and Services.

Sutherland, Edwin H. 1939. *The Principles of Criminology*, 3rd ed. Philadelphia: Lippincott.

——. 1947. *The Principles of Criminology*, 4th ed. Philadelphia: Lippincott.

Sutherland, Edwin H., and Donald R. Cressey. 1978. *Criminology*, 10th ed. Philadelphia: J.B. Lippincott.

Sykes, Gresham M., and David Matza. 1957. "Techniques of Neutralization: A Theory of Delinquency." *American Sociological Review* 22:664–70.

Sviridoff, Michelle, and James W. Thompson. 1983. "Links Between Employment and Crime: A Qualitative Analysis of Rikers Island Releases." *Crime and Delinquency* 29:195–212.

Thornberry, Terence P., and R.L. Christenson. 1984. "Unemployment and Criminal Involvement: An Investigation of Reciprocal Causal Processes." *American Sociological Review* 49:398–411.

Thornberry, Terence P. 1987. "Toward an Interactional Theory of Delinquency." *Criminology* 25:863–91.

Thornberry, Terence P., Alan J. Lizotte, Marvin D. Krohn, Margaret Farnworth, and Sung Joon Jang. 1991. "Testing Interactional Theory: An Examination of Reciprocal Causal Relationships Among Family, School, and Delinquency." *Journal of Criminal Law and Criminology* 82:3–35.

Toby, Jackson. 1957. "Social Disorganization and Stake in Conformity: Complementary Factors in the Predatory Behavior of Hoodlums." *Journal of Criminal Law, Criminology, and Police Science*. 48:12–27.

——. 1980. "The New Criminology is the Old Baloney." In J.A. Inciardi, ed. *Radical Criminology: The Coming Crisis*. Beverly Hills: Sage Publications.

Turk, Austin T. 1969. *Criminality and the Legal Order*. Chicago: Rand McNally.

——. 1976. "Law as a Weapon in Social Conflict." *Social Problems* 23:276–92.

——. 1986. "Class, Conflict, and Criminalization." In R.A. Silverman and J. Teevan, eds. *Crime in Canadian Society*, 3rd ed. Toronto: Butterworths.

Walsh, Dermot. 1986. "Victim Selection Procedures Among Economic Criminals: The Rational Choice Perspective." In Derek B. Cornish and Ronald V. Clarke, eds. *The Reasoning Criminal: Rational Choice Perspectives on Offending*. New York: Springer-Verlag.

Warr, M. 1991. "America's Perceptions of Crime and Punishment." In J.F. Sheley, ed. *Criminology: A Contemporary Handbook*. Belmont, Calif.: Wadsworth.

Weir, A. 1973. "The Robbery Offender." In F. Feeney, and A. Weir, eds. *The Prevention and Control of Robbery* I, Davis, CA: University of California.

West, Donald J., and David P. Farrington. 1977. *The Delinquent Way of Life*. London: Heinemann.

Weston, Greg. 1992. *The Stopwatch Gang*. Toronto: Macmillan Canada.

Wilkinson, Paul. 1977. *Terrorism and the Liberal State*. London: Macmillan.

Williams, F.P., and M.D. McShane. 1988. *Criminological Theory*. Englewood Cliffs, N.J.: Prentice-Hall.

Wilson, William Julius. 1987. *The Truly Disadvantaged: The Inner City, The Underclass, and Public Policy*. Chicago: University of Chicago Press.

Wolfgang, Marvin E. 1958. *Patterns in Criminal Homicide*. New York: John Wiley & Sons.

Wolfgang, Marvin E., and Franco Ferracuti. 1967. *The Subculture of Violence: Towards an Integrated Theory of Criminology*. London: Associated Book Publishers Ltd.

Wright, James D., and Peter H. Rossi. 1985. *The Armed Criminal in America*. Washington, D.C.: U.S. Government Printing Office.

———. 1986 *Armed and Considered Dangerous: A Survey of Felons and Their Firearms*. New York: Alding de Gruyter.

Yeager, Matthew G., Joseph D. Alviani, and Nancy Loving. 1976. "How Well Does the Handgun Protect You and Your Family?" *Handgun Control Staff Technical Report 2*, Washington, DC: United States Conference of Mayors.

Young, Jock. 1988. "Risk of Crime and Fear of Crime: A Realist Critique of Survey-Based Assumptions." In Mike Maguire and John Pointing, eds. *Victims of Crime: A New Deal?* Philadelphia: Open University Press.

Ziegenhagen, Eduard A., and Dolores Brosnan. 1985. "Victim Responses to Robbery and Crime Control Policy." *Criminology* 23, no. 4:675–95.

Zimring, Franklin E., and James Zuehl. 1986. Victim Injury and Death in Urban Robbery: A Chicago Study. Journal of Legal Studies 15:1–40.

GLOSSARY OF TERMS

A.A.:	Alcoholics Anonymous
A.R.:	armed robbery
AWOL:	absent without leave, on the run from prison
ACID:	LSD
ALLIGATOR CLIPS:	clamps with teeth that look like an alligator's mouth and that are used to hold objects together. Used by some robbers to attach stolen licence plates to their own car for quick release.
ARTILLERY:	heavy, large-calibre guns such as machine guns
B. & E.:	break and enter, burglary
BANDIT:	robber or bank robber
BANDIT PACK:	quantity of bills that contains an explosive device that activates when the robber leaves the store or bank. The pack explodes seconds or minutes later, giving off smoke and staining the stolen money with ink. In the United States, the packs frequently give off tear gas as well.
BEEF:	a contentious issue, an area of disagreement, a grudge between two people. A "beef" also refers to the criminal charge.
BIKERS:	members of a motorcycle club, normally a criminal gang. Also known as an outlaw gang.
BIT:	one's prison sentence or the time remaining to be served. A "small bit" is a short sentence of incarceration.
BOOSTER:	professional thief, usually a shoplifter
BURN OR BURNT:	to be caught or arrested. To be seen by the victim or witness, usually before the act. To be informed on.
CAN:	prison or a jail cell
CASE:	to check out a target before the robbery
CHUMP:	stupid person, a sucker
CHUMP CHANGE:	small amount of money
CHUNK:	gun
COOL CAR:	the getaway car not used in the robbery. Usually parked a safe distance from the target.

COLD COCK:	getting caught "cold cock" figuratively means to get caught with one's pants down. This means to be apprehended in the act and with incriminating evidence.
COP A PLEA:	plead guilty for considerations, plea bargaining
COWBOY:	to act "cowboy" is to act aggressively, to show off, or to take risks
COWBOY M.O.:	robbery in which the bandits burst into the store or bank and leap over the counter. An aggressive-style robbery.
CROWN (ATTORNEY):	prosecuting attorney acting as the Queen's (the Crown) representative in criminal prosecutions in Canada
CUT:	one's share of the loot, also called one's "end"
D-CAR:	detective car, undercover car
D-TOX:	detoxification centre for alcoholics
DEAR JOHN LETTER:	letter from a former girlfriend or wife saying goodbye
DICK OR DICK CAR:	detective or detective car
DOG DAY AFTERNOON:	term used to refer to a bad day. A number of inmates made reference to the movie of the same name, which deals with a bank robbery that results in a hostage-taking incident.
END:	person's share of the money
FAT:	to be fat with money means to have plenty of money
FEDERAL EXPRESS:	U.S.-based parcel delivery company that describes itself as the world's largest next-day delivery service. The term is used by criminals to describe someone in a hurry such as in the course of a robbery. To be "Federal Express" is to be as fast as possible.
FENCE:	someone who receives stolen goods for resale
FINGER:	to "finger" someone is to inform on them
FINK:	informant. To "fink" is to inform.
FLUSH:	to be "flush" is to have plenty of money
FRONT:	this term refers to drugs advanced by a supplier to a dealer (up front) without payment. An

	agreement is made that the money will be paid after the drugs have been sold.
GHOST CAR:	undercover police car
GRASS:	marijuana
GUCCI SHOES:	an expensive and stylish pair of shoes. The term is used metaphorically to describe a bandit who commits a robbery with class.
HARD TIME:	refers to the emotional problems inmates may experience serving their prison sentences.
HEAT SCORE:	anything that brings police attention. For example, a partner who spends money extravagantly or talks too much about his or her crimes is a "heat score."
HEIST:	robbery
HOT CAR:	stolen car used in a robbery
J.P.:	Justice of the Peace
JOINT:	refers to a prison and to a marijuana cigarette
JUNK:	heroin
JUG:	bank
KIT:	bank-robbery kit usually consisting of guns, a mask, bullet-proof vest, make-up and disguises
KITE:	prison term that refers to a note. It is frequently from an informant to the prison administration.
NICKED:	to be arrested
NICKELS AND DIMES:	this term refers to small quantities of drugs that used to sell for five dollars (nickels) and ten dollars (dimes) before inflation. The term has a general application to small quantities of drugs or money.
OUTLAW:	term used to describe a criminal. Used more specifically to refer to an escaped criminal.
ON THE RUN:	to be AWOL. On the run from the law. Escaped from prison and being sought by the police.
P.C.:	protective-custody section of the prison usually reserved for informants and some sexual offenders who are despised by other inmates. Also holds police officers and other law-enforcement persons convicted of criminal offences for their own protection.

PATCH:	to fix something that is wrong. To settle a dispute between criminals. The term also refers to a deal that informants make with the police in exchange for something.
PEN:	penitentiary, prison
PIECE:	a gun
POP:	refers to a beer. To "pop" someone is to shoot them.
PINCH:	to be "pinched" means to be arrested
PRELIMINARY HEARING:	(pre-lim) the court hearing to determine whether there is sufficient evidence to send the accused to trial
PUP:	a pushover, no stamina. To "pup out" is to give up easily without a fight.
RAT:	informant
ROOKIE:	someone who is young and inexperienced and prone to make mistakes, such as a young bank robber
ROUNDER:	a recidivist, an inmate who has been around prison before, an ex-convict
RUNNER:	inmate who is known to run. An escape artist or "go boy."
SCREWS:	prison guards
SHANK:	knife made in prison from any available materials
SHOOTING UP:	mainlining or using a syringe to insert drugs intravenously
SKUNK:	police officer
SPEED:	methamphetamine. An illicit drug.
SOLID:	having a solid reputation, a trustworthy person. A criminal who will not inform on others, who keeps his or her word.
SPINNING:	driving around trying to lose anyone who may be tailing you. Manoeuvring to avoid surveillance.
SQUARE JOHN:	person who is not criminally aware. The term is also used to describe someone who has landed in prison but has little prison or criminal knowledge.

STOOL PIGEON:	a police informant
STRAIGHT:	"going straight" is attempting to lead a law-abiding life. A "straight" person is someone who is not a criminal. It is also used to refer to someone who is uninformed or criminally naive.
TAIL:	to be "tailed" is to be followed by the police. To be under surveillance.
TEMPORARY ABSENCE:	a program that allows temporary absences from prison on humanitarian, medical, or rehabilitative grounds
TOP DOG:	the person in charge or with the most status
TRUCK:	an armoured vehicle. Also called a candy truck because it holds the money (candy).
UNDERWORLD:	loosely defined term that refers to a criminal subculture and the milieu in which criminals associate
UTTERING:	passing false cheques
UNAUTHORIZED WITHDRAWAL:	tongue-in-cheek term for a bank robbery. Usually applied to note-pushing.
WASTE:	to kill someone. "Wasted" means to be drunk or stoned on drugs.
WELL-HEELED:	having plenty of money
WALL:	prison wall, incarceration, prison
WEED:	marijuana

INDEX

J
9/04

Homer

BLACKWELL INTRODUCTIONS TO THE CLASSICAL WORLD

This series will provide concise introductions to classical culture in the broadest sense. Written by the most distinguished scholars in the field, these books will survey key authors, periods, and topics for students and scholars alike.

PUBLISHED
Homer
Barry B. Powell

IN PREPARATION
Classical Literature
Richard Rutherford

Classical Mythology
Jon Solomon

Ancient History
Charles W. Hedrick

Ancient Rhetoric
Thomas Habinek

Ancient Comedy
Eric Csapo

Ancient Fiction
Gareth Schmeling

Augustan Poetry
Richard Thomas

Roman Satire
Daniel Hooley

Sophocles
William Allan

Euripides
Scott Scullion